The Biopic and Beyond

Celebrities as Characters in Screen Media

Melanie Piper

BLOOMSBURY ACADEMIC

NEW YORK • LONDON • OXFORD • NEW DELHI • SYDNEY

BLOOMSBURY ACADEMIC
Bloomsbury Publishing Inc
1385 Broadway, New York, NY 10018, USA
50 Bedford Square, London, WC1B 3DP, UK
29 Earlsfort Terrace, Dublin 2, Ireland

BLOOMSBURY, BLOOMSBURY ACADEMIC and the Diana logo are trademarks of
Bloomsbury Publishing Plc

First published in the United States of America 2022
Paperback edition published 2024

Copyright © Melanie Piper, 2022, 2023

For legal purposes the Acknowledgments on p. viii constitute an
extension of this copyright page.

Cover image © Elvira Blumfelde / EyeEm / Getty Images

All rights reserved. No part of this publication may be reproduced or transmitted
in any form or by any means, electronic or mechanical, including photocopying,
recording, or any information storage or retrieval system, without prior permission
in writing from the publishers.

Bloomsbury Publishing Inc does not have any control over, or responsibility for, any
third-party websites referred to or in this book. All internet addresses given in this
book were correct at the time of going to press. The author and publisher regret any
inconvenience caused if addresses have changed or sites have ceased to exist,
but can accept no responsibility for any such changes.

Library of Congress Cataloging-in-Publication Data
Names: Piper, Melanie, author.
Title: The biopic and beyond : celebrities as characters in
screen media / Melanie Piper.
Description: New York : Bloomsbury Academic, 2022. | Includes
bibliographical references and index. |
Summary: "An examination of how contemporary film, television, and fan media
transform celebrities into fictionalised characters"– Provided by publisher.
Identifiers: LCCN 2022004321 (print) | LCCN 2022004322 (ebook) |
ISBN 9781501361494 (hardback) | ISBN 9781501393990 (paperback) |
ISBN 9781501361487 (epub) | ISBN 9781501361470 (pdf) | ISBN 9781501361463
Subjects: LCSH: Characters and characteristics in mass media. |
Celebrities in mass media. | Biographical films–History and criticism.
Classification: LCC P96.C43 P57 2022 (print) | LCC P96.C43 (ebook) |
DDC 809.927–dc23/eng/20220210
LC record available at https://lccn.loc.gov/2022004321
LC ebook record available at https://lccn.loc.gov/2022004322

ISBN:	HB:	978-1-5013-6149-4
	PB:	978-1-5013-9399-0
	ePDF:	978-1-5013-6147-0
	eBook:	978-1-5013-6148-7

Typeset by Integra Software Services Pvt. Ltd.

To find out more about our authors and books visit www.bloomsbury.com
and sign up for our newsletters.

In memory of Holly Belle.

Contents

Acknowledgments		viii
Introduction: Any Resemblance Is Completely Intended		1
1	Re-creating the Public	13
2	Creating the Private	31
3	The Illusion of Access	53
4	Beyond the Biopic: Sketch Comedy	69
5	Beyond the Biopic: Celebrities Play Themselves	95
6	Beyond the Biopic: Real Person Fan Fiction	123
Conclusion: Defined by Docucharacter		149
Bibliography		160
Index		170

Acknowledgments

Thank you to the School of Communication and Arts at the University of Queensland for support throughout the life of this research. This book would not exist without Lisa Bode and her encouragement, guidance, and overall cheerleading in all the time I've known her as a teacher, colleague, and friend. Thanks to current and former SCA faculty whose knowledge, feedback, and/or offers of employment also made this book possible, particularly Frances Bonner, Jane Stadler, Ted Nannicelli, Alex Bevan, Jason Jacobs, and, obviously, Lisa (again, always!). Eternal gratitude to Professor Tom O'Regan, who left us far too soon: the world will always be a less thoughtful place without him. Dennis Bingham and P. David Marshall's feedback was instrumental in shaping the direction of this book.

Thank you to the team at Bloomsbury, particularly Katie Gallof, Stephanie Grace-Petinos, and Erin Duffy, for seeing something in this project and their patience and help in getting it there.

Love and thanks to friends past and present who, whether they know it or not, had some part in helping to make my brain work the way it does when it comes to these things: Sare, Max, Krista, Kris, Liz, Emma, Riya, Ed, Cam, Bec, and Jordan. Thank you to my parents, Donna and Colin Piper, for their support, patience, encouragement, and for always being there for every decision I wanted to make, and, most importantly, for tolerating the bad ones.

Introduction: Any Resemblance Is Completely Intended

Picture a celebrity in silhouette.

You can see their outline clearly, a backlight behind them obscuring the finer details of their face. You can make out some of the things that are recognizably them, that strike you as familiar, as something that you know. Maybe it is the particular shape of their hair; the familiar lines of a body that you have seen pictured so many times, something about the way they hold themselves, the way they walk. You know them. You can tell it is who you think it is.

But what about the details? These might be familiar to you as well, but perhaps your memory is a little fuzzy when you are unable to see them clearly in front of you. This is where you begin to fill in the blanks, to project what you think you know onto the darkness in front of you. Who do you want them to be? What expression do they have on their face? Their hair, that familiar shape: is it the same color as it was in your favorite movie role of theirs? Or how it looked in that one picture from the red carpet a few years before? Are they styled the way they were when they were younger, back when you thought their career was more interesting? Or are they disheveled, caught unaware in a paparazzo's lens? Are they a genius? Are they a fool? Are they holding it together or coming apart at the seams? What have you made them out to be?

This is how real public figures become characters in screen narratives: a boldly sketched outline of what we recognize and know, with colors and shades filled in by what we imagine, what we want, and what suits the purposes of a story being told. The persuasive recognizability of the former allows for liberties to be taken with the latter. When we see the picture as a whole, the cohesive filling-in of a factual outline with shades of fiction, we are able to gain access to a version of the celebrity that we could not get close to with the original. We can see the facial expression as it has been filled in. We can know what they are thinking, what they are feeling, and how they act when there is no camera to catch them.

This character is a version, a liminal entity walking a thin line between fact and fiction, but we can allow ourselves to suspend disbelief, to treat them as if they are a representation of the real thing. If we are so persuaded, what we see projected into that outline, in the blank spaces of the silhouette, might start to shape how we see the original, untouched version of the celebrity as well.

This book breaks down the process of the outlining, the shading, and the fleshed-out simulation of access that transforms public figure into a fictionalized character in film and television forms such as the biopic and docudrama. Films based on true stories populate our multiplexes alongside blockbuster franchises and adaptations as stories with an existing audience, and movies and television series based on actual events from the best of true crime to the British Royal Family populate our Netflix front pages. Like franchises, adaptations, reboots, and remakes, based-on-a-true-story projects can be a relatively low-risk venture that does not go out into the market as a completely unknown quantity. The speed with which real events are being fictionalized is closing, with biopics being made about still-living people with greater frequency, and films based on historical events crafted in ways that resonate with the present moment (Sheehan 2013).

However, it is not only the biopic or the based-on-a-true-story miniseries that turn public figures into characters. These kinds of characters, the bold outline filled in with a variety of colors and shades, can be found in satirical impersonation and sketch comedy, RPF (real person fiction) fan fiction, or cameos and semi-autobiographical narratives where celebrities play themselves. Variations on the theme can be found in online memes, fake or parody Twitter accounts, and animated sitcoms. All of these forms of screen media (whether the cinema screen, television screen, computer screen, or smartphone screen) can take the cultural meaning and the fact of a public figure and re-make it to signify something new, or to shed light on the person being represented. Sometimes we cannot help but think of Joe Biden as the prankster sidekick to a long-suffering Barack Obama in the Biden Bro memes, or Donald Trump in the guise of a pouting Alec Baldwin in a *Saturday Night Live* sketch, or Mark Zuckerberg as Jesse Eisenberg's aloof, friendless billionaire in *The Social Network* (2010). But what is the process at work that cements those intertextual connections between the real and the interpreted in our brains?

In all these different forms, the common thread is some basis in an actual person that has been made into a character. So should we consider these ubiquitous based-on-a-real-person media forms from the perspective of their characters in order to understand them? In his work on the biopic as a film genre,

Dennis Bingham (2010) writes that "[t]he appeal of the biopic lies in seeing an actual person who did something interesting in life, known mostly in public, transformed into a character" (10). The process of a public figure becoming a screen character in the biopic has both filmmakers and audiences engaged in a process of discovering what it may have been like to be this person, to be their audience, and to understand something about the nature of that person's time, place, and role as a cultural figure and a human being (Bingham 2010: 10). If so much of the appeal of the biopic (and, as this book considers, other media that transforms real people into characters) depends on this adaptation to character, then a character-focused approach to based-on-a-real-person media is apt. This approach can shed light not only on exactly how this transformation of actual person to character occurs, but also on what the character offers audiences that the actual public figure does not. In using a character-focused approach, the aim of this book is to further critical consideration of the biopic and other fact-fiction media that has attempted to disabuse the literalist interpretation of these kinds of texts in terms of their factual accuracy or truth. Additionally, the character-focused approach of this study engages more with the imagined and fictional elements of such media.

Conceptions of truth and fact in the contemporary cultural moment are tinged with phrases like "alternative facts," "post-truth," "truth is not truth," and "feels over reals." There is no better time to look at how characters based on real people permeate media culture and the possibilities for these characters to engage and inform audiences through affective responses. Whether that response is sympathetic allegiance with a dramatic biopic character, mocking laughter in response to a satirical impersonation, or desire for the idealized version of a celebrity in a work of fan fiction, the ways audiences engage with characters based on real people supplement and shape cognitive understanding of factual historical and cultural narratives that the real public figures represent. This book makes no definitive claim to be an exhaustive consideration of all possible permutations and creative tools at play in the ways real people are adapted to characters on screen. It does not, for example, consider how non-celebrity, "accidental" public figures (such as an Erin Brockovich or a Captain Chesley Sullenberger or a Jeff Bauman) become screen characters in biopics or docudramas about the events that made them publicly notable. Much of the analysis of this book involves close reading of case studies chosen for illustrative purposes. While the analysis of these case studies may be specific to each of the individual works under consideration, it is my intention that they serve as a kind of fleshing-out of a template being proposed here. The aim of this book is to begin to think about media that turns public figures into characters as based in a consistent strategy deployed across media forms for the purposes of similar outcomes: whether they be audience enjoyment, knowledge formation and information distribution, or thematic commentary on the contemporary or historical moment. Consider the ideas proposed here as a template for beginning to think about characters in fact-fiction media in a way that they have, so far, been largely unaddressed. In order to address the variety of media forms that characters based on real people can take, I propose an ontological category that can encapsulate the process by which the transformation from actual public figure to fictionalized character takes place. I term this category, the celebrity outline filled in with various shades of detail, as the docucharacter.

Defining Docucharacter

Like the term "docudrama," docucharacter indicates the fusion of material of the real with the codes and conventions of a fictional form. Rather than indicating the fictional, or purposefully shaped, elements of the form with the term "drama," here the work of creative interpretation of fact is indicated by the word "character." Murray Smith, in his foundational work *Engaging Characters*, which breaks down what exactly we mean when we say we "identify" with characters in film and television, offers a basic definition of what a fictional character is: "a fictional analogue of a human agent" (1995: 7). Smith's work on our engagement with fictional screen characters is valuable to the consideration of characters based on real people, and it begins with this very basic definition. If a purely fictional character, one that makes us believe they are a living entity whose life on screen is worth our time and attention, can be considered the fictional analogue of a human agent, then a character based on a real person that also makes us believe those things can be thought of as a fictional analogue of a *specific* human agent. What Smith describes as the "structure of sympathy" (1995: 5) sets out three levels of how we "identify with" characters. The first of these is "recognition," where we recognize the character as being a distinct character, an analogous human, and make assumptions about who they are based on our existing knowledge of cultural and cinematic archetypes or stereotypes. This is the first step in crafting a character with which audiences can readily engage. In the case of a docucharacter, this recognition stage relies on us recognizing the character as the real person they are intended to represent, and triggering our memory and understanding of everything we know about that person and what they mean as a cultural figure. Here is where the "docu" portion of the docucharacter becomes vital in adapting a public figure to a fictionalized character.

The use of the "docu" prefix indicates that docucharacters are partially composed of some of the hallmarks of documentary as Garry D. Rhodes and John Parris Springer describe them. In the docucharacter, there is an element of the "objective recording of the world" and a basis in "*real* people, places, and events, and [a] stated aim ... to record or document a segment of the real world" (2006: 4, emphasis in original). Rhodes and Springer describe docudrama as the intersection of fictional form and documentary content in film, and it is clear that biopics and other screen media based on real people and true stories fit this description. The documentary content is the true story, and the fictional form is the "based on," the stylistic treatment of factual content. Documentaries, of course, also give their real stories and true-life content a stylistic treatment: narratives are assembled by the way footage is edited together, there are choices made about what gets left out and what makes it in from all the facts known, documents held, and footage shot. The documentary, however, is not granted the "artistic license" of the docudrama or biopic, the freedom to compress and compose, to just plain make up dialogue and scenes and characters in order to fill in the blanks. Because the docudrama is understood to be a fictional (or, at the very least fictionalized) form, genres such as the biopic are not intended or assumed to be purely objective recording of fact as a film that uses the documentary form to present documentary content. Just as the stylistic assembly of the documentary shapes a truth-telling form, facts and the material of the real exist and are integral to the creative form of the docudrama.

Docudrama is a mode of representation, a way of telling stories, and not a genre in itself (Lipkin 2011). The mode of docudrama, Steven N. Lipkin argues, relies on recognizable elements of the real—such as archival footage, or the integration of widely known factual detail—that "ground docudramatic representation in the actuality it represents" (2011: 3). For the docucharacter, these are the bold strokes of the outline; the recognizable shape waiting to be filled in. Take *Jackie* (2016), for example. In this character study biopic of Jacqueline Kennedy in the days following President John F. Kennedy's assassination, several sequences intercut archival footage of the actual Kennedys with the cinematic footage of Natalie Portman as Jackie Kennedy in a re-staged version of events. The re-staging of events is done to match the existing footage as closely as possible: through costume, production design, actor blocking, and cinematography. The effect is the illusion of presenting the real and the re-staged footage, shot more than fifty years apart, as a seamless, continuous representation of the event. The continuity of the edited footage proposes that what we see in long shot in the archival footage is existing knowledge of the public life of the Kennedys. What we see in close-up—the re-staged version, featuring Natalie Portman in a memetic performance that we recognize as "Jackie"—is part of a reality that the cameras could not capture. Based on the way the docudramatic mode grounds dramatized representation in the realm of the actual, Lipkin argues that docudrama works as a means of persuasion. Lipkin writes that "warrants" (such as *Jackie*'s integration of archival news footage and re-created performance) anchor the drama to recognizable actuality and form the basis of a credible re-staging of public memory. In turn, this re-staging and its resemblance to what the audience remembers argues for a particular point of view on the memory in question (2011: 3). In using the "docu-" prefix in the term "docucharacter," I propose that the docucharacter is also a persuasive entity that uses a basis of recorded or recognizable fact to propose that its representational analogue of a specific actual person is a plausible one.

It is important to note Lipkin's distinction between genre and docudrama as a mode of representation. As will be discussed in more detail in the following chapters, much of the existing scholarship on the biopic has worked to counter critical and scholarly derision of the form based on its loose treatment of fact and liberal use of artistic license when it comes to representing history (Bingham 2010: 147). From this starting point of needing to establish the legitimacy of the biopic in film studies, it is necessary that the biopic must first be established as a genre—and it is this task that most of the foundational literature on the biopic has undertaken, and a task at which they have succeeded. If we accept this premise that the biopic is indeed a film genre, then in conjunction with Lipkin's definition of docudrama, the biopic can be further articulated as a genre that utilizes the docudramatic mode of storytelling. With this book, as I examine media forms beyond the biopic to investigate how they transform real people into characters, this idea of the docudramatic mode is one that I argue can be adapted to these other forms. For example, sketch comedy featuring celebrity impersonations could be thought of as a docucomedic mode, and fan fiction that sees audiences re-writing versions of their favorite celebrities could be thought of as a docufantasy mode. It is the adaptability of "docudrama" as a mode of storytelling that the "docucharacter" term attempts to encapsulate and transcend categories of genre and media form. All of the forms studied in this book share the common equation of characters that have some basis in the material of the actual, supplemented, and augmented by the codes and conventions of fiction and invention.

To more fully establish what constitutes the material of the actual when it comes to creating a fictionalized version of a celebrity, Richard Dyer's (1987) concept of the "star image" is useful in considering the breadth of material that can be used to create the foundation of a recognizable characterization. Dyer defines the star image as the widely dispersed and intertextual makeup of "everything that is publicly available" about a celebrity, including performances, appearances, photographs, profiles, interviews, gossip, what they have said about themselves, and what others have said about them (1987: 2–3). Throughout this book, I use the terms "public image" and "celebrity image" interchangeably to refer to the same concept as the star image. I make this change in terminology in order to include a broader range of celebrities (such as politicians, comedians, and CEOs) that the term "star" does not quite apply to or typically connote as it does with film stars in Dyer's work. When Dyer first articulated the concept of the star image, the on-demand information archive of the internet was not a factor in the collation, storage, and navigation of the intertextual collage of an individual celebrity's public image. The vast body of archived information available about a public figure to anyone who cares to Google further complicates the dispersed and intertextual nature of the celebrity public image in the twenty-first century. Textual fragments as temporally and contextually diverse as fan gossip, promotional press conferences, officially sanctioned magazine profiles, and the celebrity's social media presence co-exist simultaneously on the same basic distribution platform: all accessible through the desktop or mobile web browser. The wealth of information that is potentially recognizable to an audience opens up numerous possibilities for how to construct the public self of a docucharacter.

To understand how the textual object of the public image works as the foundation of a rounded fictionalized character, sociologist Erving Goffman's theories of *The Presentation of Self in Everyday Life* ([1956]1990) are useful to consider. Goffman's theory of self-presentation facilitates an understanding of how we are conditioned to look behind a celebrity's presentation of self to uncover what is at the core of their "real" self. Much in the way Murray Smith's definition of character can be taken literally when considering characters based on real people, Goffman's dramaturgical metaphor for self-presentation can be applied literally in this context. In Goffman's metaphor, everyday socialization requires an individual to perform a character: the public presentation of self. Who that individual truly is, their inner, private self, is defined by who they are as the performer behind the character (Goffman [1959] 1997: 23–4). In the context of everyday socialization, in order to successfully navigate a social interaction, the ideal situation would be for us to "know all the relevant social data" about who we are interacting with: what they are thinking, and how they really feel about us. This knowledge would give us the most factual, objective picture of what is happening in the interaction (Goffman [1959] 1997: 21). However, the social data that Goffman refers to exists in the realm of the private selves of others, invisible and unknowable to us. In the absence of this information, we need to interpret what information *is* available in the public performance of others (dress, appearance, gesture, facial expression, vocal tone, and so on) as "predictive devices" that hint at the underlying fact of the social interaction (Goffman [1959] 1997: 21). As with characters in drama, we have to rely on what we see on the surface when attempting to interpret the motivations or true feelings of another individual's self-presented character in order to understand how these motivations or feelings factor into the character's narrative actions. In everyday life's narrative, however, there are perhaps fewer external cues that are deliberately designed to clue an observer into an individual's private self than there are in the performance and presentation of drama. In the life narratives of public figures, the external appearance presented to the general public is the source of the "relevant social data" that audiences and fans rely on to navigate their individual para-social relationship with the celebrity.

As noted above, Dyer's concept of the star image comprises innumerable texts that arise from a range of contextual settings. To navigate the public performance of celebrity and how it is adapted to docucharacter, Goffman's articulation of region behavior is another useful concept to consider. In keeping with the metaphor of dramaturgical performance, Goffman describes the "front region" as "the place where the performance is given": on stage, to be observed by an audience ([1956]1990: 109–10). Therefore, by contrast, the "back region" or "backstage" is the site of a knowing contradiction of the front region performance: the place where the performance is constructed. Backstage is where "the performer can relax; he can drop his front, forgo speaking his lines, and step out of character" (Goffman [1956] 1990: 114–15). In these terms, much of what constitutes the celebrity public image can be considered front-stage performance. Even those texts that purport to offer a glimpse of the celebrity's "real," backstage, or inner self (such as a tell-all memoir, confessional interview, or makeup-free Instagram selfie) are intended for public consumption and performed for an audience. The actual backstage self is who the public figure is outside of the presence of a wider public audience: in their home, at a social event without cameras, on the set after the director calls cut. The inner self is, in a simplified conception of selfhood that accepts identity as a fixed and knowable entity, who they are under these layers, the self guiding their public performance through its various contexts. It is his or her subjective interiority, thoughts, motivations, feelings, and emotions. The docucharacter incorporates these multiple levels of celebrity selves: the public self, comprised of textual fragments of the public image; the backstage self, presented through fictionalized representation of the public figure when they are outside of the public eye; and the inner self, where the docucharacter's interiority is made visible on screen. It is the latter parts of a public figure's identity that are not completely visible in the data of the public image and must be speculated upon, extrapolated, and invented in order to fill out the image in the fictional frame.

It is this invention of the backstage self and the inner self of the docucharacter which comprise the "character" part of the term. To return to Murray Smith's structure of sympathy and levels of character engagement, if re-presenting a celebrity's public image on screen facilitates recognition of the character as the real person it represents, then representing the back-region or backstage self of the docucharacter facilitates alignment and allegiance with the character. According to Smith, after spectators recognize characters as individuals, we can "access... the actions, thoughts, and feelings of characters" (1995: 6). As film and television spectators, we are able to witness character actions and behavior not only in front and back regions, but the fictionalized frame allows us to access emotional states and inner thoughts through performance cues and the projection of interiority into screen space as subjective sequences such as flashbacks or dreams. In the process of alignment, the spectator forms judgements about the character, their actions, and reactions, in relation to their (the spectator's) own ideological points of view or sympathetic responses to the character. This spectatorial reaction to the character is what Smith terms "allegiance," the third level of his structure of sympathy (1995: 6). As both a cognitive and affective response (Smith 1995: 62), the allegiance of sympathetic or antipathetic reactions to characters is key to spectatorial engagement with a film's narrative. In order to generate the allegiance response, the spectator must have the aligned access to the backstage and inner selves of the docucharacter. As this hidden, off-screen, interior world of the public figure's self is not fully contained within the text of the public image, the private self must be imagined and created. This creation is what brings the docucharacter into the realm of the fictional, supplemented, and supported by the recognizable actual.

By engaging with the material of the actual, docudrama and similar storytelling modes deploy what Jane Roscoe and Craig Hight term "factual discourse" (2001: 7). Roscoe and Hight propose that the perception of factual and fictional discourses as binary opposites is not useful for thinking about documentary or its derivative forms (like docudrama or mockumentary) that engage with both factual and fictional discourses. Rather, Roscoe and Hight argue for the existence of a "fact-fiction continuum," with individual texts "constructing relationships with both factual and fictional discourses" on their own terms (2001: 7). Similarly, it is useful to consider the docucharacter's relationship to factual and fictional discourses as taking place on a spectrum. As will be explored throughout the study of the biopic and the presence of the docucharacter in forms beyond the biopic, the position of a docucharacterization along the fact-fiction continuum is dependent upon factors such as genre, form, audience, and mode of production. For example, the docucharacterization of Captain Chesley Sullenberger in *Sully* (2016), a film based on the Miracle on the Hudson pilot's memoir and made with his cooperation, is understood to be far more engaged with factual discourse on the fact-fiction continuum than a satirical piece of fan fiction that depicts Donald Trump and Vladimir Putin in a master/slave relationship. It is through these varying degrees of engagement with factual discourse and the depth of the structure of sympathy that modulates the degree to which the resulting creation functions as an analogue of a literal human agent. As Naomi Jacobs points out in her work on the historical figure in literary fiction, characterizing a public figure can "transform the persona into a three-dimensional sculpture or, alternatively, exaggerate and exploit its cartoon qualities" (1990: xvi). With this book, as I establish the docucharacter as a way of thinking about fact-fiction media, I propose that it is a term equally applicable to the construction of both two- and three-dimensional renderings of public figures in fictionalized contexts.

To return to the term docudrama as the etymological basis of the term docucharacter, Lipkin writes that docudrama is the "fusion of documentary material (its 'actual' subject matter), and the structures and strategies of classic Hollywood narrative form, including character development, conflict, and closure" (2011: 2). I propose that it is the former which represents the public self of the docucharacter, and the conventions of the latter that shape what the speculated private self of the docucharacter is and how it is represented. In the later chapters of this book, I will further elaborate on how the "structures and strategies" of forms beyond classic Hollywood narrative construct the "character" elements of the docucharacter.

There are three common tropes or processes of the docucharacter across media that will form the guiding structure for undertaking a character-based approach to fact-fiction media throughout this book. These are:

1. Docucharacters persuade us to accept them as stand-ins for the real person they represent by re-creating the recognizable public selves of celebrities.
2. Docucharacters create a version of the unseen private self of celebrities in the form of a speculated or invented inner life of a fictionalized character.
3. By operating in a fictionalized frame, docucharacters offer audiences the illusion of access to engage with public figures and celebrities, and to witness a simulated version of the celebrity's private self that is otherwise unreachable.

The first three chapters in this book will explore these tropes further, using examples from contemporary biopic and docudrama film and television in order to establish the validity of the docucharacter using its most prevalent—and widely considered—forms. Chapter 1 will consider how strategies of docudramatic representation re-create the known public self of a celebrity in order to persuade us to accept them as a close enough approximation of the real thing. I will consider how archival footage and re-creation that resembles the original event works as a means of persuasion in the FX limited series *The People v. O.J. Simpson: American Crime Story* (2016), and look at how mimetic performance in *Bohemian Rhapsody* (2018) grants the film some permission for artistic license when it comes to plausibly re-arranging facts. In Chapter 2, I will look at how the private selves of public figures are imagined and invented on screen through strategies of extrapolating from the known public image, using the example of the characterization of Facebook CEO Mark Zuckerberg in *The Social Network* (2010) as an in-depth case study. Chapter 3 rounds out the consideration of the docucharacter approach to biopic and docudrama by looking at how the re-creation of a known public self and creation of an imagined private self afford audiences with access to an imagined version of a public figure, through the filmic language of subjective access to and affective engagement with screen characters. This will be illustrated with how the ambiguities of character-study-style biopics are navigated through the dialogic relationship between audience subjectivity, and the subjectivity of on-screen characters using the examples of *Chappaquiddick* (2017) and *Jackie* (2016).

In the latter three chapters of the book, I turn to media beyond the biopic to demonstrate how this character-focused approach to fact-fiction media translates to other forms. Chapter 4 applies the docucharacter approach to satirical sketch comedy. To do so, this chapter will look at the ways former vice-presidential candidate Sarah Palin has been re-presented in *Saturday Night Live*'s sketches, in contrast with the HBO docudrama film *Game Change* (2012). Chapter 5 stays with a primarily comedic context as it considers the celebrity-plays-themselves cameo and long-form television narratives featuring fictionalized versions of celebrity selves. Focusing on stand-up comedians playing versions of themselves, this chapter will also consider the ways the fictionalized version of a celebrity self is understood in tandem with the public persona, using a case study of Louis C.K., *Louie* (2010–2016), and C.K.'s sexual misconduct scandal. Finally, Chapter 6 will move away from the direct consideration of film and television works to consider the docucharacter in the audience practice of RPF fan fiction. Here, I will return to the earlier example of *The Social Network* to look at how fans have constructed docucharacters of both the real people the film represents and the actors who play them.

Keep the image of the celebrity in silhouette in your mind. Start to think about what makes up the outline, how those lines are drawn, and what makes them so familiar. Think about the color and the shade, the details and where they've come from. Did you take a guess? Have you made the details up completely? What is this creature now, this mess of line and shade and shadow and light? Now we can think about what makes that character come to life.

1

Re-creating the Public

In *Casting JonBenet* (2017), the hybrid documentary-docudrama explores the unsolved 1996 murder of the child beauty queen JonBenét Ramsey through interviews with actors auditioning for parts in a screen re-enactment of the crime. The interviews with the actors speculate upon the characters they are auditioning to play; the roles they may have had in the crime; and the various speculations, conjectures, and theories surrounding the case. The film culminates with a re-enactment sequence that sees these multiple possible narratives about the case played out over each other. Here, the various characters in the drama—John Ramsey, Patsy Ramsey, Burke Ramsey, and JonBenét herself—are distilled down to their most basic signifiers of actuality: costumes that replicate what they were known to be wearing when the crime took place. For example, Patsy Ramsey is signified by a short-sleeved red turtleneck and black slacks, replicated over and over to be filled by the various actors who have auditioned to play her. The actors have different body types, even different hair colors that do not match the actual Patsy's, but nevertheless, this shell of costume attempts to connect the speculative narratives that are played out over each other to a shred of actuality: the photographic evidence of how Patsy Ramsey was dressed the night her daughter was murdered. It is these connections to actuality that are central to connecting a creative work based on a true story to the truth upon which it is based, and the truth that it claims to represent. The foundations upon which the docucharacters are based are the elements of documentary: the actual celebrity at the source of any fictionalization of a public figure.

To consider how screen texts beyond the biopic are transforming the public selves of private figures, it is first necessary to consider the biopic itself. The largest body of scholarly and critical consideration of screen media based on true stories and real people focuses on the biopic as a film genre and docudrama as a mode of presentation, and therefore gives us a starting point to establish the purposes of a docucharacter: to re-create the known public self, to create the unknown private self, and to permit simulated access to the public figure that is otherwise unavailable outside the fictional frame. This chapter focuses on the first of these purposes of the docucharacter and will examine how the known public self of a biopic subject is re-created on screen. Here, I will consider the persuasive work the mode of docudrama does in triggering existing audience memory and knowledge about the biopic subject to create the screen character as a plausible stand-in for the actual public figure being represented.

As discussed in the Introduction, the "docu" prefix in the term "docucharacter" refers to the factual material that connects the character based on a real person to the actual person as a real-world referent. In Steven N. Lipkin's (2011: 2–3) writing on the docudrama as a persuasive mode of representation, he argues that in its performance of memory, the docudrama uses tactics such as indexical resemblance to actual people and events, use of actual material (such as archival footage), and the interaction of actual and created material in sequence or within the same screen space. These "warrants," or connections to actuality, "link and authenticate the evidence and the claims that docudramas forward" (Lipkin 2011: 3). By "performing the past" in ways that are either recognizable and congruent with public memory, or in ways that can be compared with an original referent for accurate resemblance, the docudrama works to persuade its viewer that the representations of actual people that it puts forth are a cohesive, plausible stand-in for actuality. In other words, if a biopic subject is constructed in such a way that it matches the audience's existing image of that public figure, then the creative and created elements of the biopic can be more readily accepted as plausible. It is an act of authentication that, as Murray Pomerance (2013: 26) notes, allows the viewer for a moment to see not a representation of or reference to an event, but the actual. The viewer is temporarily taken back in time to the actual historical event represented, and its afterimage of actuality lingers over the fictionalization it merges into. This chapter will address how the docudramatic mode of representation integrates the actual with the fictionalized in an attempt to persuade the viewer of a consistent story world that bears a plausible resemblance to our own historical world. First, an example from the limited television series *The People v. O.J. Simpson: American Crime Story* (2016) will illustrate how the interaction of actual and staged footage and the staging of footage designed to resemble actuality works as a docudramatic warrant that blends fact and fiction to re-create public events. I will then move on to a more character-focused consideration of the same concept through the example of *Bohemian Rhapsody* (2018), and how its re-creation of actuality works to authenticate an otherwise factually rearranged version of its protagonist Freddie Mercury.

Re-purposing and Re-presenting the Real

Recent approaches to contemporary biopic have touched on the centrality of the connection between the actual event or person being represented, and its representation. Rebecca A. Sheehan (2013) identifies a trend that has developed since around 2005 where the biopic historicizes the present by depicting still-living public figures. Films such as *Fair Game* (2010); *W.* (2008); *The Queen* (2006); and two films which will be given further consideration later in this book, *The Social Network* (2010) and *Game Change* (2012), are a contrast to the once common perception of the biopic as reserved largely for recounting the closed narratives of the dead (Sheehan 2013: 35). Sheehan also notes the concurrent trend of biopics about historical figures that bring the past into the present, constructing the life of a public figure on screen in ways that resonate or draw parallels with issues in the political or cultural context of the film's release (2013: 35–6). Films, such as *Milk* (2008), *Good Night, and Good Luck* (2005), and *Selma* (2014), exemplify this category, as does this chapter's first example for analysis, *The People v. O.J. Simpson*. Both strands of the contemporary biopic work to historicize and comment on what is still unfolding, and the characters at the center of these narratives serve as metonyms for a larger story or broader cultural context. Rather than the classical Hollywood biopic that argued for the historical importance of its individual subject, these kinds of contemporary biopics argue for a particular point of view on a topic, using the generally known facts of a public figure's life as its foundational material. Particularly in the case of biopics that depict still-living public figures, or that dramatize events in the recent past, the contemporaneously viewing audience would be assumed to have a readily accessible memory of the actual to compare to the representation. The re-creation of iconic still images or the interaction of archival footage and dramatized material bring existing public memory into the fictionalized frame of the docudramatic representation. I will discuss this further in a moment with a consideration of the Bronco chase sequence in *The People v. O.J. Simpson*.

Sheehan categorizes these kinds of films—particularly those about still living figures—as "'instant' biopics" and attributes their rise to the current cultural moment that places a premium on instant information. Rather than the biopic telling the story of an individual's prized place in history once that history has passed and that prized place been established, the instant biopic undertakes a form of mediation similar to television or the internet, where these films "respond to and emerge from anxieties particular to the moment in which they are produced" (2013: 36). The instant biopic becomes less about telling the life story of its subject or commenting on the importance of that life story, but rather using the basic facts of that person/persona as a recognizable vehicle to deliver a broader cultural commentary. A film like *Game Change*, for example, is less about the lives of Sarah Palin and John McCain and more a comment on the celebritization of US politics and the effect of the 24-hour news cycle and social media on how presidential elections function in the modern era, using these figures and part of the story of the 2008 US presidential election to illustrate its point about this moment in time. The relatively brief temporal distance between the event and its cinematic remediation in films such as these serves to illustrate "the collapsed distance between the actual and information that attains its own reality" (Sheehan 2013: 36). The value placed on instant information in contemporary media and culture can sometimes prioritize the speed at which the information is given over the accuracy of the information—as Sheehan puts it, the value of instant information "invites representation to trump reality" (2013: 38). What we hear first about an event may be inaccurate, but it may make for a better story than the actuality. The invitation for representation to trump reality translates to the realm of fictionalized versions of real people and events through the kind of access afforded to the audience by the fictionalized version. Reading about an unfolding disaster or tragic news event from the Twitter account of an ordinary person on the ground gives a version of events that may be lacking in factual accuracy but provides insider access. The same could be said of reliving a cultural memory through the lens of fictionalization only a few brief years after it has happened, before its place in the broader timeline of historical consequence has become a complete narrative or fully contextualized.

The second trend of contemporary biopic that Sheehan identifies does permit some contextualization of historical events through temporal distance, but the parallels that they invite us to draw between history and the current moment or the way these representations of past events are constructed with parallels to contemporary events in mind also gives them a sense of being unfinished and unresolved. By alluding to the idea that history repeats itself, or that the represented issues and cultural concerns continue in the public zeitgeist, these kinds of films (or, in the case to be discussed here, television series) construct history as an ongoing working through or battle against recurring problems. *The People v. O.J. Simpson* offers an example of this in the way its mid-1990s historical setting draws direct parallels with the context of its 2016 airing. The issues the series raises surrounding race relations in America, police corruption, the ubiquitous nature of celebrity and blanket media coverage, and the sexist double standards that women in positions of power are subject to are as prescient and ongoing in the contemporary moment as they were in its historical moment. By aligning the past setting of the docudramatic content with the present context of the docudrama's production and consumption, its historical narrative remains somewhat unresolved, despite the twenty-plus years between the events and their adaptation to the screen since the problems at the root of the series thematic concerns are ongoing.

The impact of the thematic parallels between the history represented in the docudrama and the present moment for which it is produced is heightened by the effects of recognition of the past and the plausibility of its dramatization. Through the repurposing of archival footage, and the re-creation of events that bear a visual resemblance to the archival footage, *The People v. O.J. Simpson* makes use of docudramatic warrants that anchor its re-presentation of history to the actuality it claims to be showing its audience a new, "insider" view on. On June 17, 1994, O.J. Simpson's Los Angeles freeway chase in a white Ford Bronco was watched by over 95 million Americans in what has been declared one of television history's most memorable moments (Jones 2016). In the first season instalment of FX's anthology series *American Crime Story*, the Bronco chase is the centerpiece of the second episode in the chronicle of Simpson's double homicide trial and its resonating effects on American culture. Throughout the run of *The People v. O.J. Simpson: American Crime Story*, publications such as *Vanity Fair*, *Rolling Stone*, and *Vulture* fact checked each episode, as has become a regular occurrence in the online reception of films and television shows based on true stories. These blogs show that there is a spectrum of factuality: some elements true, some true but changed for dramatic purposes, some known to be fabricated, some whose truth status cannot possibly ever be known. But how does what we see on screen persuade us to accept it all as equally plausible? As Lipkin (2011) writes, one of docudrama's persuasive strategies is the interaction of actual and re-created material, and the indexical resemblance of re-created material to its real-world referent. Here, I consider *The People v. O.J. Simpson*'s representation of the Bronco chase to illustrate how the seamless blend of archival footage and re-creation of the real sets the stage for a plausible representation of public memory.

The first appearance of archival footage comes within the first two minutes of the episode. Tom Brokaw, anchoring NBC News's coverage of Simpson's double homicide charge, is seen on television in a convenience store, shoppers frozen in place as they watch the announcement. Brokaw's actual image and voice, from twenty-two years before the FX series was broadcast, recur throughout the episode in similar scenes of stunned reaction, both for the general public and the behind-the-scenes world of the narrative's public figures. In the first appearance of the NBC News broadcast, the audio of Brokaw's voice continues to play as the scene cuts from the speechless members of the public in the convenience store, to members of the Los Angeles District Attorney's office, including Marcia Clark (Sarah Paulson) and Gil Garcetti (Bruce Greenwood), watching the same broadcast. This piece of archival footage works to trigger audience memory. For many viewers, at least in the target audience of the United States, the Bronco chase is a kind of flash-bulb memory, a "Where were you when… " moment that has an experience to recall. For many viewers, they *were* some version of the shoppers in the convenience store. The recognition of that public reaction and its seamless transition into what the general public were not privy to—the behind-the-scenes reaction to the news coverage in the district attorney's office—are unified by the re-purposed archival footage. Since the former is recognizably accurate, linked to the latter by an objectively true piece of archival footage, the latter is purported to be equally believable.

A similar strategy of linking a public event with a behind-the-scene's reaction to it is seen a short time later in the episode as Garcetti gives a press conference about Simpson's disappearance. Camera flashes strobe as Garcetti directly addresses the viewing public through the broadcast cameras, and what we see, as the twenty-first-century viewer, cuts to Garcetti's grainy image through the camera viewfinder. As with the actual archival footage of Brokaw's news broadcast, the audio of this re-creation of Garcetti's press conference bridges to a behind-the-scenes moment of Johnnie Cochran's (Courtney B. Vance) staff watching Garcetti's press conference. Within the docudramatic fiction, the re-creation of the actual news event (the performance of the press conference) is given equal status to the actual footage of the news event (Brokaw's broadcast). Both create bridges between public events, public memory, and the unseen moments behind the public memory. When a shot of the television screens in Cochran's office is shown, the re-created press conference is altered to appear as though it is actual broadcast footage, with chyrons proclaiming the press conference to be live, and network logos superimposed in the lower right corner of the screen. The footage resembles the actual news footage of the Brokaw broadcast, giving it the status of archival footage within the story world, despite its obviously re-created and performed nature, signaled by the presence of the actors playing real people, rather than archival footage of the real people themselves.

This is likewise the case as the audio of the press conference again connects another behind-the-scenes moment as we see Chris Darden (Sterling K. Brown) listening to the press conference on the radio in his car. He arrives at his father's house and rushes in to turn the television on. Again, we see a television screen playing the re-created press conference footage with on-screen graphics that mimic actual archival footage. Darden watches the television, and the scene cuts again, to a different television showing the press conference, same re-created event, different network branding. Robert Shapiro (John Travolta) and Robert Kardashian (David Schwimmer) are watching this screen. As insiders who know Garcetti and Clark, who know the inner workings of what is going on, characters like Darden and Shapiro are able to give commentary on the events that gets at the motivations of the public figures on screen, that is able to give insight into their state of mind. This sequence of multiple spatially disparate reactions to a temporally continuous re-created news event illustrates how the re-creation of the public event or public image facilitates what is unseen. The viewer can witness a plausible simulation of what might have been happening in places like Johnnie Cochran's office, or Chris Darden's family home, or the Kardashian house. They can access a simulated version of the interiority of the public figures involved, either directly through the expression of their thoughts, or indirectly through other characters with insider knowledge. The recognizability and believability of the re-created public event act as a means of persuasion to accept these unseen and unknowable events as a plausible truth claim of equal status.

Archival footage again plays a role in the episode during the sequences of the Bronco chase. Rather than mocking up re-created news events to give them the same status as archival footage, as is done for the press conferences earlier in the episode, in this instance the archival footage of the event is seamlessly blended with its re-creation. The visual resemblance between the two gives the sense of the archival footage capturing the event as it exists in public memory: in long shot, from a distance. When the re-creation is integrated with the archival footage, the film is moving in for a close-up (in some cases, literally) to capture what cameras did not or could not access at the time.

The Bronco chase begins in the episode by one such moment that cameras were not present to capture: the identification of O.J. (Cuba Gooding Jr.), driven by Al Cowlings (Malcolm-Jamal Warner), by a young couple driving on the freeway. The authorities are notified, and patrol cars swarm with lights and sirens, closing in through typically congested Los Angeles traffic. There is an initial standoff between the police, Cowlings, and Simpson, and the Bronco gets away as Simpson holds a gun to his own head. The outcome of this escape is next seen in the recurrent context of television being watched, of the characters based on real people engaging in the act of witnessing events from the outside in the same way the general public did. Simpson's family is watching television, with the audio of the re-created Garcetti press conference playing in the background, when Robert Kardashian arrives to tell them he has reason to believe that O.J. has committed suicide. The family's grief is interrupted by seeing the white Bronco on television. Here, the recognizable archival footage of the actual Bronco chase, shot from a helicopter, is integrated into the scene. Similar to the function of the re-created press conference footage in temporally uniting spatially discrete locations through the act of watching the public face of the event on television, archival footage of the Bronco chase connects multiple behind-the-scenes reactions to the events, allowing a re-creation of public memory to lay a foundation of plausibility for a behind-the-scenes narrative.

The viewers of *The People v. O.J. Simpson* become united with the characters on screen and their viewing of events on television when archival footage is, for the first time in the episode, played directly to the twenty-first-century viewer rather than seen in the context of screens within the screen space. A brief excerpt of archival footage of NBC's coverage of the NBA finals, anchored by Bob Costas, is played, giving the audience a first-person experience of watching the news coverage. For many viewers, this could be a first-person re-experiencing of the news coverage. The insertion of the Costas footage is vital, not only in reorienting viewers as the footage follows an act break/commercial break in its original broadcast on FX, but in contextualizing the seamless cut long shot of public memory to the close up of speculative, otherwise unseen and unknowable insight that follows.

There is a further first-person experience of the news coverage with NBC's footage of the Bronco chase. Brokaw's anchor narration describes Simpson's intentions and desire to see his mother and sets the scene of the number of patrol cars following Simpson and Cowlings in the Bronco. The archival helicopter shot reframes and zooms in to focus on the Bronco alone as a rising low-pitched note of nondiegetic score crescendos as the scene cuts directly from the archival footage to the "nine black and whites" Brokaw describes in re-created, dramatized footage. There are subtle differences between the archival evidence of the helicopter news footage of the actual Bronco chase and its dramatized version. In the re-creation, the police units are following the Bronco much closer than they appear in the helicopter shot. This could be read as a subjective insight into Cowlings' and Simpson's state of mind, with the space between the Bronco and the police compressed to give a sense of the inescapability of their situation. It could be an artifact of shooting with a telephoto lens that compresses space between the foreground and background of the frame. Or, it could simply be a question of the realities of production. Closing down the I-5 freeway in Los Angeles to film the re-created chase is an impractical task, so a smaller road space must be used: it is worth noting that the freeway in the re-creation is three lanes wide, whereas the freeway in the archival footage is five. Despite these differences between actual and re-creation, the way the footage is assembled— the bridging score, Brokaw's reference to the police cars and the direct cut to the image of them, the creeping zoom in the archival footage before cutting to the "close up" of what is happening in the re-creation—makes the case for persistent, plausible connections between the actual event and its dramatization. Public image and public memory is re-presented by the inclusion of its actual archival trace, replicated in a visually evocative re-creation, and augmented by the language of cinema. The effect is to ask the viewer to recognize what they already know, or that can be easily verified, and incorporate the behind-the-scenes moments that have been created for dramatic purposes into their developing understanding of the event.

This consideration of *The People v. O.J. Simpson* has largely focused on the events being represented, rather than the people, and the ways that the re-presentation and re-creation of actual events can serve as the replication of public image or public memory. In order to shift focus to begin considering how the re-creation of public image facilitates the creation of a character based on a real person, I turn now to the example of the Freddie Mercury biopic *Bohemian Rhapsody*. While *The People v. O.J. Simpson*'s weekly fact-checks represent a relatively balanced combination of fact and fiction that are granted equal status within the frame of the docudrama, *Bohemian Rhapsody*'s navigation of the actual and the invented prompted a much more contentious reception upon the film's release. Rami Malek's performance as Queen front man Freddie Mercury was praised as not simply an impersonation or recognizable representation of Mercury, but as a resurrection. At the same time, the film faced numerous criticisms of its tenuous relationship to fact, particularly in terms of its timeline of events. A convergence of these two disparate treatments of public self and public memory occurs in the film's framing device, the re-creation of Queen's 1985 Live Aid concert.

Re-creating and Re-configuring the Real

A particularly useful approach to considering the true/untrue nature of the docucharacter is Custen's (1992: 11) view of the biopic character as an intertextual Frankenstein's monster made "of bits of previous incarnations of already-lived lives," both of the actual person that the film depicts, and other similar depictions that have appeared on screen before. Beyond understanding characters adapted from known personas as the merging of public and private selves, the construction of these various aspects of self in the screen character must be approached as an intertextual, intersubjective creature. The end result on screen draws from a body of sources as varied as the body of the star image that forms its initial blueprint. To the already-lived screen lives that Custen identifies as comprising the biopic character, I would add that the collaborative nature of the contemporary biopic—as opposed to the biopic as a largely studio-controlled form in the Classical Hollywood era that Custen studies—necessitates that the lives of the people responsible for bringing the character to the screen are a significant factor in constructing the character. Writer, director, performer, and the myriad others working in the collaborative process of producing a film can contribute to the formation of the character drawing from their own experience, or the experiences of people they know.

Thinking about the "character" portion of the docucharacter and how its interior life is shaped from this mash-up of already lived lives, both imagined and real, is perhaps getting ahead of myself into the topic of the next chapter, where I will discuss the creation of the docucharacter's private self in more detail. For now, returning to considering the re-creation of the public self through multiple lives, or versions of the same life, in multiple texts, Márta Minier and Maddalena Pennacchia (2014) touch on intertextuality in similar ways to Custen as they attempt to articulate exactly what the source text is for the adaptation of a biopic subject. In approaching biopics as adaptations, Minier and Pennacchia build on Linda Hutcheon's theory of adaptation to consider what the "adapted text" is in the case of a biopic (2014: 7). The life being retold can take many textual forms that serve as the starting point for the biopic narrative: one or more biographies or other books written by third parties, autobiographies, memoirs, a piece of the body of work, interviews, diaries, or a combination of such sources. The various parties responsible for adapting the life of a public figure to the screen may be working from different source texts in the process of their collaboration. For instance, the screenwriter could be basing the script on the narrative of a third-party biography, while the actor bases their performance on the physicality exhibited in a particular interview (Minier and Pennacchia 2014: 8). The result is the screen life of a public figure drawn from an intertextual and transmedia body of sources, generated not only by the public figure and their publicity machine, but third parties with their own agendas and imperatives. What Minier and Pennacchia articulate as the biopic source text, then, is remarkably similar in its scope to Richard Dyer's (1987) idea of the star image as consisting of everything publicly available about a star. The broad scope of sources available to choose and combine for the screen adaptation of a public persona contributes to an understanding of biopics as adaptations, as it clearly permits the tenet of adaptation that calls for "repetition without replication" (Hutcheon 2006: 7; Minier and Pennacchia 2014: 8). There is obviously a lack of replication in the case of a biopic subject being played by an actor, since, as James Naremore (2012: 38–40) writes, even an accurate impersonation of a known figure cannot completely erase the fact that it is an impersonation: indeed, a too-accurate impersonation may have an alienating effect. But in the narrativization of the life, or a portion of the life, of a public figure, there is a lack of replication of the specifics of the source itself, due to its vast, widely dispersed nature. This lack of replication is compounded by the constraints of the feature film format, dependent on elements such as length and the classical Hollywood three-act storytelling structure.

Returning to the example of *Bohemian Rhapsody*, the source texts compiled into the screen adaptation include Queen's songs, music videos, television appearances, and live performances. As source texts with an often-iconic visual record, these are a particularly persuasive and recognizable means of re-creating the public image of a celebrity in the visual medium of a biopic. Rather than being deemed unsettling in the mimetic copying of recorded gestures and mannerisms, Malek speaks about invoking the "spirit" of Mercury, capturing his essence as "[the] refusal to be stereotyped [and the] refusal to conform" (Savage 2018). Similarly, reception of Malek's performance suggests that there is a pleasure in the way Malek brings the character of Freddie to the screen, with viewers of side-by-side comparison footage of the two responding to the performance as a resurrection, rather than simply an impersonation ("Live Aid": 2019). Viewer comments of comparison YouTube videos also express a kind of amazement (and again, pleasure) at the technical accuracy of Malek's embodied re-creation of recorded footage, such as the Live Aid concert sequence. The mimetic resemblance of the re-created public self to its original—particularly in the case of an iconic public figure such as Freddie Mercury, and a widely viewed event such as Queen's Live Aid performance—endears the audience to the screen character as aligning with the public figure in their memory. As Belén Vidal writes, the body of the actor is a central locus of audience expectation in the biopic, and that for disbelief to be suspended, the actor's resemblance and embodied performance need to conform with the audience's existing knowledge of and emotional response to the biopic subject (2013: 11). This plausible resemblance of both the actor to the biopic subject and the visual staging of re-created events lends a sense of believability to help overcome any slips of factuality or outright fabrication. Both fact and fiction are given the same status within the diegesis of the film: the re-created and the created are blended seamlessly, and for the viewer without a significant amount of background knowledge in the subject, a whole, rounded character comprised of both fact and fiction is portrayed.

The desires of filmmakers, viewers, and the perpetuation or subversion of dominant cultural narratives about a public figure all become a factor in the reconstruction and reinterpretation of the public figure. While not directly about the biopic, Roberta Person's work on the memorialization of Frank Sinatra is relevant to consider here in its argument that "multiple and competing representations of historical figures circulate simultaneously" (2014: 205). In the course of adapting a real person to the screen, these multiple representations may exist within a single film, such as in *I'm Not There* (2007) with its six diverse actors embodying the figure of Bob Dylan, or *American Splendor* (2003), which features both the actual Harvey Pekar and Paul Giamatti's performance of him. Alternatively, they may exist across screen works that represent the same person, such as multiple versions of Barack Obama circulating in films like *Southside with You* (2016) and *Barry* (2016), satirical impersonations of him on shows like *Saturday Night Live* and *Key and Peele* (2012–15), and the actual still-circulating media image of Obama himself. Through the selective construction of a memory comprised of particular elements of the wider star image, "different representations originate from different players, serve different purposes, and appeal to audiences differently situated within the hegemonic system by virtue of their different economic and cultural capital" (Pearson 2014: 205). When fictionalization in representing a public figure enters as an additional factor in the construction of the person as memory (whether of the distant past, as with a figure such as Sinatra who is often remembered as specific to a particular time even though he lived well beyond that era, or recent past and ongoing present, as with many of the major case studies in this book) there exists further opportunity for the various stakeholders in the construction of the image to circulate multiple and competing representations of the subject.

The ways that re-creation of public lives in the biopic speaks to how culture wishes to remember a subject is often manifested in re-creation based on mimesis of expectation. Michael Sicinski (2012) contextualizes early twenty-first-century biopic in similar ways to Rebecca Sheehan's idea of the instant biopic and the prioritization of instant information over accuracy. Sicinski categorizes the "New Biopic" and its mimetic imperative as analogous to the concept of "truthiness," where facts can be spun to fit an existing ideological viewpoint (2012: 2). Truthiness, as popularized by fake pundit Stephen Colbert on the premiere episode of *The Colbert Report* in 2005, is the state of thinking with the gut rather than the head, and of believing something is true simply because it feels true. Sicinski argues that truthiness manifests in the contemporary biopic out of a desire for transparency and truth in art that does not exist in American politics and culture at large. The result, though, reflects "the world as we think we know it to be" (2012: 1), with a focus on the pleasure of recognizing a faithful copy of a public figure capable of disguising the textuality of the film (2012: 2). The truthiness of the contemporary biopic presents a version of the self that claims to be rendered coherent through the assemblage of a sequence of biographical facts. Sicinski claims that, with rare exceptions, the "New Biopic" does not leave room for realistic nuance or historical and cultural contextualization, only serving up the representation of a public figure in ways close to how the culture at large already sees and recognizes them (2012: 3). I would argue that there has perhaps been some development in the arena of "Character Study"-type biopics which does introduce some nuance to the representation of public figures by focusing on restricted time frames within the story of a life, rather than attempting to narrativize an entire life within the space of a single feature film. I will consider this in more detail in Chapter 3, when discussing the kinds of simulated access afforded by the biopic and other fictionalizations of actual public figures. Sicinski is correct though, in the role that mimetic performance and visual re-creation play in making any attempt at an alternate reading of a public figure as a screen character seem plausible and acceptable. The centrality of mimesis in Sicinski's "New Biopic" is brought into sharp focus through the example of *Bohemian Rhapsody*.

Bohemian Rhapsody takes numerous liberties with its subject, Freddie Mercury and Queen. The film's disregard for factuality was a topic of criticism against it, particularly surrounding its alterations to the actual timeline of events depicted (largely to do with Mercury's HIV diagnosis) in order to give more of a dramatic weight to the film's closing sequence: an extended re-creation of Queen's 1989 performance at Live Aid. While the film faced criticisms about its lack of historical and factual accuracy, it was simultaneously praised for Rami Malek's highly mimetic performance of Mercury, for which Malek received the Academy Award for Best Performance by an Actor in a Leading Role. It is the physical and performative resemblance of Malek to Mercury that enhances the plausibility of the film's portrait of Mercury and, therefore, makes its factual inaccuracies particularly grating to viewers and critics with background knowledge of the historical fact. Because the re-presentation of Mercury's public image closely resembles its real-world referent, the private self of Mercury that is crafted for the film subsequently becomes more plausible and acceptable as truth. The fictionalized representation—the docucharacter—is an entity that the viewer has more (simulated) access to than the actual Mercury: on screen, Malek's performance is present, with both public and private selves visible and comprehendible. This is how the biopic potentially invites representation to surpass reality, in its accessibility and simplification.

The issue of using a real person's public image as the basis for a screen character that bears their name and likeness in service of a fictionalized or factually inaccurate story raises questions about right to privacy and libel. Although this book does not focus on these legal concerns of adapting real people and events to the screen, existing writing on the legal and ethical issues at stake here exemplifies the complicated nature of merging the known and the unknowable in the docucharacter. Scripted and narrative screen media, whether on film, television, or the reception text of fan fiction, has an inherent degree of fictionality by virtue of its media form. In his work on the legal concerns of adapting real stories and people to the screen, John T. Aquino writes that "[to] tell a good story, it is sometimes necessary to lie—who wants to get mired down in 'details'?" (2005: 3). At the same time, however, mainstream commercial film and television texts that make some claim to truth or factuality must work within the boundaries of what is a legally acceptable lie since, despite its intrinsic fictionality, "the medium of film is lifelike and apt to be mistaken for reality," if not literally, then in the claims to truth it makes (Aquino 2005: 24). In the United States, laws concerning defamation rest their burden of proof on "what a reasonable person might infer and not what the author intended" (Aquino 2005: 30). It is here that the unknowable nature of a public figure's inner self and how it is presented on screen becomes a consideration. Would a reasonable person assume that the private moments of a public figure adhere to strict accuracy? Unlikely, considering the out-of-the-public-eye nature of such moments: the filmmakers cannot represent them with strict accuracy since they do not know what happened. The representation of what *is* known, however, colors and shapes these moments to enhance their plausibility. Even while a truth claim is made, there is a disavowal of it due to the nature of filmic storytelling and the need to represent a public figure and the events of their life in ways that "make the action convincing and believable" so that the audience can "*connect* with what they are seeing" (Aquino 2005: 2, emphasis in original). Questions of what is or is not defamation in how the construction of docucharacter plays along the fact-fiction spectrum, and how that construction of character becomes enmeshed with the actual celebrity's public image are no doubt in play during the production process of these characters. In the reception process, the answers given to these questions by filmmakers and other creators shape the simultaneously true and untrue nature of creative works based on actual people. In the case of a film like *Bohemian Rhapsody*, where the primary figure of the biopic is deceased but their associates (in this case, the remaining members of Queen) are involved with the production of the film, there is the further complication of a sense of endorsement of the portrayal concurrent with the subjective memory of people who knew the biopic subject and have a stake in the way they themselves are portrayed as characters in the biopic.

The crux of how *Bohemian Rhapsody* re-arranges the real by re-presenting it through mimetic resemblance is in the Live Aid concert sequence which book ends and serves as the climax of the film. One of the criticisms of the film regarding its accuracy was the re-arranging of the timeline of events, particularly surrounding Mercury's HIV diagnosis, and an invented breakup of the band with the Live Aid performance serving as a reunion. These exercises in creative license work to recontextualize and give the re-created Live Aid sequence a degree of backstory and narrative meaning not present in the original event. In the context of the film's rearranged narrative timeline, the Live Aid performance acts as both a reunion and a swan song, a dual performance of Mercury's mortality and immortality.

On the surface of the re-creation Malek's performance is a study in the mimesis of gesture and timing, his physicality, prosthetic-altered appearance, and costume a trigger for audience memory or a visual image able to stand up to scrutiny when held against the original, as evidenced by numerous fan-made side-by-side comparison videos on YouTube. In these side-by-side comparisons, footage from the film is synced up with footage of Queen's actual Live Aid performance. Malek's physical performance copies Mercury's almost to the second, with gestures and movement replicating what exists in the original. In terms of cinematic style, while the performance matches the existing one in the archival footage, a wider variety of coverage and available shot choices, such as close-ups on the other band members, or a close-up on "Freddie's" hands on the piano with his face reflected in the instrument's surface enables this mimetic re-creation of actuality to be injected with flourishes of cinematic style that speak to the factually altered understanding of the character the film presents. While the resemblance of the re-creation to the actual attempts to "vouch" for the accuracy of the rest of the film—a question of "If this looks so much like the real thing, then surely everything in the film must have an element of truth to it?"—how facts are arranged in order to construct characters can alter the way the re-creation of actual events is read in the context of the film.

Because biopics do not exist in a vacuum and contribute to the way we understand their subjects as cultural figures, there can be big-picture effects from how life narratives are transformed on their way to the screen. The authentication of mimetic accuracy can not only create a plausible foundation upon which some artistic license is taken in a film but can lend credibility to the truth claims that the biopic makes. After all, the entirety of a film based on a true story is marketed as "Based on a True Story": there is no deliberate distinction within the text of what is based on verifiable fact, what is based on rumor, or what is entirely invented. The varying sizes of kernels of truth are all granted equal status throughout a biopic, which can have ramifications for the ongoing re-evaluation and re-interpretation of a public figure's star image as films about those individuals become part of that star image. One example of how the film's factual inaccuracies transformed the cultural meanings of Freddie Mercury as a queer icon comes from *Vox* columnist Aja Romano (2019). Romano argues that in the film, Freddie's relationship with his former partner Mary Austin (Lucy Boynton) is foregrounded, with his queerness relegated to tropes of the extravagant, the isolated, and the predatory. When the film changes the timeline to include Freddie's HIV diagnosis before the Live Aid concert, and to break Queen up in order to bring them back together for Live Aid, the performance is recontextualized to cast Freddie as a kind of martyr: he has sacrificed his potential life in a stable, heteronormative existence outside of the band for the good of the music, much of the value of which comes from his authentic, queer self. Here, through the factual inaccuracies present in the narrative adaptation of a life to the form of the biopic, more than simply creating emotional stakes for the film's climax, the cultural meaning of Freddie Mercury himself is transformed as his public image is subject to recurrent cinematic tropes surrounding queer representation—the influence of already lived lives and how they are presented on screen through not only tropes of queer representation, but the representation of artists and musicians, making their mark on how Freddie becomes a screen character.

With a foundation in plausibility, the representational mode of docudrama that grounds a fictionalized story in factuality can work to render its creative decisions in bringing the private lives of public figures to the screen as believable. How the various transmedia sources of a celebrity public image can be extrapolated into a believable back-stage self of a docucharacter will be considered as the next feature of what docucharacters in the biopic—and, by extension, other screen media forms—are able to do to the celebrities upon which they are based.

2

Creating the Private

It is a matter of public record that multiple lawsuits were brought against Facebook CEO Mark Zuckerberg in relation to the contested foundational years of the social media giant. This is the kind of public record and known fact that is re-created and re-presented in films and television shows based on true stories in order to anchor them to the actuality they represent, and to construct a plausible possible version of the world as we know it. What is not part of the public record, however, are the inner motivations of the parties concerned and the finer details of moments beyond what the deposition transcripts reflect. The core of what happened, why it happened, how it happened, and the emotional experience of those involved are not part of the public record. These things are perhaps, ultimately, unknowable, given the ambiguous and contradictory nature of the inner self and the conflicting stories of the parties involved when billions of dollars are at stake. However, through the adaptation of the major players of these lawsuits in *The Social Network*, the known is re-presented in a way that shows us the possibilities of the unknown and the unknowable, with explanations suggested for why things are the way they are. This is how the adaptation of a real person to a character moves beyond the simple re-creation of what is publicly known, to the creative augmentation of replicated history with the processes of fleshing out a character, and creating a plausible version of an unknown private self. This chapter will look at *The Social Network* to consider how a private self is created for a public figure such as Mark Zuckerberg who, at the time of the film's release, did not have a highly visible public self-performance, and whose public image has been indelibly shaped by the private self created for him by his docucharacterization on screen. *The Social Network* uses the docucharacterization of Mark Zuckerberg to make a statement about what his story can say about our culture at large, using an imagined version of his private self and speculated motivations to render on film a portrait of our shifting information economy.

In making such a statement it is the work of the biopic, and, as this book investigates, the creation of a docucharacter in any screen form, to supplement the known with a plausible version of the unknown. One example of this direct juxtaposition of public and private in *The Social Network* is the sequence of flashbacks during Eduardo Saverin's (Andrew Garfield) testimony about his and Mark Zuckerberg's (Jesse Eisenberg) first meeting with Sean Parker (Justin Timberlake). We see the dramatized interpretation of Eduardo's testimony in the deposition, the public moment, verifiable through recorded information. Intercut with Eduardo's testimony are his flashbacks to their first meeting with Sean. Through the focus on Eduardo's reactions throughout the dinner montage and the narration from his testimony, we get the sense of Eduardo's dislike for Sean, his skepticism of Sean's ability to know what's right for Facebook, and his perception that Mark was completely enchanted by Sean. The scene gives us access to Eduardo's subjective experience of the memory, an emotionally colored view of the events of public record. There is the suggestion of explanation for Eduardo's side of the story, as he sees it. In the aftermath of betrayal, he sees Sean as having taken Mark away from him and their partnership in Facebook: the deciding factor in influencing his friend to cut him out of the business completely. These are the unknowables of the real Eduardo Saverin, the things that can only be speculated upon, drawn from the framework of factual information that is used in crafting the film's adaptation of its characters and their lives.

The Social Network serves as a useful case study in the creation of the private selves of public figures, with its deployment of character subjectivity in the form of multiple points of view of events. Additionally, the film has a significant online fan presence, allowing for a direct consideration in the latter part of this book, where we move beyond the biopic, of how mainstream biopics and real person fan fiction similarly adapt real people to characters in their respective forms. *The Social Network* as a case study also allows for the consideration of the ways in which a public figure with a comparatively limited visible public presence, and who did not deliberately seek fame as an actor, musician, or even a politician would, is open to a broader degree of interpretation in its dramatization. This interpretation, however, remains built on a foundation of factuality to argue for the interpretation as a plausible portrait of its subject. The plausibility of the characterization contributes to how the general public has largely gotten to know these public figures through the lens of their dramatized versions.

As discussed in the previous chapter, in his book *Bio/Pics*, George F. Custen compares the biopic character to a Frankenstein's monster comprised of "bits of previous incarnations of already-lived lives," not only the life of its subject but public lives that have been dramatized before it (1992: 111). It is not only the fragments of textual lives that comprise the biopic character, however, nor are pieces of other lives the only intertextual fragments that contribute to the overall make-up of a biopic character. As the contemporary biopic has progressively become a director's genre with films often helmed by high-profile auteurs (Bingham 2010: 18), characterizations are shaped by the lives of their creators, both that of their directors and other key collaborators such as actors and writers. Textual elements of genre and narrative construction provide the means of crafting the character. Within the parameters of the contemporary Hollywood biopic narrative, the character's authors use intertextual fragments of the source public persona to shape the private self behind the public image. In order to examine *The Social Network* as a specific case study, I will first consider Dennis Bingham's (2010) categorization of the neoclassical biopic and the ways this intertextual mash-up of various past stages of the biopic's generic evolution influences the creation of a private self for a public figure.

Neoclassical Biopic and the Private Self

Bingham's *Whose Lives Are They Anyway* (2010) features the examination of a film that is not strictly a biopic, but, as Bingham argues, has nonetheless had significant influence on the development of the contemporary biopic. *Citizen Kane* (1941) features a fictional protagonist that is popularly understood as based on a real public figure: newspaper magnate William Randolph Hearst. In this way, it does not fit with the trait Custen identifies as a central commonality among all biopics, that the film is "minimally composed of the life, or the portion of a life, of a real person whose real name is used" (1992: 6). However, the influence of *Citizen Kane* on contemporary biopics such as *The Social Network* lies in its use of an investigatory device that enables its subject to be reconstructed by the memories of multiple characters with differing points of view.

In defining his category of the post-2000 neoclassical biopic, Bingham cites *Citizen Kane* in conjunction with Custen's work on the subjects of classical Hollywood biopics. Custen, drawing on the work of Leo Lowenthal on magazine biographies in the early-to-mid twentieth century, frames his examination of biopic subjects in Lowenthal's terms of "idols of production"— military leaders, statesmen, inventors—and "idols of consumption"—actors, musicians, entertainers. Custen writes that Lowenthal argues that the shift in focus from biographies of the idols of production to the idols of consumption indicates a shift in American values, from "community" to "consumerism," an indication of the beginnings of our mass consumer culture (Custen 1992: 32–3). Custen identifies a similar shift in biographical subjects in his study of Hollywood studio era biopics, and Bingham argues the idol of production film has undergone a contemporary resurgence. The neoclassical idol of production biopic, Bingham writes, is reinvented "with a warts-and-all or *Citizen Kane*-like investigatory tinge" as opposed to its largely celebratory form in the classical era (2010: 6). Bingham cites *The Aviator* (2004) and *Kinsey* (2004) as two examples of such films, and, in later published writing, includes *The Social Network* as another example of the neoclassical biopic (Bingham 2013: 251). In order to consider how the tenets of the neoclassical category shape characterization, I will elaborate on how *The Social Network* fits in this category by looking at it in conjunction with Bingham's first two examples of *The Aviator* and *Kinsey*.

Like *Citizen Kane*'s biography-through-investigation that attempts to uncover the "real" Kane through the mystery of his last word, "Rosebud," both *Kinsey* and *The Social Network* use investigatory devices that attempt to uncover the truth of their subjects. As in *Citizen Kane*, this truth often comes from the subjective point of view of the investigation's sources. In *Kinsey*, it is the recurring sequences of Alfred Kinsey (Liam Neeson) acting as a practice subject for his research assistants as they are trained in conducting sexual history interviews. These interviews frequently lead into flashbacks narrated by Kinsey's responses. In *The Social Network*, subjective truths are uncovered through legal depositions that invite the multiple viewpoints of its conflicting characters. The influence of the melodramatic warts-and-all mode is also a common thread among these films. In *Kinsey*, melodrama manifests in the depiction of the damage Kinsey's work causes in his personal relationships with his wife, children, and staff; in *The Aviator* through the foregrounding of Howard Hughes' mental illness and scandalous relationships with famous women; and in *The Social Network* through the depiction of the destruction of Mark's personal relationships with Eduardo and Erica, key characters in his small circle of college friends.

The investigatory or warts-and-all skew of the early twenty-first-century idol of production biopic in films like *The Aviator, Kinsey*, and *The Social Network* speaks to contemporary practices of consuming the lives of the famous. Screen narratives of idols of production are currently shaped by the prevalent celebrity discourses of gossip and scandal and the search for who the celebrity "really" is in the contemporary culture of democratized celebrity. Any known person can potentially be treated as a celebrity, subject to media inquiry and gossip about their private life, and how the individual became famous is irrelevant. Graeme Turner writes that gossip functions in "integrating the celebrity and the stories about them into one's everyday life" (2004: 107). In a cultural context where all types of celebrities are treated similarly, regardless of how they achieved their fame or what it is that they are known for, even the once celebrated "great men" of history—or, in the case of *The Social Network*, the contemporary moment—can be brought down to the level of the everyday through the dramatized exposure of their private lives. To return to Lowenthal's terms, the idol of production figures that were once emblematic of community values are now subject to the prevailing consumer culture of the idols of consumption. Additionally, the media discourse of celebrity "encourages us to think in terms of 'really'—what is [the star] 'really' like?" (Dyer 1987: 2). As scandal is taken as a marker of authenticity, a sign to the "really" of the celebrity (Desjardins 2004: 35), the investigatory biopic structure that uncovers and presents what is perceived as the authentic truth in the form of scandal satisfies both of these dominant elements of contemporary celebrity discourse. It is the appearance of bringing the private self into the realm of the public: a strategy seen in the previous chapter through the discussion of the re-created events of the O.J. Simpson trial in *The People v. O.J. Simpson* and the narrative weight of Freddie Mercury's backstory in the recontextualized Live Aid sequence of *Bohemian Rhapsody*. The warts-and-all investigatory mode that Bingham articulates acts as a narrative frame in which to merge public and private, where secrets or hidden selves can no longer be contained to backstage space and are brought into the front stage frame for public consumption. The investigation, the basis of which largely stems from known fact, is a narrative device that uncovers the unknown in the form of a speculated private self of the character.

In addition to textual characteristics such as the investigatory narrative device and the exposure of the "true" self through a warts-and-all or scandalous approach to characterization, the neoclassical biopic can integrate the textual/extra-textual influence of the auteur. In addition to integrating influences from the stages of the biopic that reflect classical form, critical investigation, and warts-and-all melodrama, *The Social Network* marks itself as part of the history of biopic transitioning from a producer's genre to an auteur director's genre. The film is written by Aaron Sorkin and directed by David Fincher, and both bring reputations of distinct author functions to the work. In *How Did They Ever Make a Movie of Facebook?* (2011), the making-of documentary that accompanies the initial DVD release of *The Social Network*, Sorkin and Fincher, along with principal actors Eisenberg, Garfield, and Timberlake, are seen deconstructing the script page by page during the rehearsal process. Writer, director, and actor are all depicted as engaging in collaborative authorship as they discuss the pertinent traits and motivations of the characters, engage in debate and argue for their own views on how the characters can be read, performed, and eventually interpreted by the audience.

Sarah J. Heidt (2009) notes in writing on director Julian Schnabel's personal investment in his adaptation of *The Diving Bell and the Butterfly* (2007) that in portraying real people on screen there is the potential "of *mis*representation in an adapted memoir, of partialities that might lead to a subject's being remade in a recollector's or creator's own image" (Heidt 2009: 144, emphasis in original). While the degree of authorial appropriation in *The Social Network* may not be to the same degree that Heidt writes of in Schnabel's appropriation of another's memoir in telling a story that is personal to him, the influence of the filmmakers' personal connection to the material is evident in the way they speak about the characters extra-textually. In interviews and film commentaries, Sorkin, Fincher, and Eisenberg all speak of finding their way of relating to Mark as a character (and, subsequently, Zuckerberg as a person) by viewing him as a creative artist. Even within this similar approach, there can be conflict. Sorkin views Mark through the lens of the writer as someone with a creation that others attempt to take credit for (Sony Pictures 27). Conversely, Fincher views Mark through his experiences as a director, as someone with an idea who needs to convince the right people, rather than Sorkin's understanding of creation as a solitary effort (Sony Pictures 2010: 21). As *How Did They Ever Make a Movie of Facebook?* shows, Sorkin and Fincher agree that their conflicting points of view on the character are forged by their personal connections to the material, and the film's structuring investigative device that allows for multiple points of view on Mark/Zuckerberg can contain these divergent interpretations.

Bingham's (2010) study of the biopic as a genre charts the development of a number of evolutionary stages, all of which, he argues, have a tangible influence on the contemporary era of the neoclassical biopic. What is largely left unaddressed in Bingham's genre study, however, is what the consequences are of this intertextual mash-up of genre stages for how biopic subjects are constructed as cinematic characters. I argue that through the integration of conventions from particular stages of the biopic's evolution, *The Social Network* places its characters on narrative trajectories guided by the conventions of classical Hollywood biopic lives, but presented in a way that permits a subjective construction of the character. As a result, the character is posited as a possible, plausible interpretation of the public figure, rather than a definitive characterization that claims to be who they really are. This merging of classical Hollywood narrative tropes with contemporary subjective character construction is representative of the way that the merging of public and private in biopic character is an interpretive process. Multiple possible versions of a public persona as character exist, and how they are conjured into being depends on who is doing the adaptive and interpretive work of constructing the character. Before beginning an in-depth consideration of how these elements of the neoclassical biopic work to construct Mark Zuckerberg as a character, it is first necessary to consider what, exactly, the public image is that is being re-created: the source text that serves as the foundation of the created private self of the character. Therefore, I now move on to a consideration of the figure of the celebrity CEO and the public persona of Mark Zuckerberg in particular.

Mark Zuckerberg as a Public Source Text

In viewing Zuckerberg as a celebrity text ripe for adaptation, it is necessary to consider what the figure of the celebrity CEO means for how his public image and its popularly circulating narratives are constructed. Eric Guthey, Timothy Clark, and Brad Jackson argue that, like celebrities from the entertainment arena, the business celebrity can act as "a forum… for concerns and debates about what it means to be an individual in a complex, modern society" (2009: 5). As Craig Batty (2014) argues, characters are vital for the way we understand media narratives, and, subsequently, Guthey, Clark, and Jackson's assessment of the celebrity CEO demonstrates how celebrity personas can function as media characters without being purposefully crafted as characters in drama. Through their roles as prominent figures in the business world, celebrity CEOs "function both to highlight and to smooth over some of the key cultural and ideological tensions generated by the dominance of business institutions in contemporary society" (Guthey, Clark, and Jackson 2009: 4). The public persona of the CEO itself acts as a character in media narratives, a means for understanding cultural concerns about topics such as technological innovation, globalization, and income inequality. In the specific case of Zuckerberg, rather than acting as a metonym for the dominance of corporate institutions in general, he functions as a metonymic representation of Facebook specifically and the concerns it raises over everyday aspects of privacy, connectivity, and communication.

The work of Jo Littler (2007) is useful for a consideration of what the relationship between Zuckerberg and his company does for understanding Zuckerberg as a persona. Littler writes that the function of a celebrity CEO is to act as the individual narrative of the company brand, embodying the values and aesthetic of the company (2007: 230). In acting as the face of the company, the celebrity CEO gives consumers and potential stockholders an individual to attach the brand to (Littler 2007: 235). One example Littler cites is Richard Branson, whose persona as "young and casual" corresponds with the Virgin brand, and the marketing of these qualities as "revolutionary" through the way Branson embodies them (2007: 237). This conflation of persona and brand functions in the same way an actor or athlete endorsing a product gives consumers a known individual to attach to and associate with a particular brand of fragrance or sneakers. In the case of the celebrity CEO, however, the corporate brand they are endorsing is their own. The company is their work and what brought them to the attention of the public, therefore furthering the conflation of corporate brand with celebrity image. The company image and the celebrity image thus work to shape each other.

In the case of Zuckerberg, there is both conflation and contradiction between his public persona and Facebook as a brand. Zuckerberg has been described as "a wary and private person" who rarely speaks to the press and reluctantly speaks in public (Vargas 2010), at odds with the way Facebook encourages and in some cases requires its users to openly share personal information. A *60 Minutes* interview with Zuckerberg in 2008 shows him as somewhat stiff, awkward, and evasive in his presentation. He is surrounded, however, by an anti-establishment aesthetic of youth and openness. There is significant focus on the graffiti-decorated Facebook offices, Zuckerberg's casual clothing, and the fact that he works from a non-descript desk among the company's other software engineers. A second *60 Minutes* profile on Zuckerberg aired in 2010, coinciding with the release of *The Social Network* and the increased interest in uncovering the "real" Mark Zuckerberg prompted by the film. This profile is clear to point out Zuckerberg's changed self-performance, noting that he is more at ease and confident in front of the camera. While Zuckerberg's media presentation skills in the time between the two *60 Minutes* profiles may have evolved, the elements connecting Zuckerberg's identity to the Facebook brand identity have not changed. Although the new, larger Facebook office eschews the graffiti aesthetic of the previous one, the word "hack" is prominently painted on one wall, and Zuckerberg still works from a desk among other staffers in the open-plan office, wearing jeans, a t-shirt, and sandals. The consistent element between these two profiles is the conflation of Facebook's brand identity with Zuckerberg's public image. Both paint Zuckerberg as the young, anti-establishment, practical, new breed of tech billionaire, and thus paint Zuckerberg and Facebook at the forefront of the Silicon Valley tech revolution.

At the time of *The Social Network*'s production, little had been seen of Zuckerberg's self-performance in popular media beyond the 2008 *60 Minutes* profile, largely allowing the Facebook brand and its success to speak louder than its CEO. This lack of a highly visible Zuckerberg public self-performance is cited as one reason *The Social Network* was able to take such a degree of creative interpretation of Zuckerberg in creating the character of Mark. As *New York* magazine journalist Mark Harris notes of Zuckerberg's largely absent and impersonal public self-performance and its appropriation to cinematic dramatization, "[o]ne of the problems with so self-consciously presenting yourself as a blank slate is that you invite others to draw all over you" (2010: 3). I would argue that Zuckerberg is not an entirely blank slate, as elements of his backstory do exist on the public record, however minimal the finer details of his embodied self-performance may be. We know that Zuckerberg's origins are as an upper-middle class Jewish kid from the New York suburbs who made his way to Silicon Valley via the Harvard dorm room where he created a social network that became unimaginably successful. His lack of highly visible self-performed media presence (*c.* 2010) is notable, however, for the way the gaps in the story invite others to fill in the blanks. There is room on the slate to flesh out the public persona with assumptions based on narrative archetypes and cultural stereotypes that can be extrapolated into the fictionalized context of the biopic and accepted by the audience as plausible.

Those drawing over the spaces in Zuckerberg's blank slate do not exactly have an infinite palette of colors to use if what they paint is to seem like a plausible extension of Zuckerberg's public persona. Third parties extrapolating and interpreting Mark Zuckerberg as a celebrity text, such as those writing about him in a non-fictional context, the filmmakers of *The Social Network*, and the general public who are the potential audience of both, bring their own assumptions and expectations based on existing knowledge of the source. If we regard Zuckerberg's public image as a text, then those seeking to fill in the blanks of his minimal self-performance "use cultural models and stereotypes to 'fill out' the information provided by the text" (Smith 1995: 19) to compose a more fully realized character. For a simplified example, it is not such a stretch for *The Social Network* and its audience to approach the character of a nineteen-year-old Harvard student who builds a social networking platform from his dorm room with assumptions based on narrative archetypes of the "nerd." From "nerd," the assumptions about the archetype extend to character traits like "socially awkward" and "has trouble getting girls."

These assumptions based on pre-existing notions of character form the basis of Murray Smith's "recognition" stage in his theory of how we engage with screen characters. In the fiction film, the spectator uses what information is provided in the text upon the introduction of a character to "produce hypothetically fuller versions of the character than the text, taken as an object, actually puts before us" (1995: 120–1). In the biopic, this initial introduction to the character often takes place before the spectator even enters the cinema, as they bring any pre-existing knowledge they have of the public figure to the film. Smith's theory of this process of character recognition could be likened to Erving Goffman's description of the understanding of another individual's self-presentation in everyday socialization, where one must rely on the given external cues of others to interpret the possible reality of the situation ([1959] 1997: 21). For example, if a Harvard administrative board member is confronted with a student who is rude and sarcastic to the members of the board (as depicted in the film), the administrator could process the external cues of the student's gesture, expression, and appearance to make assumptions about the cause of their rudeness. A student dressed in a hoodie and shorts, who fidgets, and whose face is blank and sentences clipped may be assumed to not care about the board's authority because the student thinks he is smarter than them. Whether that is true or not, the administrator can never know, but the assumption guides their understanding of the situation and how they behave in return. In both theories, we take the information that is initially presented to us and process it in ways that extrapolate possibilities from fact in order to more fully understand that fact in the moment, regardless of whether those possibilities turn out to be actualities. As I will explore later in this chapter, *The Social Network* builds on the assumed traits of Zuckerberg's public persona to construct much of the core of Mark's motivation as a character. If a contradictory, highly visible media image existed of Zuckerberg as, for example, an easy-going, popular party guy, the film's claim of the driven, friendless, lonely billionaire would not be accepted as a plausible private self that corresponds with the known public persona. The relative lack of the highly visible media image allows greater space for the audience familiar with what exists of the public image to find plausibility in the creative interpretation of what is known. This is in contrast to a film like *Bohemian Rhapsody* which, as discussed in the previous chapter, has a dual audience of both dedicated fans of Queen well versed in the band's history who are resistant to factual inaccuracies, and a less-informed audience that may be more willing to accept the mimetic re-creation of a known public image as plausible.

As Zuckerberg's public media image lacks a highly visible self-performance, much of what constitutes this image is made up of what others have written and said about him and his actions as the figurehead of the Facebook brand. While Zuckerberg may embody some elements of the Facebook brand and tech billionaire ethos, such as the casual office environment he inhabits, there are contradictions between Zuckerberg and his social network that are deeply embedded in his public image. Others write about Zuckerberg as a private person, and he confirms that image through the lack of highly visible self-performance. Facebook, on the other hand, is built on its users engaging in public self-performance and freely sharing their personal data. Particularly at the time of *The Social Network*'s release in 2010, much of the circulating public narrative of Zuckerberg as a celebrity text stemmed from changes in Facebook functionality and user backlash to those changes. In May 2010, five months before the film's initial release, a Quit Facebook Day campaign circulated in reaction to further changes in the site's privacy policy. Another change to the privacy policy triggered a campaign for a coordinated boycott of Facebook on June 6, 2010 (Smith 2010). These changes made privacy settings overly complicated and set many privacy options to public by default. Problems arose from users posting sensitive information—such as complaints about their boss, boasts about calling in sick to take the day off, and admissions of cheating on their spouse—without knowing that their posts were available to public view (Boggan 2010). Prior to 2010, Facebook had other issues with maintaining the privacy of its users, including not giving users control over who could see their activity following the introduction of the news feed feature in 2006; the Beacon ad system that tracked user activity and purchases on partner websites in 2007; and a formal complaint filed against Facebook with the US Federal Trade Commission by the Electronic Privacy Information Center in 2009 after the removal of some privacy settings and a default of public to others (Schwartz 2012). As Daniel Schwartz notes, Zuckerberg's response to many of these situations was to admit Facebook's mistake, make changes to satisfy users, and then make similar mistakes months later. Zuckerberg's and Facebook's normalizing of, and persistence with, this kind of information sharing early in Facebook's development may be a contributing factor to the acceptance of similar practices now. An ad system like Beacon, while controversial in 2007, has become the norm a decade later with Facebook and other platforms such as Google basing their revenue model around collecting data on user searches, interaction with content, and purchases to customize advertising. Likewise, Facebook's loose treatment of user data with issues such as the 2018 Cambridge Analytica scandal has persisted and reinforced this perception of Zuckerberg's contradictions when it comes to his own privacy and the privacy of his platform's userbase.

The disparity between Zuckerberg's behavior regarding his own privacy and the privacy of his company's users is an example of something in his public image that has undergone extrapolation and interpretation in the process of creating a private self for Mark Zuckerberg, the screen character. The conflict between public action and the behavior of the inner self as a personality trait is echoed in *The Social Network*'s Mark. He is the college student who has trouble socializing yet creates a tool with the initial purpose of connecting and cementing the social circles of college students. Due to Zuckerberg's lack of a publicly performed media self, it would not be unreasonable to assume that the average viewer of *The Social Network* comes to the film with much of their pre-existing knowledge of the story stemming from their use of Facebook. Any controversies they may know about are the ones that affect them the most: the privacy concerns, rather than the legal battles over Facebook's contested creation. The recognition of existing ironies and contradictions in Zuckerberg's media image could feasibly make the audience more receptive to a Mark character whose story is also based on ironic contradictions, albeit contradictions with a different premise that gives a new spin to a known story. Mark's personality contradictions in the film perhaps offer an origin story for the real Zuckerberg's contradictions between his privacy and that of his users, and the way these narratives play out in the media and wider public sphere.

With these ideas of Zuckerberg's public image, largely constructed by others and represented by Facebook as a stand-in for his own embodied self-performance established, I now move on to examining how the process of extrapolation and interpretation makes visible the character of Mark's private self: a version of a private self created for the purposes of the biopic narrative. By considering the source text of Zuckerberg in conjunction with the framework of the neoclassical biopic as a mode of storytelling, I examine why and how creating a version of the private self is necessary in order to render a public figure as a screen character in the contemporary Hollywood biopic.

Motivating Mark: Creating the Screen Character

I return to Bingham's (2010) neoclassical biopic category and the various stages of the genre's evolution that comprise the category's influences. A dominant trope of the classical-era biopic that Custen (1992) identifies which endures in contemporary biopic and is a vital component in shaping the private self from a public persona is the personalized motivation. In *The Social Network*, character motivations are crafted from classical Hollywood tropes, with these motivations, in turn, driving narrative events and character behavior, such as why Mark was driven to create Facebook and how he behaved when met with its success. Custen draws on archival research of production documents related to many of his Hollywood studio era sample of films to argue that studio heads, particularly Twentieth Century Fox's Darryl F. Zanuck, played a significant role in shaping the conventions of the classical Hollywood biopic. One convention Custen credits Zanuck with enforcing in Fox biopics is the "personalizing of history." According to Custen, Zanuck insisted that the biopic subject "had to have a clear motivation for the decisions that brought him or her greatness. Actions had to be communicated to the audience in a telegraphic scene or two which served as an explanation of the forces that drove the person to achieve his or her unusual destiny" (Custen 1992: 18–19). Through this clear communication of the biopic character/subject's motivation for greatness, the audience could make a personal connection with the screen version of the famous subject and provide an understandable hook on which the audience could hang their sympathies. In line with Batty's (2014) argument about how characters guide audiences in making sense of media, this purposeful construction of the biopic character as someone the audience can readily understand aids in the process of following the film's explanation of the importance of the person, their time, and place. On the origins of this kind of character construction in the biopic, Custen points out that the means of personalizing the biopic subject were guided by Zanuck's perceptions of what the audience would accept as "understandable" motivation for unique achievement. Therefore, by constructing the famous subject's life as something explainable and recognizable through the depiction of their home life and romantic and familial relationships in addition to celebrating their unique achievements, biopic lives were presented as greatness and fame arising from the circumstances of normalcy (Custen 1992: 19).

In the case of *The Social Network*'s depiction of Mark Zuckerberg, it is important for several reasons that the film draws upon these classical conventions. Mark is portrayed as having difficulty with emotional expression, often leading to an aloof and condescending treatment of others. As I will discuss, much of Mark's motivation in the film stems from trying to win back his girlfriend, Erica (Rooney Mara). The fact that Mark is battling against his own personality and trying to compensate for his difficulty with relationships through his talents as a hacker and programmer sets up a sympathetic struggle that can potentially endear the character to the audience despite his lack of emotional expression. The motivation for Mark's achievement is crafted from classical cinematic tropes that position him as an outcast underdog figure, creating possibilities for the audience to become invested in Mark's success. We as an audience know that Mark will succeed in his business venture—we are, after all, at the very least aware of Facebook's existence in our world—but his success on a personal level, his struggles with his own personality and the problems he has with relationships, remain the unknown story of the private self that we need to discover through the film. The audience has an opportunity to become invested in and sympathetic toward a character who may otherwise present as unlikeable.

In the terminology of Murray Smith's structure of sympathy, *The Social Network* creates an "alliance" with Mark by granting the audience both "spatio-temporal attachment," where the audience witnesses Mark's actions and reactions, and "subjective access," where the audience has direct access to Mark's interiority through techniques such as voice over or dream sequence, or indirect access to his interiority through the emotional tone of the film (Smith 1995: 142). The film also grants the audience a similar alliance with other characters, creating differing understandings of Mark and his actions. For example, scenes focused on Cameron and Tyler Winklevoss (Armie Hammer), and Divya Narendra (Max Minghella), where they speak about Mark as having deliberately stolen their idea for a Harvard social network, introduce a different perspective of Mark as calculating, dishonest, and deliberately manipulative, rather than the solitary creative genius that may be Mark's image of himself. Smith argues, however, that alliance with a character does not automatically create "allegiance" (1995: 222). Allegiance is based on the audience's affective response, such as sympathy, empathy, or judgment, to the character. Mark's classical personalized motivations are an attempt to create a positive response with that allegiance, to explain the actions that lead to his fame and success in ways that are familiar to the audience from their past exposure to cinema. As I will discuss in detail in a moment, Erica is the girl Mark is working to win back, a basic story premise that, in the hands of another genre, could make for a classic romantic comedy. This familiarity and easy recognition can potentially evoke sympathetic allegiance in the reception of Mark's often morally ambiguous behavior throughout the course of the conflicting points of view of the film's characters.

To illustrate the possibilities of sympathetic audience response to Mark, I draw on the example of the conflict between Mark and the Winklevoss twins. It can be a satisfying experience for the audience to become invested in Mark's underdog success over the Winklevosses throughout the film. That the spectator has been aligned with Mark up until the point of the introduction to Cameron and Tyler serves to highlight the differences between Mark and the twins. Once the spectator has been aligned with one character, as Smith writes, "the recognition of any new character may be subject to the effect of mediation produced by the alignment" (1995: 144). Thus, Mark's self-perceived inferiority in comparison to men like Cameron and Tyler (as established in the opening scene, which I will discuss in detail further on in this chapter) is projected onto our recognition of them. The twins, with their classic all-American athletic looks, blond hair, and chiseled jaws (as embodied by Armie Hammer, himself a member of old money establishment thanks to his namesake great-grandfather, petroleum magnate Armand Hammer), represent the best kind of self-proclaimed "gentlemen of Harvard." Mark, on the other hand, is the anti-authoritarian rebel, his family history absent from the film's story, a seemingly self-created man at the age of nineteen who rejects the Harvard establishment, first through his disrespect for its systems—technical, security, academic, and disciplinary—then by literal rejection as he drops out to pursue Facebook's success. *Revenge of the Nerds* (1984) is often invoked in pun headlines about both Facebook and *The Social Network* for a good reason. Here Mark is the typically downtrodden, rejected nerd who ends up controlling the prized idea despite the entitled and privileged Winklevosses' best attempts to take it from him.

The provision of a personalized motivation for Mark's success provides an emotional hook that allows the audience to become invested in his journey. Additionally, it allows the audience to forge a connection with or understanding of a version of a public figure whose real-world counterpart does not have a similar kind of personalized presence. Jonathan Bignell (2010) writes that the basis for making meaning from a screen character based on a public figure is to draw on the audience's existing knowledge of the subject's media image. Films that can rely more heavily on re-creating a recognizable facsimile of the public image (such as those discussed in Chapter 1) use the audience's prior knowledge and opinions of the public figure in conjunction with the affective codes of fictional drama in the depiction of the subject's private self to foster an emotional investment in the biopic character (Bignell 2010: 59). With *The Social Network*, however, the film's central character, despite having created what is arguably one of the most significant media tools of the twenty-first century so far, at the time of the film's production and initial release comparatively lacked this immediately recognizable self-performance with which audiences can connect. Zuckerberg is, as previously noted, vulnerable to creative interpretation of what is known in order to depict the unknown of his private self and driving motivations. Therefore, the personalized motivation created by classical biopic tropes shapes how this creative interpretation manifests on screen.

In *The Social Network*, much of the creative interpretation of Mark's motivations is encapsulated by a character who does not have a real-world counterpart. This character is Erica Albright, Mark's girlfriend whom we meet, along with Mark, in the film's opening scene. The Mark first introduced in *The Social Network* is the pre-Facebook Mark who is wholly unknown to the average viewer, rendering the audience's lack of immediate recognition of the public figure in the screen character less of a vital component in comprehending the character. Mark's lines of personalized motivation that eventually lead to public recognition, as well as the character traits of his social and emotional shortcomings, are established immediately in this opening scene. The film begins with Mark and Erica sitting across from each other at a table in a crowded student bar, engaged in a conversation that the audience is dropped into even before the Columbia Pictures logo has begun to fade from the screen. Their rapid-fire exchange pursues numerous different conversational threads that overlap and change quickly.

Demonstrating the influence of the biopic-as-auteur-genre developmental stage in the neoclassical biopic, the pace, structure, and verbosity of the dialogue are a signature of Aaron Sorkin's writing that makes no pretense to naturalism. Therefore, from the very beginning, the audience is introduced to these characters as obviously written characters. They do not speak the way real people do, let alone the way real nineteen-year-olds do. It signals to the audience that these people are characters, these are dramatized events, and the sheer written-ness of the characters attempts to distance Mark from Zuckerberg as a creatively interpreted version. The content of the dialogue introduces one of Mark's lines of motivation: the desire to distinguish himself from the already distinguished Harvard herd, to gain the acceptance of the elite networks of the Harvard final clubs. Erica's question of which club would be the easiest for Mark to get into, and Mark's offended reaction that she would ask which is the easiest and not the best demonstrates both Mark's high personal standards as well as the expected difficulty he would face in being accepted to a final club. He lacks any of the traditionally acceptable skills to help him distinguish himself at Harvard—rowing crew, singing in an acapella group—and does not fit the classic profile of the final club member as the next generation of the WASP old money establishment.

The way Mark and Erica's conversation unfolds introduces the audience to many of Mark's core character traits. Erica's reactions to Mark offer an understanding of what he is like as a person. Erica's echoing of Mark's words and doubling back on topics shows that despite her obvious intelligence, Erica is unable to keep up with Mark's train of thought, revisiting topics and ideas that Mark has already abandoned. The intelligence of the dialogue becomes a character trait of Mark's. It flatters the audience member who can keep up and, through Erica, offers a warning to those who cannot. Sorkin consciously rejects any attempt to write naturalistic dialogue for young characters, and instead writes them the way he usually writes his (typically middle-aged) characters (Sony Pictures 2010: 25). In doing so, Sorkin creates a thematic parallel between the opening dialogue and the film as a whole: old versus new, young versus old, who gets ahead and who ends up being left behind. In this scene, the immediate introduction of these elements of characterization and specifically highlighted character traits give the audience a feel for what the film is about thematically.

Throughout the opening scene, Erica implies that her frustration with Mark is the norm when carrying on a conversation with him, such as when Mark tries to stop her from leaving and she snaps in frustration that the conversation "is exhausting. Dating you is like dating a Stairmaster." This exchange establishes that Mark's traits demonstrated by the conversation—such as his intelligence, by being several steps ahead of Erica, and his impatience and condescension when she fails to keep up with him—are everyday aspects of his personality. Their unequal positions in the exchange, as well as Mark's projected sense of superiority at their unequal positions, cause the conversation to devolve into Erica ending the relationship. At this point, she acts as a foreshadowing of both

Mark's future success ("You are probably going to be a very successful computer person"), and to put a name to the lack of social skills that are depicted as being another of Mark's motivations in the creation of Facebook ("You're going to go through life thinking that girls don't like you because you're a nerd... that won't be true. It will be because you're an asshole"). After she leaves Mark, she becomes a cinematic trope, "the girl that got away," and a catalyst for Mark's subsequent actions that lead to the creation of Facebook. Mark's major lines of motivation as established by this opening scene could be labeled as two well-trodden Hollywood cinematic tropes: the triumph of the underdog and winning back the girl. By giving Mark motivations that the audience will at the very least recognize, if not sympathize with, his future actions are explained in cinematic terms. Cinema constructs the private person that drives the public persona: Zuckerberg has become a character.

Erica's role as the embodiment of a classical winning-back-the-girl trope is cemented by her further appearances later in the film. Erica first reappears when Mark sees her in a restaurant after TheFacebook (as the earliest incarnation of the platform was named) has become successful on the Harvard campus. He approaches her with an attempt to reconcile, but Erica dismissively rejects him. Mark's immediate reaction is to begin expanding TheFacebook to other Ivy League colleges and publicizing it at Boston University, where Erica is (as Mark derisively notes in the opening scene) a student. Erica's final appearance comes in the closing moments of the film. Mark sits alone in a deposition room after being informed his lawyers are going to settle the lawsuit with Eduardo. He looks up Erica on Facebook, and, finding her profile listed, sends her a friend request. Under title cards that proclaim both the screen's and the real world's Mark Zuckerberg to be the world's youngest billionaire, he repeatedly refreshes his browser window, waiting for a response that never comes before the image cuts to black. The audience is left to decide for themselves what constitutes Mark's success, given the reasoning that the film has presented for why Mark created Facebook to begin with. What worth does overwhelming financial success have without the tangible social connections that Mark was trying to create? The end point of Mark's (on-screen) story is yet another familiar trope as he becomes a *Kane*-like figure. *The Social Network* leaves the audience with the impression of Mark as a man who only seems to have it all, left alone and attempting to recover an earlier, pre-success, state. The Zuckerberg of the real world has a continuing story, however, now shaped for better or worse in the public imagination by the phantom of Mark in the deposition room waiting for acceptance that will never come.

If this is how *The Social Network* creates the private self of Mark, through the tropes of classical Hollywood cinema, then how does it re-create the known public self of Mark Zuckerberg in order to ground the character in plausibility? It may seem a difficult task, given Zuckerberg's lack of easily recognizable public self-performance. The answer, however, lies in the role of the celebrity CEO as the embodiment of their brand and the audience's immediate recognition of Facebook. Thus, Facebook becomes transposed onto the character of Mark as the recognizable public self, a stand-in for Zuckerberg's public self-performance. As well as serving as the foundation of recognition and understanding for the audience's approach to Zuckerberg, Facebook becomes much of the core of Mark's self-identity. An example of the way Facebook serves as the recognizable public self for which the film creates a behind-the-scenes private moment happens when Mark's roommate Dustin (Joseph Mazzello) presses Mark for information on the relationship status of one of his classmates. In a scene reminiscent of the origin story of a song in a musician biopic (such as the writing of "We Will Rock You" as depicted in *Bohemian Rhapsody*), Dustin's queries lead Mark to have the sudden flash of inspiration for the "Relationship Status" and "Interested In" features of the Facebook profile. It is an inspiration so overwhelming that Mark stops speaking to Dustin mid-sentence and flees from the room, proceeding to run through the snow back to his dorm, dressed in his trademark but weather-inappropriate Adidas sandals, cargo shorts, and hoodie. This behind-the-scenes moment reveals something about the "real" person behind the public face, showing how Mark is perpetually in his head, how his creative thinking and obsession with the site instantly transforms an off-hand remark from Dustin into one of Facebook's most well-known features, and how his total dedication to the project leads him to run through the snow to immediately execute the idea and get the site running.

How the film intertwines Facebook and Mark's self-identity is perhaps best demonstrated later in the film by the phone call between Mark and Eduardo after Eduardo freezes the Facebook bank accounts following his ill-fated trip to the temporarily relocated Facebook headquarters in Palo Alto. When Mark begins his conversation with Eduardo, his initial expression of anger in the dialogue stems from the consequences Eduardo's actions have for the site. The loss of money means the loss of access to additional servers, which can potentially lead to the site crashing and damaging the fledgling social network's reputation for never facing downtime. Mark first presents this as a slight to "everything I have been working on." Eduardo corrects him: "Everything *we* have been working on."

It is only after Eduardo's correction that Mark switches to "our" and "we," forced to acknowledge Eduardo's contribution to placate Eduardo rather than Mark expressing his true perception of Facebook as an extension of himself. However, the real indicator of Mark's investment in Facebook as a means of self-definition in this scene comes as Mark's anger quickly and seamlessly shifts from addressing the problems that Eduardo's actions could cause for Facebook to addressing the problems that the failure of Facebook could create for Mark. He tells Eduardo, fast and angry:

> I am not going back to the Caribbean night at AEPi... Did you like being nobody? Did you like being a joke? Do you want to go back to that? ... Do you know how embarrassing it was for me to try to cash a check today? I am not going back to that life.

As Facebook has become the means for Mark to achieve a level of social acceptance and status closer to what he feels he deserves, Mark has begun to revise his self-image by how Facebook has enabled him to be perceived by others. He is no longer a "joke," and now that he has lived the possibilities of what social acceptance can be, he fears returning to his pre-Facebook life. Eisenberg's openly emotional performance—in the raised volume of his voice, his flustered pacing through the frame, the visible shake of the hand that tightly grips the phone, and emphatic gesturing with his free hand—is a stark contrast to his often-affectless performance as Mark and reveals the importance of this moment to Mark. He sees Eduardo's actions as an attack on the stability of the company and, in turn, an attack on the stability of Mark's current self-identity. It is at this moment that he finally breaks, his disengaged, above-it-all demeanor giving way to an open display of reactionary anger, fear, and panic. In this way, through narrative, performance, and cinematic style, *The Social Network* offers up Facebook itself as the public Mark Zuckerberg that the audience will be most familiar with and that most plausibly corresponds to the private Mark Zuckerberg that the film constructs.

Through this examination of *The Social Network* as an example of the contemporary neo-classical biopic that marries public and private selves through an investigatory narrative framing device, I have demonstrated how the film grants spatio-temporal access to recognizable elements of Zuckerberg's image through Mark's attachment to Facebook as well as the extrapolated private self of Mark as a screen character through his classical Hollywood-influenced motivational tropes. It is useful to return once more to Custen's idea of the biopic character as a Frankenstein's monster of intertextuality, pieced together not only from the life of the subject but also from the past screen incarnations of the lives of other public figures. *The Social Network* is illustrative of the other multiple lives contained within the biopic character adapted from an actual public figure. These multiple lives can consist of conflicting points of view of characters within the diegesis, and the real people from which they are adapted, that are introduced by the investigative narrative device of the neoclassical biopic. The lives of the character's collaborative authors manifest in the character in the ways that writer, director, and actor form connections to both public figure and character throughout various stages of production. Biopic characters are also invested with the lives of their audience in the reception of the film, as viewers rely on their existing knowledge of the biopic subject and their means of connection to the film's characters as they attempt to navigate an ambiguous representation of the docucharacter's actions. This idea will be pursued in the following chapter by considering what this fictionalized frame surrounding fragments of actuality permits, in the form of granting access to witnessing events and subjective interiority otherwise inaccessible outside of the realm of fiction.

3

The Illusion of Access

The famous photograph of Jackie Kennedy standing next to Lyndon Johnson while he takes the oath of office following President John F. Kennedy's assassination can tell us something about her. There is much to be read in her facial expression as she stands, shell-shocked, bloodstains on her pink Chanel suit. Her lips are parted, jaw slack, face lined, and weary. We can speculate on her state of mind, the obvious trauma she has experienced. But without the frame of fiction, without re-creating that moment for the purposes of screen drama, we cannot get closer to that moment. We cannot step into it in full living color, we cannot witness the before and after of what the camera shutter captured in 1963, we cannot feel what Jackie might have been feeling. While the cinematic re-creation of events in the biopic does not get us all the way there— it is not, after all, a literal time machine or virtual reality experience, and the technology to actually live another person's life does not yet exist—it can bring us close to witnessing a version of events, and of feeling what is potentially the emotional truth of history in ways that the third-party observation of historical photographs, footage, or writing cannot.

If we consider "docudrama" as a mode of presentation that merges the documentary evidence of fact-based material with the codes and conventions of cinematic drama, then it is necessary to consider what the consequences are of that merging for the ways that we can access, understand, interpret, and experience that foundational fact-based material. Sonia Amalia Haiduc (2020) approaches the tensions between factual truth and dramatic invention specifically through the lens of melodrama. Haiduc argues that melodrama, with its focus on the individual, the personal, the moral, interiority, and the embodied, can be deployed in the biopic to offer an "emotional truth" that can sometimes co-exist with, and sometimes be at odds with, the factual truth of the biopic's subject matter (2020: 24). The key to this emotional truth, Haiduc argues, is the embodied performance of the actor on screen. When considering the unique abilities of cinema and cinema viewing as an experiential act of meaning-making, Vivian Sobchack's (1992) work on the phenomenology of film also places embodied experience as the locus of cinema's language. In the biopic, embodiment works on multiple levels of meaning-making: there is the embodiment of historical events and people by actors and the embodiment of the viewer in their act of viewing the film. As Sobchack argues, embodiment of the film viewing experience is not something that is only done through the senses of sight and hearing, but through emotional, bodily, and cognitive processes in the act of sense-making (1992: 6). Film viewing is an experience, and through the experience of viewing, the viewer simultaneously engages in the experience of what is being viewed. This chapter will consider how cinema's capabilities for witnessing and experiencing can be applied to the biopic, and what the emotional and affective dimensions of the cinema viewing experience have on the ways we make meaning from celebrities adapted to screen characters.

If, as Dennis Bingham writes, "[t]he appeal of the biopic lies in seeing an actual person who did something interesting in life, known mostly in public, transformed into a character" (2010: 10), then what that transformation into a character makes possible is central in considering the phenomena of the docucharacter in not only biopic, but other media forms. Seeing a public figure adapted to a character has both filmmaker and audience engaging in a process of discovering what it may have been like to be this person, to be their audience, and to understand something about the nature of that person's time, place, and role as a cultural figure and a human being (Bingham 2010: 10). The processes discussed in the first two chapters of this book—re-creating the known public self and creating the unknown private self of the biopic subject—are the foundations of this process of discovery and experience. Without being a recognizable and plausible stand-in for an actual public figure or of actual historical events, the kind of simulated witnessing and experiencing afforded by the language of cinema loses some of its efficacy. To return to the silhouette analogy I raised in the introduction, if the overall shape of the figure we are looking at is not recognizable or acceptable, we are not as likely to accept how it has been rendered once we begin to see the embellishments of tone and color. When what we see on screen is not "believable" or allows us to properly suspend our disbelief, we cannot be fully drawn into the cinematic experience of meaning-making: we can become too distracted by what *doesn't* make sense. Although we are consciously aware that we are watching a film, and watching an actor playing a public figure on re-created sets, wearing re-created costumes, edited together with archival footage that may not be a perfect visual match, we need to be able to forget that conscious experience and accept the biopic's performance of fact *as if* it *could be* true in order for it to achieve its full experiential impact.

Screenwriting scholar Craig Batty (2014) writes that characters are key to how we experience and make sense of media, in both fiction and non-fiction texts. Batty argues that it is through the agency of character that the spectator can follow a story and through the emotional arc of a character, that "we are able to feel what the narrative is trying to suggest; we are offered a way of reading the text" (2014: 36). Batty's thought is perhaps a more simplified encapsulation of Smith's arguments for the importance of character and understanding character engagement, in that characters are how "narrative texts solicit our assent for particular values, practices, and ideologies" (Smith 1995: 4). Unnarrativized fact does not hold the same kinds of engagement and understanding as facts that are structured as a story. Batty gives the example of a news report about rising fuel costs to illustrate this point, writing that "we do not care about how much the price of petrol has increased over the past twelve months: we care about how it has affected us, and our ability to pay for it" (2014: 39). The space between knowing a fact and understanding its relationship to our lives and the world at large is what Batty, using a term from Keith Bettie, calls an "information gap" (qtd in Batty 2014: 40). This gap, Batty argues, can be filled not only with the characters of a strictly factual narrative (such as the news report about fuel costs highlighting a man-on-the-street interview illustrating how rising prices have affected one consumer's life) but through the fictionalization of real people and events. Within the frame of fictionalization, this gap in knowledge can be filled by the ways a story offers possible explanations for actual human actions (Batty 2014: 40).

The key, then, to audiences developing knowledge and understanding of the world around them by watching fictional media based on real events is through characters based on real people and the possibilities for these characters to engage audiences and elicit an affective response. Whether that response is sympathetic allegiance with a dramatic biopic character, mocking laughter in response to a satirical impersonation, or desire for the idealized version of a celebrity in a work of fan fiction, the ways audiences engage with characters based on real people supplement and shape cognitive understanding of factual, historical, and cultural narratives that the real public figures represent.

Character subjectivity is a particularly concrete example of how a character-based approach can shed light on the creation and interpretation of meaning in the biopic. Vincent M. Gaine has argued that through the selective construction of biopic narratives, they can be represented as the subjective experiences of their characters, rather than claim to be the definitive, objective telling of events (2010: 3). The role of memory in structuring a biopic narrative is one particular device that shapes the way characters are constructed. For example, in its reflexive awareness of the way history can become myth, *Jackie* dwells in the disjointed, disoriented mind of Jackie Kennedy in the immediate aftermath of her husband's assassination and her work to control and perpetuate the story of the Kennedys' Camelot. In *Lovelace* (2013), the Rashomon-like structure of the life of porn actress Linda Lovelace illustrates the divide between the public and private selves of celebrities as two versions of events comprise the film: the sanitized public face of Lovelace's career as filtered through the point of view of Linda's husband, porn producer Chuck Traynor, and the darker private version of events from Linda's point of view as Traynor's coercion and violent physical abuse shapes her career. In *The Social Network*, character motivation and self-identity plays a part in the conflicting points of view at stake in lawsuits related to the creation of Facebook. In *Game Change*, the 2008 US presidential election is revisited as the memory of a key Republican strategist, framing its take on Sarah Palin within the point of view of a frustrated insider who helped orchestrate a failed campaign. Understanding not only how character memory is constructed, but how these memories construct other characters based on real people, works to elucidate meaning from the text. Subjective constructions of real stories and characters based on real people can help in creating the illusion of access to actuality. The audience is brought into the story through the experiences of the characters, either through witnessing the acts of a public figure as a close participant in events, or by gaining access to a constructed subjective interiority of the known public figure themselves.

Just as whole narratives can be constructed subjectively; there can also be select moments in biopics where a character's subjective interiority takes over the diegetic screen space. In *Hitchcock* (2012), which presents the life of Alfred Hitchcock during the production of *Psycho* (1960), the audience witnesses hypothetical conversations between Hitchcock and murderer-with-mother-issues Ed Gein. The film uses Gein as the inspiration for Norman Bates in a framing device for the film, and Gein recurs throughout as a kind of muse in the process of bringing *Psycho* to the screen. These are not literal, actual conversations that Hitchcock had and are not presented as such in the film. Rather, they are an embodied enactment of what the film proposes as Hitchcock's internal monologue, interior conversations he has with the figment of Gein, or perhaps visual and auditory hallucinations brought on by the pressures of the production. In *The Iron Lady* (2011), Margaret Thatcher's descent into dementia is represented on-screen by enacting her fractured frame of mind through, once again, embodied conversations with other characters who are not physically present, as well as the use of sound and editing to convey to the audience the sense of pieces of memory being thrown like shrapnel as Thatcher's cognitive abilities explosively deteriorate. In *Confessions of a Dangerous Mind* (2002), the story of game show producer Chuck Barris' involvement with the CIA as a covert assassin that may or may not have actually happened, the limits of time and space are bent to treat Barris' story as if it were true, while questions as to whether or not it actually is go unanswered. The elastic nature of the film's stylistic treatment of time and space suggests that what we see on screen could only be played out in the mind of Barris the character. Unrestricted access to character subjectivity in films such as these gives insight into the character and the real person they represent and guide the interpretation of the thematic content of the film and the filmmaker's point of view on their biographical subjects. It is, as Batty suggests, as the audience gains direct access to how the character experiences what is happening, the process of affective understanding of the character supplements cognitive comprehension of the narrative.

What, then, is the potential appeal of gaining this kind of simulated access to the imagined backstage and interior selves of a public figure? How does this reflect the role of the celebrity in contemporary culture? Charles L. Ponce de Leon writes that celebrity culture operates on the principle of finding the "real self" behind the purely textual figure of Dyer's star image (2002: 5). Ponce de Leon argues because of its association with factual discourse, news media claims to be able to deliver the accurate inside story of a public figure. Even with this association with factual discourse, though, celebrity news can be based on as much of a fiction as a film star's on-screen performance (Ponce de Leon 2002: 5). While public interest in the private lives of celebrities is not a new phenomenon, as discussion of the public and private lives of celebrities has become normalized in news discourse as the boundaries between entertainment and news have become increasingly blurred in television, print, and online media (Marshall 2014a: 154–6; Turner 2016: 93). The normalization of celebrity as news has led to traditional news figures, such as politicians, being viewed more through the lens of celebrity culture (Marshall 2014a: 157). Additionally, the venues of celebrity news have moved more from the fringes of niche entertainment media, such as the shift in celebrity gossip from women's magazines to mainstream online blogs and network newscasts, to the social media identities of celebrities that are instantly accessible from our smartphones whenever and wherever we wish (Turner 2016: 93). The contemporary mediascape is so saturated with discourses of celebrity culture that it can be near impossible to escape its most pervasive public images.

Amanda Retartha (2014) cites Joseph Roach in discussing the way audiences can have an overwhelming familiarity with a celebrity, while at the same time remaining impossibly distant from knowing the celebrity: what Roach terms "public intimacy" or the "illusion of proximity" (qtd. in Retartha 2014: 2). The knowing-unknowable nature of audience relationship to celebrity is perhaps most apparent in discourses of gossip. Much like the docucharacter, celebrity gossip uses the material of the real as the basis for speculation about a celebrity's private life and private self. For example, a paparazzi photograph and comments from an "eyewitness source" about Angelina Jolie visiting a new rental property with her children following her divorce from Brad Pitt generates gossip blog speculation about her state of mind: relaxed, doing well, and moving on with her life (Bueno 2016). The facts of what Jolie has done in this example are knowable: she has filed for divorce from Pitt, she is looking for a new place to live, she has her children with her, she spent time walking on the beach barefoot after touring the rental property. What is happening inside Jolie's head, how she and her children are coping with the situation, and what her plans are for the future are inherently unknowable to the distanced public, and can only be imagined and speculated upon, turned into a narrative for mass consumption and entertainment.

The real and not-real, knowable and unknowable nature of celebrity is addressed by Richard Dyer, who compares celebrity to a kind of fiction in that "[s]tars are, like characters in stories, representations of people" (1998: 22). Similarly, Joshua Gamson compares engagement with the "celebrity text" to "a movie based loosely on a true story, or a soap opera: you wait to see 'what's going to happen next,' the next plot element to develop, the next tidbit to be offered up" (1994: 174). What Dyer and Gamson go on to say shortly after making these points is particularly pertinent when considering the role of celebrity discourse in the appeal of the docucharacter. Dyer writes that "unlike characters in stories, stars are real people" (1998: 22). Gamson identifies the pleasures of celebrity gossip as "its freedom from but resemblance to the truth" (1994: 177). Here lies the appeal of engaging with the docucharacter. Like the star image, the docucharacter is also the representation of a real person, and like the speculative discourse of gossip, there is a degree of freedom from absolute truth that is granted to a fictionalized character. A selectively constructed character created for the purposes of a singular narrative simplifies what John Ellis describes as the "incoherent" and "incomplete" nature of the public image (1991: 304) and attempts to reconcile the disparity between what is known and what is unknowable within the frame of a single character. As a textually constructed entity, the public persona and identity of a known individual could be argued to be as much a construct of language as a fictional character (Jacobs 1990: xvi). By embellishing the public persona with various fictionalized inner selves, the possibility exists to "rehumanize" the textual public image (Busse 2006a: 256). This rehumanization process adds the "fullness and plausibility" that we seek from fictional characters through melding "verifiable facts and created factoids" that are given equal status in the adapted text (Jacobs 1990: xvi–xvii). As Retartha argues throughout her work on imagined celebrity selves in fan fiction and literature, "in narrative space, the unfulfilled need [to breach the illusion of proximity] is both worried, like a sore tooth, and potentially satisfied" (2014: 4).

In cinema, the effect that Retartha notes in literature is replicated and, perhaps, magnified by the illusion of witnessing that film creates. Richard Allen's theory of projective illusion articulates the process of viewers' "suspension of judgment that the character is a character" and experience of the character as a person (embodied by the actor), an emotional being with which to have an affective engagement (1995: 129). In the case of a character that is purely fictional, the only reference for accepting the illusion of the character as a living entity is the actor. However, in the case of a character adapted from a known, publicly visible person in the real world, there exist additional extratextual reference points of the public image. The extent to which the viewer has an awareness of or familiarity with the public image has the potential to vary widely between individuals, thus varying the individual response to the adapted character. Allen's idea of projective illusion compares the experience of film spectatorship that willingly sets aside the medium awareness of cinema to the experience of a dream or daydream. In the experience of film as a projective illusion, there is the possibility for a kind of experiential wish fulfilment similar to that of a dream, with the caveat that in film spectatorship the viewer is awake and fully aware that what they are experiencing is not actually happening to them (Allen 1995: 125). The fact that a story adapted from the real world that the viewer may already be familiar with, featuring an imagined access to public figures they may already know, further facilitates the process of experiencing the adaptation as a kind of wish fulfilment of subjective proximity to a famous figure. While the viewer has an awareness that the character adapted from a public persona is a dramatization, the projective illusion of cinema coupled with an existing knowledge of the real-world referent depicted on screen can facilitate a desire to suspend knowledge of the illusion and experience the film as a representation of what the person is really like, and how things really happened. While this need and desire to know a celebrity might seem more obvious with traditional objects of fantasy such as movie stars and rock stars, in this book I am also dealing with types of celebrity that are not quite on the same level of desirable objects. While the desire for proximity may not be the same between the actual Mark Zuckerberg and Jesse Eisenberg for fans of the actor who plays Zuckerberg in *The Social Network*, a desire to breach the front-stage frame of public performance exists, regardless of who the performer is. In some of the case studies considered throughout this book, such as politicians, or a somewhat enigmatic figure like Zuckerberg, public awareness of the constructed nature of the public performance of celebrity breeds the same desire to know the real and the authentic, to know what is "really" going on with a public figure or the institutions they represent.

In order to illustrate in more detail how the biopic can create this illusion of access and what it can do for our understanding of its subject through witnessing and experiencing a version of actual events and public figures, I will be looking at two films that tell the tales of two Kennedys. The first, *Chappaquiddick*, gives its audience access to a version of events from the disputed facts and motivations of Senator Edward Kennedy's culpability of the death of Mary Jo Kopechne in the Chappaquiddick car crash in 1969, and both invites and encourages viewers to understand the character through their emotional responses. The second, *Jackie*, sets aside the disputed facts and conspiracy theories surrounding the 1963 assassination of President John F. Kennedy to witness and experience the event and its aftermath from the point of view of his wife, projecting her fractured subjectivity into the screen space for the audience to experience in the process of cinematic sense-making.

Feeling Facts: Witnessing the Events of *Chappaquiddick*

Chappaquiddick begins by using the documentary evidence of the real in order to extrapolate motivations for its central character, Ted Kennedy, the youngest son of the Kennedy political dynasty. A photograph of the actual Kennedy family paired with archival voice over announcing the deaths of each of the older

Kennedy sons who were in turn charged with advancing the family's political ambitions until responsibility progressively fell to the next son in line following a tragedy: Joseph P. Kennedy Jr., killed in action during the Second World War; John F. Kennedy, President of the United States, assassinated in Dallas in 1963; and Robert F. Kennedy, former Attorney General and Senator who was assassinated during his 1968 presidential campaign. The camera pushes in on the photograph, focusing on the young Ted Kennedy, responsibility zeroing in on him with each of his brothers' deaths. This use of the actual is paired with a mock-up of the actual as Jason Clarke, playing Ted, delivers an interview about JFK's legacy in relation to the space program. The fact of Apollo 11's mission to the moon coinciding with the Chappaquiddick incident in July 1969 is woven throughout the film, juxtaposing the expectations placed upon Ted after his brothers' deaths with his own floundering sense of identity and behavior in the face of a crisis. *Chappaquiddick*'s writers Taylor Allen and Andrew Logan intended the film to be a character study of Ted Kennedy and did not intend to engage with any of the conspiracies surrounding the event (Wilkinson 2018). The film chooses one set of facts to present, and its focus is on speculation surrounding the why of the events, rather than the how or what. In this case, much of the "why?" question surrounds the exploration of Ted Kennedy as a person—or, more specifically, Ted Kennedy as a screen character functioning to make a comment on Ted Kennedy as a person, and a broader commentary about how powerful people can control scandal narratives.

The version of facts the film chooses to represent takes out some of the more speculative gossip-type discourse surrounding the event. For example, there is no indication of a romantic or sexual relationship between Ted and Mary Jo in the film. Rather, the film attempts to humanize Mary Jo in what little screen time she has. The role is played by Kate Mara, in an interesting casting choice with a layer of extra-textual meaning that she brings to the character given her performance of another cast-aside victim of the political machine as Zoe Barnes in Netflix's *House of Cards*. Even if the viewer is not familiar with that reference, however, Mary Jo is depicted as still shaken by the assassination of her former boss, Robert Kennedy, the year before, and at somewhat of a loss with what to do with her life, dominated by a reluctance to become involved in a national political campaign again. The relationship between Ted and Mary Jo is introduced as being a professional one, as he asks her to work for him. The loss of identity that they are both experiencing in the wake of Bobby's death, however, allows the actual historical event that exists outside of what is shown on screen to act as a kind of shorthand for bonding the two characters together in a shared mourning and re-evaluation of their lives. Witnessing the event with this version of facts providing context establishes a limited number of possible interpretations of Ted—as a screen character—and the actions and behaviors he exhibits following the accident. If there was, for example, an obvious romantic relationship established between the two at the beginning of the film, then the audience's simulated access to the event would be shaped by a different version of the story: Ted might have a motivation to contribute to Mary Jo's death, or perhaps even deliberately cause it, if there was a danger of the relationship becoming public.

Rather than a more cut-and-dry scandal narrative, the film forges a connection between Ted and Mary Jo in terms of a shared crossroads in their life, with Ted's reluctance to run for President and Mary Jo's reluctance to continue working in national politics. The crossroads prompted by one Kennedy tragedy—RFK's assassination—is repeated for Ted with the accident, and unresolved as another Kennedy tragedy for Mary Jo. The way the film juxtaposes the two characters for the remainder of the film gives an emotional resonance to the filmmaker's thematic intentions of considering how often women become disposable to men with the power to make anything go away. Through the film's emotional cues, the viewer's witnessing and experiencing of this version of the story is guided toward a particular response and understanding of the historical narrative. Without the kind of simulated access to people and events permitted through the fictional frame of the screen biopic, the audience would not have these opportunities to see unseen events played out as they might have been.

This is particularly notable in the access we are granted to Ted's actions following the accident and its juxtaposition with Mary Jo's struggle to stave off drowning and escape the submerged car. When Ted's car flips off the Dike bridge and into the water, the film cuts to black for several seconds. We hear Ted calling out for Mary Jo, but when the visual image resumes, we see him already sitting on dry land before he leaves and returns to the beach house where his friends and some of Bobby Kennedy's former staffers are holding a party, not stopping for help along the way. When he does get help, in lieu of explaining what happened, he simply says "I'm not going to be president." When he returns to the site of the crash with his cousin Joe Gargan (Ed Helms) and friend Paul Markham (Jim Gaffigan), his only action is to lie on his back on the bridge, murmuring "What have I done?" and "She's already dead," while the other two men frantically dive into the pond in an attempt to retrieve Mary Jo. It is the *lack* of witnessing the complete aftermath of the accident, of the narrational structure of the film withholding information from the viewer, that opens Ted's reactions up to the viewer's interpretation. Is it shock? Indifference? A calculated move to allow Mary Jo to die so he has a concrete reason to never be able to become president, as his father expects him to be? When Ted returns to the mainland, we witness his actions in not reporting the accident as he had promised Joe and Paul he would do. Intercut with Ted taking a bath, calling his father, and creating an alibi by having someone see him at his hotel, is Mary Jo's fight for survival trapped inside the submerged vehicle, breathing in a small air pocket, her face barely above water. As we see Ted slip below the surface of the bath water, a controlled, safe environment, we also see Mary Jo's frantic pounding on the car doors and the windshield, trying to find a way out. With the crosscutting between these two scenes, it is ambiguous whether this is Ted's subjective imaginings as he holds himself underwater, or if this is an omniscient point of view that the audience holds. Is he plagued with guilt? Is he trying to feel what Mary Jo felt? Is he trying to harm himself? Clarke's blank-faced performance as Ted Kennedy in this scene allows the audience space to project any pre-conceived notions they may have of the event onto the character's motivations, or to interpret Ted's behavior (as a screen character, and, in turn, perhaps the actual Ted Kennedy) through the lens of the visceral emotion and physical response conjured up by Mary Jo's panic and abandonment. The soundtrack gives us Mary Jo's subjective sense of being underwater, the sound muffled as she bangs on the windows, her voice calling out for Ted echoing and forming a sound bridge back to the shots of Ted submerged in his bath. The viewer is aligned with and has access to Mary Jo's experience in this moment, whereas Ted is more distant and unreachable, his face betraying little of his interiority. Our understanding of the events in experiencing Mary Jo's struggle can work to color our emotional response to Ted's actions (or inaction), and our moral judgment of what he has done and how he actually feels about it. We are feeling our way through the facts as they are presented to us.

Whatever understanding of Ted's actions that the audience gleans from witnessing his reactions and feeling Mary Jo's fight for life carries throughout the film as the aftermath is played out. His apparent lack of his own sense of agency in the shadow of his family legacy has him wavering between raw emotion, such as when he calls Mary Jo's family to inform her of their death; a duty to do the morally right thing, such as when he tells his father that he must tell the truth about the fact that he was driving; and participation in a self-preserving cover-up, such as his attempts to get Mary Jo's body returned to her family as quickly as possible in order to avoid an autopsy. By having access to a version of a public figure's public and private behaviors within a single screen story, the audience sees every disparity or congruence that exists between the two. With a character whose behavior and motivations are somewhat complex or ambiguous, such as the character of Ted Kennedy in *Chappaquiddick*, the ways the audience interprets those spaces between public and private can be guided by the emotional or affective reactions they have toward the screen story and its characters. An individual viewer's response to interpreting the version of history presented on screen can also be shaped by their existing knowledge and ideological underpinnings. In the case of *Chappaquiddick*, for example, while screenwriters Allen and Logan and director John Curran express their own political leanings as liberal and their intentions for the film to be a character study of Kennedy, the film's reception was open to interpretation by others with different political opinions. Conservative commentator Rush Limbaugh was a particularly notable example of a figure on the right who embraced the movie and saw it as a deeply critical exposé of the event (Wilkinson 2018). The process of being granted simulated access to a version of events through the fictional frame and interpreting the facts presented through not only the affective response created by the text, but also the emotional responses of the individual viewer, can potentially foster a deeply subjective and personal understanding of the actual events and people represented. The fictional frame of a real story and real people adapted to screen media allows the audience not only to witness a re-created or simulated version of actual events, but also to feel the facts of those events in ways that can shape the viewer's understanding of those facts.

The ways that films and other screen media based on real events offer access through fiction is to place the viewer inside a simulated version of an actual person's experience. Through the fictional frame, we can be granted not only to witnessing events play out, and witnessing public and private behaviors, but, through the language of cinematic style, we can gain access to a character's interiority and shape our understanding of facts in experiential ways. I will now consider how the illusion of access consists of not only the viewer being "present" for a version of events, but also the possibilities of getting close to the experience of a screen character based on a real person. To do this, I will draw on the example of Pablo Larraín's *Jackie*.

Stylizing Subjectivity: Experiencing *Jackie*

Jackie Kennedy's presence at her husband's assassination has largely been relegated to still and silent images of history. The pink suit she wore on November 22, 1963, is iconic, but the visuals are what is most prominent about Jackie Kennedy on that day: arriving at Dallas Love Field, riding in the motorcade, the Zapruder film showing her climbing onto the trunk of the convertible after the President was shot, standing beside the new President Johnson on Air Force One as he took the oath of office. *Jackie* attempts to return Jackie Kennedy's voice to her (via Natalie Portman) from that period of time in the immediate aftermath of JFK's assassination. Through the investigatory framing device of an interview (given to an unnamed journalist played by Billy Crudup but based on an actual article written by Theodore H. White for *LIFE* magazine), the audience is, similarly as *Chappaquiddick*, able to witness the disparities between the private, human behavior of a public figure and the carefully controlled image they orchestrate for public consumption. *Jackie* could be considered a character study biopic much in the same vein as *Chappaquiddick*: its narrative is based in a restricted time frame and does not attempt to chronicle the life of its subject on a broader scale. Rather, the way the public figure's actions and behavior are presented during a specific, pivotal moment in their history is intended to make a larger commentary on them as both a public person, a private human, and a potential legacy. Similarly, there is some ambiguity in the protagonist's motivations and contradictory public/private behavior, although unlike *Chappaquiddick*, *Jackie* offers the audience a more direct subjective access to its subject's state of mind. Through the investigatory device of the interview, Jackie moves between telling her own subjective experience and withdrawing it from the record with firm instructions to the reporter, cleaning up the official version of events and approving the completed article in order to put forth the version of her husband's legacy that she wishes to perpetuate. The film also, by framing much of the film as Jackie's recounting of memory to her interviewer and through its stylistic choices, works to align the viewer's experience of the film with Jackie's subjective state of mind.

One notable example of how the film stylistically communicates Jackie's subjectivity to the viewer is through sequences full of abrupt cuts, temporal ellipsis, and unfinished dialogue. This style recurs during moments where Jackie appears to be at her most untethered and lost to her grief—over the loss of her husband and her own public/private identity—and trauma. The abrupt gaps in time mimic the lost memories of dissociation and trauma, and the difficulty that Jackie is having in processing events through a mental fog is replicated in the audience experience of being jolted through time and attempting to find narrative and spatiotemporal coherence in these sequences. For example, on the Air Force One flight back to Washington, Jackie's fractured thought patterns dominate the sequence, as she jumps across topics ranging from the caliber of the bullet that killed her husband to preliminary plans for the funeral to refusing to sneak out the back of Air Force One away from the cameras or change her clothes for the benefit of the watching public, to wanting to know the details of what Kennedy's autopsy will entail. There is an isolation in her trauma, a confusion in the abrupt cuts, dialogue sound bridges, and temporal gaps that mimic the jumbled short-term memory that often follows the aftermath of trauma. As Sobchack's phenomenological theory of film proposes, the viewer is engaged in an experiential processing of the information played out on screen (1992: 6). As Portman embodies Jackie's disconnected mood and thought process and the cinematic style lays out the same in its temporal disruptions and lack of unobtrusive continuity editing, the viewer becomes engaged in the experience of processing what they are seeing in the same way the screen character Jackie is experiencing it. As Jackie's cognitive and memory processes are disrupted by experiencing her husband's death, the audience has also become somewhat lost in the processing of events, and, instead, has the raw emotional cues of Portman's performance, which within the span of minutes moves between weeping as she wipes blood from her face, alone, in front of a mirror; to her shellshocked presence at Johnson's swearing in, where she flinches at the camera flashes; to her steely resolve and attempts to begin to take control of the situation as she tries to get as much information as she can and refuses to hide from the public.

There is a moment of reprieve from Jackie's fractured memories as the arrival in Washington brings Robert Kennedy (Peter Sarsgaard), who seems to anchor Jackie back to coherence and gives her someone to reveal her experience of the assassination to as the film's style returns to unobtrusive continuity editing and coherent temporal sequencing. The reprieve is temporary as the fractured editing style resumes as Jackie, Bobby, and various aides and family members are waiting together at Bethesda Naval Hospital as JFK's autopsy is conducted. Here the editing becomes even more spatiotemporally fractured, as, with a larger space to occupy than the cabin of Air Force One, Jackie moves between the waiting room and hallways of the hospital from cut to cut, with no orientation for the audience of what precedes or motivates her movements. Family members and staff try to placate her, but her questions and further calls for information go unanswered as the shot cuts before she can find out whether the doctors can make Jack look like he did, or what her children know. She is told to rest and given a pill, and in the next cut sees her near whispering a bitter stream of consciousness to Bobby about who the assassin might be. Even he will no longer provide her with the comfort of a sounding board, presumably consumed by his own shock and grief, as he tries to quiet her. In the next abrupt cut, Jackie is marching determinedly down a hallway and it is a few beats before we, the disoriented viewer, realize she is headed to the room where the autopsy is being conducted. She breaks down as Bobby pulls her away, already having seen too much, and in the next instant tries to compose herself. Her fractured memories, and our experience of them, are again restored to temporal consistency as she and Bobby again ride with Jack's casket back to the White House. This time, Jackie is anchored by a plan and yet another attempt to regain her agency and control: she is determined that in the ranks of assassinated American presidents, her husband will be remembered like Lincoln, rather than be forgotten by public memory as McKinley and Garfield were.

This stylized experience of Jackie's subjectivity is repeated in other sequences of the film, such as the spatiotemporally disconnected montage where she dresses herself up in her elegant gowns as though they are the skin of her dissolving identity as First Lady, and wanders through the White House, drinking, smoking, downing pills, gathering up possessions, hosting a phantom dinner party. Similarly, a later sequence where Jackie has a chance to openly, but privately, express her grief and fears for the future to her friend and close aide Nancy Tuckerman (Gerta Gerwig) is cut in much the same way, with abrupt elliptic cuts, the heavy orchestral score sometimes swallowing the dialogue Portman delivers through tears. Throughout the film, it is the moments where Jackie is most overcome by grief, trauma, and the sudden re-evaluation of her life and identity where her subjectivity—and, thus, through the way it is stylistically presented, the way the viewer experiences her subjectivity—becomes the most jumbled and fractured. It is through the frame of fiction, where unseen private events can be staged based upon publicly known fact to seem like a plausible stand in for the actual thing, that allows us to witness, access, and imagine the "how things might have been" to the stories and lived experiences behind public memory.

In these three preceding chapters, I have outlined the basic template for how a docucharacter is constructed, and what the construction permits. While the textual examples I have engaged with throughout have been necessarily limited in their scope, I propose that the template illustrated here can serve as a useful starting point for examining how characters are based on real public figures in docudrama and biopic in film and television. As I move into the second half of this book, and considering media beyond the biopic, I argue that this fundamental template of merging the re-created public self with a created private self in order to provide simulated access and proximity to celebrities and public figures is replicated in other forms of media that feature characters based on real people. Keep this extended consideration of the possibilities of biopic characters in mind as we move forward to considering how docucharacters are created and function in the vastly different arenas of satirical sketch comedy, celebrity self-performance in fiction, and audience-generated real person fan fiction.

4

Beyond the Biopic: Sketch Comedy

In March 2012, "Sarah Palin" made a return to *Saturday Night Live*. The impersonation made famous by Tina Fey had been something of a cultural phenomenon during the 2008 US presidential election and had only been seen twice on screen (when Fey hosted) since. The occasion was the release of the HBO film *Game Change*, and "Palin" was there to make a response on Weekend Update. Only this time, it was not either of the Sarah Palins that *Saturday Night Live* (*SNL*) audiences had come to expect. This was not Fey's version, nor was it the real Sarah Palin, who had appeared in a sketch with her doppelganger late in the 2008 campaign. Instead, this time, in a wig, glasses, and red blazer, Andy Samberg stepped in with a jumbled facsimile of Fey's performance. Samberg, who for the purposes of the sketch knew nothing about Sarah Palin aside from Fey's impersonation of her, played a copy of a copy. Using Fey's take on Palin's accent and gestures, Samberg purposefully mixed up the *SNL* Palin's catchphrases ("You can see my house from Russia!" rather than the oft-quoted "I can see Russia from my house!") with other infamous political sound bites ("I did not have sexual relations with that woman") and *SNL* classics ("Da bears"). While the point of the bit was more about making a joke of Samberg's bad performance than anything to do with the actual Palin, it cemented the status of "Sarah Palin" as an *SNL* character, complete with her own iconic lines and expected comedic behavior. It is a character that evolved alongside the media image of Sarah Palin in 2008, each shaping the other as weekly sketches responded to the latest news, and the news media and public perception responded to the sketches. This is a character that became so intrinsically linked with the public image of Sarah Palin that the HBO dramatization of the 2008 campaign, *Game Change*, couldn't go without a couple of scenes of Julianne Moore's Sarah Palin watching Tina Fey's Sarah Palin on television, scowling to herself. They were the kind of scenes that asked us to imagine that, somewhere, Sarah Palin was probably scowling at Julianne Moore too.

In this chapter, I take the first step in considering how public figures are adapted into fictionalized characters in media forms outside of the more traditionally considered biopic and docudramatic film and television. The three-step process of the "docucharacter" established so far—re-creating the public, creating the private, and providing the illusion of access—will be considered through the example of Sarah Palin by comparing adaptations of the 2008 vice-presidential candidate in comedy and drama. Here, I look at how *Saturday Night Live*'s Sarah Palin sketches re-created and re-characterized Palin's media image. Through this case study, I examine how television sketch comedy works to adapt real public figures into docucharacters, and how the known public selves and unknown private selves of docucharacters are negotiated in a comedic context. Additionally, to further illustrate the nuances of docucharacter construction across genres and forms, I compare the characterization of Tina Fey's *Saturday Night Live* Palin with the characterization of Palin as performed by Julianne Moore in *Game Change*. As well as illustrating how the differences in form between these two contexts shape the construction of public and private selves in docucharacters, I also aim to shed light on strategies for constructing docucharacter from a public figure with a highly visible co-present media image. Sarah Palin offers a prime opportunity to discuss this, in contrast to Mark Zuckerberg in the earlier consideration of creating a private self in *The Social Network*. As discussed in Chapter 2, Zuckerberg, at the time he was used as the basis for a screen character, lacked an easily recognizable public self-performance. Before considering the public image of Sarah Palin as an iconic source text and the position of the political celebrity, however, it is first necessary to consider sketch comedy and the *SNL* approach to celebrity impersonation as a form for constructing docucharacter.

Saturday Night Live and Celebrity Impersonation

Michael Upchurch, writing on the "Poetics of Sketch Comedy," argues that the comedy sketch is "a unique narrative form with its own rules and conventions" (1992: 3). As the original meaning of the word "sketch" applies to "a rough, hasty drawing which outlines major features without giving detail," so too it applies to the comedic sketch as a brief, discrete segment of comedy lasting usually three to eight minutes (Upchurch 1992: 22). The "hasty" elements of the sketch are useful in considering the format of *Saturday Night Live*, where the content of each show is written and produced within a matter of days leading up to its live broadcast. This enables the show to respond to current events, which is particularly relevant when considering its political sketches. The "outline of major features without giving detail" is pertinent when considering how the televisual form of sketch comedy shapes the way a public figure is rendered as a character. Here I refer to sketch docucharacters as *characters* rather than *caricatures* based on the literal application of Murray Smith's broad definition of character as the "fictional analogue of a human agent" (1995: 17). When considering characters based on actual people, as with the biopic, this translates to defining them as the fictional analogue of a specific human agent. While the hastily drawn outline and brief narrative time frame of the sketch necessitates a broad and cartoonish approach to its characters, I argue that it is useful to consider the sketch docucharacter in terms of how Naomi Jacobs (1990) approaches two- and three-dimensional characters in her study of historical figures in literary fiction. While the sketch character is clearly a more two-dimensional rendering than that produced in the biopic, taking a character-focused approach enables an analysis of celebrity impersonation in sketch comedy to uncover how the boundaries of public and private selves are traversed in satirizing public figures, and how the features of re-created public, created private, and simulated access are present in all forms of the "docucharacter" across media.

The degree of narrative drive in sketch comedy can be a determining factor in how fleshed out a character appears to be. Historicizing the development of the form, Upchurch outlines that as the comedy sketch translated from the vaudeville stage to the television variety show, the form of television itself became one of the possible structuring premises of a sketch and gave rise to both narrative and non-narrative forms of sketch comedy (1992: 21). The non-narrative sketch form that derives its structure from other television formats (such as the talk show, the game show, the variety show, or the news show) is a staple of *SNL*, particularly for sketches that foreground celebrity impersonation. Upchurch's work is a valuable foundation for considering sketch comedy as a form, but his focus is largely on narrative sketch, rather than the non-narrative, media-framed forms that typically showcase *SNL* docucharacters. These direct re-creations or reinterpretations of media events can lend themselves to having less of a narrative focus where the actions and reactions of characters are the primary means of propelling the sketch forward. The *SNL* media-framed sketch is more often driven by the escalation of jokes that are generated in response to intertextual references to current events or the identifiable quirks of the subject of the impersonation, rather than from the premise of the sketch. In narrative or character-based sketches, characters function to drive the premise of the sketch forward, rather than the sketch's premise acting as a frame for an impersonated character. In adhering to the sketch form's rules of eliciting laughter and remaining brief, intertextual references to people, characters, or media forms that the audience has an existing familiarity with are shortcuts to establishing the premise. This is akin to the use of recognizable stock characters or stereotypes in a more character- or narrative-driven sketch premise. Both approaches remove any need for exposition that does not further the sketch's comedic goal, and to use Murray Smith's terms, aid the viewer's recognition response to characters. To compare this to the approach to the biopic that has been considered in this book so far, this is the stage where a re-creation of the actual is used to trigger audience recognition and create a plausible foundation that connects the constructed character to the reality it aims to represent. This remains so even if the goal of the comedic sketch is to bend reality to absurd extremes in order to critique and satirize it.

Unlike the biopic, the goal of the celebrity impersonation sketch is not to construct its subject as a more well-rounded character consisting of public and private selves that offer an extended engagement with a simulated version of the actual. Rather, the celebrity impersonation in sketch comedy reduces the celebrity to a set of easily recognizable characteristics. This is most often done using signs such as dress, hair, speech, and mannerisms. There are some contexts, however, where celebrity impersonation might necessitate the creation of a rounded, three-dimensional character, at least from the perspective of the performer. In writing on the work of celebrity impersonators in theatrical contexts such as Las Vegas stage revues, Kerry O. Ferris illustrates that some impersonators acknowledge a need to replicate the imagined inner self of their character and repress their own performance of self in order to fully flesh out the recognizable public image the performer presents through physical and vocal resemblance to the impersonated subject (2011: 1198). But *Saturday Night Live*'s approach to celebrity impersonation, particularly political celebrity impersonation, does not need to develop the same kinds of "subtleties, layers, and textures" (2011: 1198) that Ferris' research identifies in stage revue performers. The stage impersonations of Ferris' study seek to faithfully replicate the celebrity in order to provide their audience with a simulated experience of their subject, rather than appropriating a celebrity persona for the purposes of comedy. The *SNL* tradition of celebrity impersonation skews more toward a two-dimensional, cartoonish rendering, with impersonated characters sometimes joining the ranks of *SNL*'s original characters in the use of recurring jokes or catchphrases—as Samberg's Weekend Update Palin sketch illustrates—and often deviating wildly from the original source of the celebrity image to take on a life of their own.

Take, for example, the "Celebrity Jeopardy" sketches that appeared regularly from 1996 to 2002 (and revived in later years, such as when Will Ferrell hosted and for *SNL*'s fortieth Anniversary special). One of the running jokes developed and repeated throughout the fifteen original sketches was that perennial contestant Sean Connery (Darrell Hammond) would mercilessly taunt host Alex Trebek (Ferrell), imply that he had sex with Trebek's mother, and misread category names in sexually suggestive ways. While this joke plays on Connery's star image as the James Bond playboy type, it devolves into absurdly petty behavior that establishes Hammond's Connery as a character that seemingly exists only to make this Trebek's life miserable: something with no connection to the celebrity being impersonated that has been generated by the repetition and evolution of the sketch throughout its numerous appearances. Darrell Hammond has spoken of the way his performance as Connery first began as a faithful replication of Connery's voice and mannerisms, but over time grew into a "bastardization" of Connery, with Hammond and the writers prioritizing what was funny over what was accurate (Miller and Shales 2014). Likewise, other celebrities impersonated in the sketch are performed as two-dimensional renderings of their most recognizable mannerisms due to the way the sketch sets up the idea of the stupidity of the celebrity contestants. The contestants usually begin the sketch with scores in the negative numbers, the categories are dumbed down, and category titles often give away the answers ("Colors that are red," "Foods that end in amburger," "Black comedians named Whoopi"), and none of the contestants seem to be aware of the rules of the game or able to sustain enough focus to attempt to play it correctly. The frame of the sketch premise even bends celebrity self-performance to fit it: Tom Hanks, the only celebrity to play themselves in "Celebrity Jeopardy," appears as equally stupid as the other contestants (if not more so) after speaking into a pen as though it were a microphone, getting caught in a plastic dry-cleaning bag, and knocking himself unconscious on his podium.

This two-dimensional treatment of celebrity impersonation as sketch character largely carries over to *SNL*'s political impersonations. Jeffrey P. Jones (2008) writes that *SNL* has an established approach to political impersonation that "is focused more on personal mannerisms and political style than on politics," which in turn results in presenting a filtered image of politicians that does not engage with "any form of meaningful political critique." Jones highlights a notable example of this in Chevy Chase's portrayal of President Gerald Ford in the earliest seasons of the show. Chase's impersonation made no attempt to look or sound like Ford, with his claim that he was the president being enough of an appropriation for the show's original incarnation as an "edgy and youthful approach to comedy and politics" (Jones 2013: 79). Such a purposeful use of political impersonation that does not truly attempt to impersonate would likely be out of place in the modern incarnation of *SNL*, where a roster of particularly skilled impressionists over the years (such as Phil Hartman, Dana Carvey, and Darrell Hammond), in conjunction with the work of the show's hair, makeup, and wardrobe departments, has changed audience expectations for political impersonation. Although examples such as Chase's Ford or Hammond's Connery may evolve into performances that bear only the most superficial resemblance to their original, they align with Jones' assertion that by being memorable and repeated, impersonations of politicians and other celebrities like these can "[play] a role in shaping public memory" of the actual celebrity (Jones 2013: 78). This was evident in the use of the "Celebrity Jeopardy" sketches as public memory when the actual Sean Connery and Alex Trebek died in 2020 within days of each other (on October 31 and November 8, respectively). In response to the news of each man's passing, and the co-incidental timing, a significant amount of response on social media such as Twitter and Reddit referenced the sketches and the comedic possibilities of the two reuniting in the afterlife via *SNL*.

As a follow-up to his assessment of the *SNL* approach to political impersonation, Jones argues in later writing that on rare occasions the good-natured parody of a politician's behavior or presentational quirks can co-incidentally create critical satire. Jones cites Ferrell's performance as George W. Bush (specifically during the 2000 campaign season) and Fey's performance as Sarah Palin as examples of instances where the "outlandish personal tics of the candidates … was exactly where the satiric critique belonged" (2013: 81). Similarly, Jason T. Peifer argues in his analysis of thematic framing in the Palin sketches that the issues the sketches make salient (such as Palin's incompetence and folksiness) are ones that are embedded in the treatment of Palin's personality, rather than based on political issues (2013: 172). Nickie Michaud Wild (2015) proposes a similar argument to both Jones and Peifer, but disagrees with Jones on one point. Michaud Wild argues that Ferrell's George W. Bush lacked any specific substantive satirical criticism, and, rather, latched onto a general "Bush as the dumb guy" narrative (2015: 500). In contrast, by addressing not only Palin's personal mannerisms and quirks but targeting specific actual instances that demonstrated her lack of experience and knowledge, the Palin sketches were more successful in highlighting her political failings (Michaud Wild 2015: 505). Michaud Wild is in agreement with Jones, however, when she notes that both the Palin and Bush campaign sketches parody and mock the personal mannerisms of their subjects in order to comment on the source public image. The role that self-performance plays in articulating the political position of a candidate (and the parody and satirical critique of the same) evolved between the years 2000 and 2008, resulting in this difference between generalized parodic commentary, and parody as a vehicle for specific satirical critique. This evolution is further demonstrated in *SNL*'s treatment of Donald Trump during the 2016 election campaign and into his presidency, which, while Alec Baldwin's Trump impersonation mocked physical idiosyncrasies, the sketches also focused on Trump's racism, policies, and lack of interest in the job of being president.

I return to Jones' assessment of Ferrell's Bush and Fey's Palin as offering satirical critique through the parody of personal quirks, and his argument that similarities between Palin and Bush are highlighted by their representation in sketch comedy. The status of both Bush and Palin as newcomers to national politics at the time of their respective campaigns, and their shared characteristics of being "dim-witted and arrogant, with a desire to charm their way into power," which both impersonations rely heavily upon, are, as Jones argues, "key to understanding them as politicians" (2013: 81). It is perhaps notable here that Jones focuses only on Ferrell's performance as Bush, when the role was eventually played by five different actors during Bush's two terms in office. This may be due to the scope of Jones' essay as largely focusing on *SNL*'s treatment of political campaigns, or it could perhaps be that other interpretations of Bush were less successful than Ferrell's, in that they did not showcase the qualities Jones highlights. For example, Will Forte, who played Bush from 2004 to 2006, presented the character as far more nervous and desperate than Ferrell's arrogant frat boy Bush with the "vapid-but-determined stare" (Michaud Wild 2015: 494). Forte's interpretation was no doubt shaped by the context of the time in which he played the character (in the midst of the Iraq war as opposed to Ferrell's largely pre-9/11 portrayal). However, Ferrell's portrayal of Bush has remained consistent when he has reprised the character, such as in cameo appearances during the 2008 and 2016 election seasons or in his Broadway play turned HBO special, *You're Welcome America: A Final Night with George W. Bush* (2009). The relative consistency of Ferrell's interpretation speaks to his George W. Bush as a sketch character that arose from a specific context and remained consistent to itself as a character, rather than changing to resemble the evolution of the actual Bush. The star image of the performer, too, is undoubtedly a factor in Ferrell's particular interpretation of Bush. Ferrell's post-*SNL* film career has seen him playing similar overly confident, dim-witted characters, such as in *Old School* (2003), *Anchorman: The Legend of Ron Burgundy* (2004), and *Talladega Nights: The Ballad of Ricky Bobby* (2006). This suggests that, much like Chevy Chase mapping his developing comedic persona as a physical comic onto his Gerald Ford character (Jones 2008: 39), Ferrell's work on *SNL* is what brought him to public attention and, thus, the types of sketch characters he played became a vital component of his subsequent film roles and overall star image.

While Chase and Ferrell's star images developed alongside their notable political impersonations, Tina Fey's public persona was already well established in the context of *Saturday Night Live* when she played Sarah Palin. Before I apply Jones' observations about *SNL* political impersonation to a detailed analysis of the Palin sketches, it is first necessary to consider not only the persona of Sarah Palin as a political celebrity source text, but the persona of Tina Fey as a lens through which Sarah Palin is viewed as a satirical docucharacter. This enables us to consider how the process of re-creating the actual is filtered through a specific comedic lens in order to create the unknown private self in this particular example of a sketch or satirical docucharacter.

The Multiple Lives of "Sarah Feylin"

Graeme Turner argues that contemporary media's proliferation of information needs to be understood through the lens of entertainment. With so much information available to consumers, Turner writes that media producers are competing for their piece of a fragmented audience, resulting in "the rise of entertainment and its ascendancy over information as the most marketable regime of content" (2016: 49). Liesbet Van Zoonen similarly argues that the prevalence of "entertainment culture" has molded the mediation of politics to the conventions of entertainment media in order to draw and sustain audience interest in complex, difficult, or boring political issues (2005: 69). This application of entertainment form to political content has contributed to the celebrification of politicians, where the focus on individual political actors and their personal narratives acts as a shortcut for constituents to make political judgments. The nature of the entertainment format necessitates that this shortcut is both "brief" and "pleasurable" (Van Zoonen 2005: 69). The blurred lines between entertainment and news and the rise of politicians as celebrities (and celebrities as politicians) mean that the individual personality of a politician is often the focus of the way they are represented and understood, rather than any substantive explanation of issues and policies being the focus of popular political narratives. Just as the celebrity CEO embodies the values of their company, the attachment of an individual personality acts as a means of branding and embodying the ideals of a political party or movement.

In this environment, upon her selection as John McCain's running mate on the 2008 Republican presidential ticket, little-known Alaska Governor Sarah Palin was immediately elevated into the public eye and understood very differently based on the ideological position of the spectator. Robert E. Denton Jr. (2010) attempts to pin down some of the labels affixed to Palin throughout the campaign. Politically, from her resume as a small-town mayor and governor, she could be called a "conservative," a "reformer," and a "maverick." Her selection as vice presidential candidate despite her lack of national experience also gave Palin the label of "gimmick" (Denton Jr. 2010: 17). Her personal narrative was as the confident, self-made working mother, the "hockey mom" and former beauty queen. In an encapsulation of the increasingly blurred nature of the political and the personal, labeling Palin as "authentic" attempts to articulate the appeal of her intersecting personal narrative and political brand (Denton Jr. 2010: 17). To the late-night sketch comedy show, however, the space between what Palin presents as her authentic self and the usually tightly controlled and managed front-stage space of political performance is where a more appealing narrative lies.

Ann McKinnon (2008) argues that even as Palin engaged in highly visible public performances of self, much of the narrative of Palin's public image during the campaign was crafted by others. Palin made a number of readily ridiculed gaffes early in the campaign, such as her claim that Alaska's proximity to Russia gave her relevant foreign policy credentials. Events such as this, McKinnon writes, led to the McCain campaign preventing Palin from speaking directly to the press or from holding press conferences, instead instituting a photographs-only media policy when she met with foreign leaders in New York in September 2008. The absence of Palin speaking directly for herself in the public eye (and her repeated mistakes and failure to project a strong impression as the possible vice president when she did) left room for her persona to be appropriated by others to fill the void. This resulted in a media environment during the campaign where, as McKinnon notes, "we have seen more parodies of Palin than we have seen the actual Palin" (2008). Sarah Esralew and Dannagal Goldthwaite Young argue that this proliferation of parodies alongside what was seen of Palin's self-performance (before the campaign's media embargo) resulted in the public attempting to understand the previously unknown Palin "using whatever relevant information they had available" (2017: 342). *Saturday Night Live*'s version of Palin was not only one of the most visible and culturally resonant commentaries on Palin, but also an embodied performance of Palin (rather than being only verbal or written commentary), thus becoming a significant part of her public image.

The visibility of Fey's impersonation of Palin readily extended beyond the television audience watching the live broadcast of *SNL* when the sketches aired. At the time, *SNL* distributed individual sketches as short video clips online via the official NBC website as well as Hulu and YouTube, making for easy shareability and encouraging viral viewership. Additionally, portions of the sketches were repurposed for news broadcasts and punditry, becoming part of the wider body of media commentary about Palin and demonstrating the fusion of entertainment and news media. As Michaud Wild argues, journalists had an easy and engaging way to speak about Palin as incompetent by reporting on the sketches and using them as a reference point for understanding Palin (2015: 505). Fey's performance subsequently became a highly visible and instantly recognizable shorthand for referring to Palin, with lines from *SNL* sketches like "I can see Russia from my house" becoming attributed to Palin herself in the popular imagination.

While the conflation of Tina Fey's performance of Sarah Palin with the actual Sarah Palin worked in shaping Palin's public image, Fey's own image does not completely disappear into her performance. Rather, much like Jean-Louis Comolli's (1978) idea of the body too much in the performance of historical fiction, Fey's image lingers in her performance of Palin. This in turn shapes how the character is viewed in ways that a lesser-known performer (such as Jesse Eisenberg was at the time of his breakthrough role in *The Social Network*) does not. In the context of *Saturday Night Live*, Tina Fey is a star, and hers is a star image that (unlike Chevy Chase and Will Ferrell) was firmly established at the time of her most notable impersonation. In particular, Fey is an *SNL* star who primarily performed on the show in her own persona, given she is most well-known for her six years as Weekend Update co-anchor and *SNL*'s first female head writer, rather than as a sketch performer who was routinely seen as multiple different characters each week. Amber Day and Ethan Thompson describe Fey's Weekend Update persona as "slightly nerdy and awkward and... politically invested," a purposeful contrast to her first co-anchor Jimmy Fallon's position as "an amiable, goofy guy" (2012: 177) and second co-anchor Amy Poehler's "quirky [and] upbeat" persona (2012: 178). Day and Thompson also note that given that Fey's Weekend Update tenure largely coincided with the George W. Bush administration, she was often politically critical and "periodically spoke her mind about larger political debate and public life" (2012: 178). By the time of the 2008 election campaign, Fey had already left *SNL* and was best known as creator, executive producer, writer, and star of the critically acclaimed *30 Rock*, a media savvy single camera sitcom loosely inspired by Fey's life as *SNL* head writer that often poked fun at NBC, the very network that aired it. With her politically engaged, acerbic "smart girl" persona, the East Coast liberal Fey is perhaps the very antithesis of Sarah Palin's folksy, small town, anti-elitist political persona and a counterpoint to criticisms of Palin's inarticulateness and ignorance about world events and foreign policy. While it may have been a noted physical resemblance between Fey and Palin that encouraged Fey's return to *SNL* for the role (Fey 2011: 201), the stark contrasts between these women and their public personas worked to call attention to the differences between the two every time they merged on screen. When Fey embodies the cheerful, folksy Palin wink, it is as though Fey herself perpetually lingers behind the appropriated persona: under the wig, under the flag pin, under the makeup, Fey remains, winking at us too. But it is only Tina, and not her character, that is in on the joke, subsequently rendering her Sarah as even more blissfully ignorant and lacking in self-awareness.

With an understanding of the *SNL* celebrity impersonation sketch, and the ways Tina Fey's persona inflected her Palin character, I move now to a detailed analysis of Fey's performance and the docucharacterization of Palin in the sketch comedy frame. Here I return to Jeffrey P. Jones' (2013) argument that *Saturday Night Live*'s method of parodying the personality and mannerisms of a public figure led to a satiric critique of Sarah Palin's specific failings. In particular, here I will apply Jones' characterization of Palin as "dim-witted and arrogant, with a desire to charm [her] way into power" (2013: 81) to an analysis of Fey's performance in "A Non-partisan Message from Governor Sarah Palin and Senator Hillary Clinton." This sketch, which aired on September 13, 2008, was the first appearance of Fey's Palin character, featured alongside Amy Poehler's

Clinton. Through this analysis, I highlight how elements of Fey's physical and vocal impersonation of Palin deviate from the source material of Palin's persona in order to shape the characterization that Jones identifies.

Re-creation, Creation, and Access in Sketch Comedy

Although it is not a direct re-creation of a media event, the "Non-partisan Message" sketch and its political impersonations operate within the frame of a media event. The premise of the sketch, as the title indicates, is a formal address to the nation from Palin and Clinton, coming together across party lines to address the issue of sexism in the campaign. While the sketch does not depict a specific existing media event, its jokes draw on intertextual knowledge of Palin's public appearances thus far, such as her speech accepting the vice-presidential nomination at the Republican National Convention (RNC), and her first national interview with Charles Gibson. The sketch also references general discourse about both Palin and Clinton's public images at the time, and how they were being spoken about in the media.

Fey's performance of Palin's mannerisms is most notably vocal, as Fey replicates Palin's distinctive accent and folksy cadence and speech habits, such as ending "-ing" words with a truncated dropping of 'g's. Fey says that, given that she is not an experienced impressionist, she began her approach to the impression with the accent and vocal inflections. Fey felt that approaching the voice best suited her skills, given her training in developing characters for theater and improvisation. From the voice, she constructed the impression and the character (*Fresh Air* 2008). One particular element of the vocal performance that Fey highlights as an insight into both the character and the real Sarah Palin is that when Palin is being "sassy" or taking a shot at an opponent, her voice pitches higher, giving the sense that she is "pretty pleased with herself" and the joke she is making (*Fresh Air* 2008). The "Non-partisan Message" sketch includes an example of this when Fey repeats a joke from Palin's RNC speech ("What's the difference between a hockey mom and a pitbull? Lipstick."). As Fey begins the joke in the sketch, her voice pitches higher and her speech slows down. The higher pitch and anticipation of the joke's setup gives the sense that Palin is indeed pleased with herself. Poehler's Clinton appears irritated and tries to cut her off by flatly repeating the punch line, "Lipstick." Palin ignores Clinton completely, and gives the punch line as though it is completely new.

Palin's self-satisfaction and steamrolling of Clinton points to Palin's arrogance, the attempt to win over the audience with her folksy humor points to her charm, and the fact that she's repeating a joke heard so many times by this point in her campaign that Clinton is annoyed and already knows the punch line points to a dim-witted lack of self-awareness.

Fey's physical performance similarly imitates Palin's mannerisms and creates her as a character. Fey has stated that as part of attempting to physically resemble Palin, she compensates between differences in their appearance by sticking her jaw out further and trying to make her mouth seem wider (*Fresh Air* 2008). Particularly in the "Non-partisan Message" sketch, Fey also tilts her chin slightly higher. This, in combination with the forward setting of Fey's jaw and the way she positions her mouth higher and purses her lips, not only achieves a closer resemblance to Palin's squarer jawline, but also signifies and amplifies Palin's arrogance and overconfidence. The actual Palin frequently displayed this facial expression during her RNC speech. There, three minutes of a standing ovation, cheering, and applause followed Palin's introduction and her entrance onto the stage. In C-Span's live broadcast of the event, the footage cuts between the smiling faces of the gathered delegates and Palin on stage where she was shown making the same pursed-lipped expression, as though she was suppressing a self-satisfied smile. Palin made this expression numerous times throughout the speech, particularly during applause breaks, and the suppression of a smile gave her a smugness that was not present in the moments when she did allow herself to smile (Republican National Convention 2008). Fey's replication of the expression gives the sense that, despite Palin's lack of national political experience, she is a politician who is comfortable in situations where she has the rapt attention of a large audience, and where she is the only one speaking and thus has some sense of control over her words. This is in contrast to her behavior in interview settings such as those with Charles Gibson and Katie Couric where the actual Palin seems significantly less comfortable. It is worth noting that Fey later carries this expression over to *SNL*'s Couric interview sketch, where the Palin character is clearly trying to bluff her way through the interview on her overconfidence and charm alone. The expression is disconnected from her garbled, nonsensical responses to questions (of which many lines were taken verbatim from the actual interview), highlighting her misplaced overconfidence.

Fey's posture at the podium in the "Non-partisan Message" sketch, however, differs from how Palin stood in a similar setting during her RNC speech. On stage at the RNC, Palin's stance is squarer and steadier, her weight distributed equally on both feet, whereas Fey's shoulders are tilted, the left side of her body angled as though she is standing with her weight on her left side with her right hip cocked. While this may be partially explained by the fact that Fey shares the podium space with Poehler, who is also standing in a slight three-quarter profile with her body leaning toward Fey, Fey's tilted posture is far more pronounced than Poehler's. It makes her Palin seem flirtier and more casual, an effect amplified by the way Fey moves her body behind the podium far more than both the real Palin and Poehler-as-Clinton do, frequently dipping her left shoulder and extending her right hip. While this mannerism is not a strict impression of Palin, it works as a means of communicating one of the signature Palin characteristics that Jones identifies in the *SNL* sketches: her desire to skate by on charm alone. This element that is subtly communicated by the position of Fey's body becomes more obvious later in the sketch, as Palin ignores Clinton's account of her struggle for the White House to wave to the audience and move through a series of flirty pin-up poses, including a pose with a mimed gun. This is also not a direct physical impression of Palin, but rather captures the essence of the substance versus style rhetoric in comparisons between Clinton and Palin. Similarly, the impression captures the essence of the role that sexism plays on the contrasting positive and negative attention given to the two based on their appearance and behavior, rather than their policies, experience, or knowledge. This is the issue at the core of the sketch's premise, and, once again, it is Palin's charm and arrogance that is given attention in Fey's body language as her Palin character responds to the topic.

This analysis of Tina Fey's performance as Sarah Palin demonstrates how Fey's replications and slight alterations of Palin in voice, facial expression, and body language work to create Sarah Palin as a sketch docucharacter. As Jones argues, the parodying of Palin's mannerisms and individual quirks, such as those discussed here, work to highlight elements of her personality and public persona which are key to understanding her as a politician: namely, charm, arrogance, and a dim-witted lack of self-awareness. There is a simultaneous execution of the "re-creation" and "creation" elements of the docucharacter, as the recognizable public persona is re-created through visual cues such as hair and wardrobe, vocal cues such as accent and speech patterns, and textual cues such as the re-purposing of actual dialogue from existing speeches or public appearances.

The Palin impersonation in the "Non-partisan Message" sketch is somewhat more generalized in its re-creation of the actual, since it is not based on replicating a specific or actual media moment. To consider how characterizations are created in sketches that are based on actual moments, it is worth considering the example of the "Vice Presidential Debate" sketch to illustrate how a sketch can offer access to a simulated version of a public figure in a comedic lens. I argue that the *SNL* sketch constructs a recognizable resemblance to an existing media event in order to present the comedic subtext of the event as the text of the sketch. This is done in ways that bring the satirically speculated interior self of the character into the realm of the on-stage public self formerly occupied by the actual celebrity persona, thus offering the viewer access to the satiric subtext of actuality, and a version of a public figure that may resemble the actual but behaves in ways the actual public figure often tries to mask.

Saturday Night Live's re-creation of the 2008 Vice Presidential debate aired on October 4, 2008, two days after the actual event. This sketch served as the third appearance of Fey's Palin impression, and featured regular cast member Jason Sudeikis as Palin's opponent Joe Biden, with a guest appearance from Queen Latifah as debate moderator Gwen Ifill. The stage set for the sketch mimicked the set of the actual debate broadcast, with moderator Ifill sitting at a semi-circular desk facing the two candidates' podiums. The blue walls of the set are adorned with symbols of the United States, its government, and its patriotic ideology, such as a bald eagle with a flag shield, a row of white stars bordering the top of the set, and lighter blue panels featuring text from the Declaration of Independence and the preamble to the United States Constitution forming the backdrop for each candidate in shots where they directly address the camera.

Much like the appearance of the set, the dialogue of the sketch mimics the actual event. Some lines are verbatim up until a point where the dialogue is augmented in ways that reveal the presumed satirical truth behind them. After Fey's Palin and Sudeikis' Biden are introduced, they approach the center of the stage (with Palin blowing kisses to the audience, as she did in the original) and shake hands. Character Palin asks (as the actual Palin did during their introduction in the debate), "Hey, can I call you Joe?" Biden responds in the affirmative, just as the actual one did. From this point, however, the sketch deviates from the original source material of the debate's transcript as Palin, still continuing to vigorously shake Biden's hand, explicitly states the comedic subtext of the original moment in order to make the satiric point: "Okay, 'cause I practiced a couple zingers where I call you Joe." Peifer identifies this technique as "refracting political realities," where the "impersonation parody can articulate the hidden subtext of a political situation in a unique way, borrowing from and reinventing a political figure's own behavior" (2013: 170). The comedic subtext of the original moment (as *SNL* sees it) is that due to Palin's previous campaign gaffes when responding to questions she was seemingly unprepared for, her debate responses have all been scripted ahead of time, down to the letter. If it had been necessary to refer to her opponent as Senator Biden, her memorization of the script could become unraveled into a similar nonsensical word salad as some of the unscripted answers in her widely seen interviews with Couric and Gibson. As it was, in the actual debate, Palin referred to Biden several times as "O'Biden," a slip that the film *Game Change* dwells on in its sequences of behind-the-scenes debate prep, which I will focus on later in this chapter in examining Sarah Palin as a docucharacter in the HBO film.

Returning to the "Vice Presidential Debate" sketch, the "I practiced a couple zingers where I call you Joe" line is one of many examples in this sketch (as well as the other Palin sketches, and other celebrity impersonation sketches based on a specific event) where humor arises from the character explicitly uttering the comedic subtext of a moment in the source material. This transforms the perceived subtext of the original media event into the text of the sketch and highlights the space between the front-stage, public self of the political performance, and the contradictory backstage self behind the political performance. That Palin has memorized the script of her debate responses, right down to the exact wording of a few soundbite-worthy zingers, is not something that the actual Palin would be expected to reveal in the public, front-stage context of the debate. In Erving Goffman's terms, it is a revelation from the backstage frame invading the front-stage space. It becomes an act of witnessing the unwitnessable, granting the viewer simulated access to an otherwise inaccessible funhouse mirror comedic distortion of the public figure. It is comedic because of the cheerful and almost unthinking way that Fey's Palin makes the revelation and makes a satiric critique as it renders the actual Palin as incapable of preparing for the debate in any way other than strictly scripted performance. With the shortened screen time inherent in the television sketch form, the shortcut to revealing the private moments behind the public media event becomes to acknowledge them directly in dialogue. This is in contrast to the ways that longer form narratives, like the biopic, stage private events for the audience to witness. In this collapsing of public performance and private thought to a single on-stage frame, the sketch achieves its intention of humor through the incongruity and inappropriateness of such an honest revelation taking place on the carefully orchestrated political stage. It is a disruption of the expected norms of the televised political debate to reveal too much, and in doing so the sketch pulls back the curtain on the real public figure through the appropriation of their performance in a media event.

The use of inappropriate utterances such as this is another example of how Tina Fey's public persona shapes the construction of the Sarah Palin sketch character. In the sketches, inappropriate utterances are a feature of Fey's Palin that mocks her developing media image as the folksy, Washington outsider maverick, who wants to "say what she's thinkin.'" Additionally, the inappropriate utterance of private thought is something embedded in Fey's existing star image through her *30 Rock* character, Liz Lemon. As the head writer of an *SNL*-like sketch comedy show, Liz is depicted as living almost entirely for her job and having no personal life. For Liz Lemon, her work is home, and her professional life is her personal life. Much of the comedy of the character stems from Liz making personal utterances that would ordinarily be out of place in a work context. The inappropriate utterance is a quality of other characters and frequent source of comedy on the show. Regular subjects of such jokes are the performer characters Tracy (Tracy Morgan) and Jenna (Jane Krakowski)—characters who are too bizarre, famous, or self-possessed to recognize the inappropriateness of their words and actions. Likewise, the inappropriate utterances of Fey's Palin demonstrate a similar lack of self-awareness, knowledge, or regard for the contextual rules of public life. Her ignorance of or apathy toward such rules brings into focus the constructed nature of political speech through the character's inability to hide the political machine. The way the debate sketch riffs on Palin's vague answers and dodging of questions is a further example of this.

In the "Vice Presidential Debate" sketch, the running joke about Palin's question dodging is set up from Fey-as-Palin's first response. When Ifill addresses her first question to Palin about the economy, Palin does not immediately attempt to answer the question, instead responding with a backwards compliment to Biden about his hair plugs. The running thread of Palin's question dodging in the actual debate and the perceived subtext behind it becomes satiric text which, as per sketch comedy conventions, is escalated (or heightened) by raising the stakes on the obviousness of Palin's refusal to answer on each repetition (or beat) of the joke. On the first beat of the question-dodging run of jokes, Fey's Palin is asked if she would like to respond to comments Biden has made about John McCain. She responds, "No, thank you. But I would like to talk about bein' an outsider." Next, when asked about climate change, Palin first gives an answer that she is unsure if "this climate change hoozie-what's-it is manmade, or just a natural part of the End of Days," before abruptly (after Fey pauses for audience laughter) redirecting the subject: "But I'm not gonna talk about that. I'm gonna talk about taxes." The third beat has Ifill asking a direct question about Palin's position on healthcare regulation. In this final escalation of the Palin-dodging-questions joke, the dodge is at its most blunt and inappropriate for the situation: a bright and cheerful, "I'm gonna ignore that question and instead talk about Israel!" Rather than the actual Palin's somewhat more subtle approach to not directly addressing the questions posed to her in the debate, *SNL*'s Palin plainly states her desire to not answer those questions and states the topics she would rather talk about instead. Needless to say, being this obvious about a political topic pivot would be inappropriate to explicitly state in an actual debate forum. The comedic intention of the sketch, however, depends on the explicit disruption of political performance norms to highlight and critique how the actual Palin avoided questions in the debate. Once again, the subtext of the actual moment becomes the explicitly stated thoughts of the sketch character's inner self as front-stage and backstage frames are collapsed for comedic effect.

There is a similar collapse of front- and backstage frames for the sketch's other characters. Latifah's Ifill, for example, opens the sketch by establishing the rules of the debate and that she "will not ask any follow-up questions beyond 'Do you agree?' or 'Your response?' so as not to appear biased for Barack Obama." The backstage truth behind the statement is revealed as she immediately throws in a promotion for her book about Obama that is due for release on inauguration day. The fact of Ifill's book is part of the material of actuality that the sketch uses not only to base the sketch in reality, but also to give a satiric critique of that reality by imagining the contradictory backstage, inner selves of its characters. As Joe Biden, Jason Sudeikis parodies Biden's quirks in the typical style of *SNL* political impersonation that Jones writes of: the largely good-natured dig, rather than aggressive satirical criticism. This is done by the heightening of familiar aspects of Biden's political persona, such as his frequent reliance on his blue-collar background and humble origin story ("I come from Scranton, Pennsylvania, and that's as hard-scrabble a place as you're going to find. I'll show you around some time and you'll see: it's a hellhole! An absolute jerkwater of a town. You couldn't stand to spend a weekend there!"). While the sketch's treatment of the Biden character is largely based in good-natured parody, there are moments of public/private collapse that create specific satirical critique. This is most notably done on the topic of marriage equality, where Sudeikis' Biden agrees that same-sex couples should be granted the same legal rights of marriage as heterosexual couples. Then, when prompted to confirm whether he agrees with Obama's contradictory position favoring civil unions, the Biden character immediately disavows his own beliefs in deference to the views of the man on the top of the ticket. Like the sketch's treatment of Palin, the Ifill and Biden characters are constructed in ways that point out the gaps between public action and private thought and endow political performance with an inherent insincerity.

SNL's re-creation of the Vice-Presidential debate and its characters serves what Joel Schechter identifies as a function of satiric impersonation, in that it "raise[s] serious doubts about the credibility of an event, a person, or a policy" (1994: 2–3). In this situation, considering the doubts about Palin's credibility that were already circulating in the media at that time, the sketch (and, indeed, Fey's other performances as Palin throughout the campaign) could better be described as cementing and comedically articulating those doubts about Palin's credibility. When the sketches present the private self behind Palin's media gaffes as the actual spoken dialogue of the sketch, key doubts about Palin such as her inexperience and lack of knowledge are articulated in ways that closely align with her public image. The close alignment with Palin's public image is done using more-or-less verbatim dialogue taken from the original event(s) the *SNL* sketches re-create, the visual re-creation of media events, and the performative re-creation of Palin's actions within them. This material of the actual, shaped by the comedic and critical intentions of the sketch and its characters, dismantles the norms of political performance by pointing out the carefully constructed frame of the public and its absurdist disruption by the private. In addition to calling Palin's credibility into question, the credibility of the political event itself is questioned in the "Vice Presidential Debate" sketch through the Gwen Ifill character's plug for her book about Obama and jokes about the incredibly low expectations for Palin's performance in the debate. Additionally, the nature of authentic political self-performance is questioned through the sketch's critique of Biden's abandonment of his personal views on marriage equality in favor of conforming to the political realities of the presidential ticket he represents.

In this case study of political impersonation on *Saturday Night Live*, I have argued that the form of the television sketch uses documentary evidence in similar persuasive ways as the docudrama: a docucomedy mode of representation. The docucomedy mode at work here aims to create a sense of verisimilitude to existing people and events to immediately signal a joke, relying on the highly visible media presences of those it impersonates in order to establish recognition (to draw on Murray Smith's terms) of a sketch character. This can be considered an explicitly intertextual, more specific version of using stock characters and stereotypes in screen comedy. Through this persuasive mode of presentation, the sketch establishes what is known in order to disrupt it with the inappropriate revelation of private thoughts and actions. These disruptions and the methods by which they occur can evolve through the repetition across multiple sketches. This repetition, in conjunction with the way an individual actor approaches an impersonation with a fidelity to accuracy in mind, can move the impersonation into the realm of being a sketch character that takes on a life of its own beyond its original source material. While this life does not have, nor does it intend to have, the same degree of fleshed-out, three dimensional being as a dramatic character might, it nonetheless can exist as a distinct entity that, through its association with the celebrity image at its source, can shape understandings of the celebrity subject. With this analysis of the adaptation of public figures in sketch comedy in mind, I continue considering the example of Sarah Palin by contrasting how her docucharacterization is transformed by a change in genre and screen context as I examine the HBO film *Game Change*.

Game Change: Palin in Docudrama

Like *Saturday Night Live*'s Palin sketches, the HBO film *Game Change*, adapted from John Heilemann and Mark Halperin's book of the same name, anchors its remediation of Sarah Palin in the replication of widely broadcast public events already familiar to the presumed audience. When compared to sketch comedy, the form of the docudrama necessarily alters how these anchoring media events are structured. The film as a long-form narrative, the dramatic intent of the film, and the broader thematic scope of the film all have a significant impact on how the existing media event is used. It should be noted that the book *Game Change* follows multiple narratives of the 2008 presidential election campaign, such as Barack Obama and Hillary Clinton's close competition for the Democratic nomination, the scandal of John Edwards' extramarital affair, and presumed frontrunner Rudy Giuliani's failed bid for the Republican nomination. The screen adaptation, however, is entirely concerned with the selection of Sarah Palin as John McCain's running mate, and the consequences of that decision for the Republican party's presidential hopes. Narrowing its focus further, rather than being presented as an objective third-party account of events the film is structured in a way that announces its version of Sarah Palin as being constructed by the subjective point of view of an insider, granting the audience access from the insider point of view.

The film is bookended by a re-creation of a *60 Minutes* interview with McCain advisor Steve Schmidt, played by Woody Harrelson, which combines the actor's performance with actual footage of interviewer Anderson Cooper. Cooper poses the question to Schmidt of whether he would still include Sarah Palin on the ticket if he were able to have a second chance at the campaign. Harrelson's Schmidt pauses, and the film then cuts to a flashback of Schmidt receiving a phone call from John McCain, asking him to join the campaign. From there, the narrative of the election, and Palin's role in it, unfolds. At the end of the film, the *60 Minutes* interview is revisited, Cooper's question repeated, and Schmidt's answer finally delivered. The bookend effect serves to structure the film as an extended flashback sequence as Schmidt considers Cooper's question, a consideration primarily informed by the points of view of Schmidt and other McCain campaign staffers, making this version of Palin one that is tied to the point of view of a specific character (or group of characters with a similar perspective) with a very specific opinion of her. By engaging the memories of both the audience and the characters in the film, it situates this representation of Palin as a reflective one informed by hindsight, rather than one that develops alongside the real-life narrative as was the case with Fey's impersonation in *SNL*'s topical sketch comedy.

This extended flashback of the film uses Palin's major media events as narrative tent poles from which connective, behind-the-scenes sequences hang, depicting the build-up to and fall-out from these events. The known public and imagined private are presented alongside each other, and the broad, intertextual body of Sarah Palin's public persona and speculated private self are presented as a single, cohesive character. As Julianne Moore embodies Palin's multiple modes of public and private self-performance, the film achieves a function of docudrama that Steven Lipkin identifies: to make visible the known but unseen (2011: 48). Through the spectator's alignment with Moore's embodiment of the character, we witness a private Sarah Palin who is emotional, unprepared, uncooperative, and focused on herself. From the perspective of the insider, we see for the first time the amount of preparation that was required to try to fill in the substantial gaps in Palin's knowledge of world history and foreign relations. We see her emotional response to the rigors of the campaign and the media's criticism of her. We see her attempts to reclaim her agency from operatives who remade her image for their own political gain. Rather than including these elements as explicit comedic text as the sketch format requires, the docudrama shows the division between public and private as discrete elements of the character. In the case of *Game Change*, this works to give an understanding of Sarah Palin that, above all else, she is a performer and a star.

To draw appropriate comparisons and highlight the formal differences between the *Saturday Night Live* sketch and *Game Change*, I will focus on the re-presentation of the debate between Palin and Biden in my analysis of *Game Change*. As with the *SNL* sketch, the set of the debate is re-created for *Game Change*. However, driven by the closer relationship to actuality that the docudrama claims, and facilitated by the higher production values and longer pre-production time the HBO film has available (as opposed to *SNL*'s necessary quick turnaround of content), the set is a much closer approximation of the actual debate set. This allows the film to successfully integrate docudrama footage with actual news footage to make it appear to be a seamless presentation of the event. Here, debate moderator Gwen Ifill is represented by actual footage from the debate, as is Joe Biden when he appears in the front-stage space of the debate. A Biden body double appears in the representation of the debate's backstage space, in an out of focus long shot that obscures his face and preserves the illusion that it could be the same Biden as the repurposed news footage, as he and Palin stand in the wings on opposite sides of the stage. Moore-as-Palin's front-stage dialogue and delivery are replicated directly from the actual debate.

The division of public and private selves within front- and backstage frames is represented in the *SNL* sketch through the inappropriateness of private utterances in the on-stage frame of public political performance. In *Game Change*'s narrative structure of public media events and the behind-the-scenes stories behind them, Erving Goffman's dramaturgical metaphor is made literal. In the vice-presidential debate sequence, the frame of public and private is demarcated by literal on- and off-stage spaces. Throughout the sequence, the façade of the public Palin remains intact and unbroken throughout the front-stage frame of the debate. The film opens space for private thoughts and moments to take place in hidden from the public, backstage spaces. Backstage sequences depicting Palin's private self bracket the event of the debate. While Palin is on stage, the sequence cross cuts to the backstage reactions of other major characters, such as Schmidt, Nicolle Wallace (Sarah Paulson), and John McCain (Ed Harris). For example, in the *SNL* sketch, elements of Palin's debate performance such as question dodging are explicitly addressed as Fey's Palin deliberately announces her question dodging strategy. In *Game Change*, the strategy is addressed in the backstage, private space of the narrative.

As the story is structured by the build up to and fallout from Palin's major media events (her RNC speech, the Gibson interview, the Couric interview, the debate, negative attacks against Obama at stump speeches, and so on), the build-up to the debate is colored by Palin's behavior and emotional state taking a downturn after the failure of the Couric interview. She is shown in debate prep as unresponsive and uncooperative, unable to understand or remember anything on which the campaign staff attempt to coach her. Frustrated and expecting the debate to be a complete disaster, Schmidt changes strategy and proposes that "the greatest actress in American politics" simply memorize scripted answers to likely debate questions rather than understand the answers she needs to give. The rote memorization is given as the reason behind Palin's question dodging and pivoting to topics other than the ones she is asked about during the debate. Rather than a point of comedic derision, as it is in the *SNL* sketch, the strategy is presented in *Game Change* as the breakthrough that saves Palin's debate performance. Through the film's simulated access to backstage space, the audience witnesses the strategy being encouraged and applauded by Schmidt and other staffers as they watch the debate.

Much like *Saturday Night Live*'s characterization of Palin as a performer through its emphasis on her desire and ability to skate by on charm, *Game Change* engages with a similar characterization through Schmidt's labeling of Palin as "the greatest actress in American politics." The characterization is evident in Moore's performance as she stands in the wings before the debate begins. Her eyes narrow at Biden across the stage, mimicking the way he stretches his arms before waving her hand dismissively, as though she is attempting to perform how a politician is supposed to (copying the more experienced Biden's actions), before rejecting it in favor of her own self-image (Palin sees herself as a political outsider, unwilling to play the usual game). She repeats Biden's name quietly to herself, trying to reinforce it to avoid the "O'Biden" flubs she repeatedly made during debate prep. The nerves and worry in her expression disappear just before she walks on stage, as she puts on a confident smile and posture moments before stepping in front of the audience and the camera, prepared to perform her memorized lines.

While *SNL* and *Game Change* propose similar characterizations of Palin through their remediations of the vice-presidential debate, differences between the forms of television sketch and docudrama film allow a more clearly demarcated division of public and private in the latter. In sketch comedy, the imagined private becomes public in the text to elicit laughter and satirize the fabricated nature of both Palin's political performance and the media event of the debate. In docudrama, the imagined private is constructed in backstage spaces to be witnessed by the audience, to give audiences access to an imagined version of events not reflected by the public historical record.

Game Change does not have the comedic intent of *SNL*, but it is not without its moments of humor. The reaction shot is a common technique of screen comedy, and it is used in *Game Change* in ways that position Palin as absurd from the film's subjective point of view of Schmidt and the other McCain staffers. There are moments in the vice-presidential debate sequence that add levity to the drama, like Palin's "O'Biden" gaffe in prep and Schmidt's handling of it that leads to a "Who's on first"-esque dialogue exchange between the two. However, *Game Change* does exclude some memorable moments from the actual debate in its re-staging. Actual moments that highlighted Palin's folksiness and maverick self-image were used to frame her as ridiculous in the *SNL* sketch, as well as in broader commentary about her debate performance, were left out of *Game Change*. Debate memes such as Palin's references to regular "Joe six packs" and winks to the camera are absent from *Game Change*'s version of the debate. By eliminating popular memory of some of the failed aspects of Palin's debate performance, the film presents an understanding of the vice-presidential debate through the lens of its insider perspective.

Because the narrative is focalized through the point of view of McCain staffers, the representation of the difficult lead up to the debate positions the debate as a victory for Palin and the McCain campaign. In a post-debate scene, one staffer reads from a poll declaring Biden the winner of the debate and is quickly dismissed by Schmidt. In *Game Change*'s backstage space of the debate aftermath, the McCain staffers celebrate, and Palin's own confidence is reclaimed through her performance. The charm and arrogance of Palin's wink (which, in actuality, took place on the debate stage) appears in a backstage scene after the debate, where Palin expresses to Schmidt the need to win the election, because she "so [doesn't] want to go back to Alaska," followed by the wink. The presence of this known front-stage gesture in this unknown backstage space suggests that at this moment in the story, Palin has reclaimed a sense of self through her public self-performance. The traits of the public Palin are shaping the way the private Palin acts. Gone is the silent, unresponsive Palin of the debate prep, and here is the confident, cocky Palin of the stage. The persona is potentially an act in every frame, with Palin's attempt to bluff her way through on charm in public and in private, the ultimate embodiment of the insincerity of public political life.

In the political impersonation sketch, through the collapse of public/private into the public utterances of the text, the focus of the private is largely restricted to the imagined subtext of the public figure's private thoughts during the actual media event. In the docudramatic film, however, the representation of and access to the private extends beyond the imagined thoughts to more private spaces and aspects of Palin's character. In the pre-debate/debate/post-debate sequence alone, Palin's husband and children are a significant presence. Palin attributes her unresponsiveness in the early stages of debate prep to missing her baby. McCain and the campaign staff work to reunite Palin with her family in an effort to improve her performance by inviting them all to McCain's home in Sedona to continue debate prep. It is a conversation before bed with her husband that encourages Palin to be herself, to follow her own instincts and disregard the way campaign staffers are pushing her. Moments such as the emotional phone call with her deployed son and praying with her youngest daughter before the debate present Palin's private life in ways that characterize her as being deeply committed to her family. Aligning the spectator with private moments such as these work to elicit a sympathetic response in the audience's allegiance to the Palin character. In witnessing the ways Palin has been separated from her family during the difficulties of the campaign and engaging with the Palin character's emotional reaction to the situation, the distant figure of the actual Palin's public image becomes relatable and humanized in ways that can potentially transcend the divisiveness of political ideology.

The space of time and location and the non-comedic imperative afforded by the docudrama allow for a more nuanced melding of public and private selves, creating a character that is more rounded, unlike the "sketched," hurried nature of the sketch character that is drawn in broad strokes and generalizations. Despite the differences in form and intention, though, both sketch and docudrama use similar textual strategies to recreate the public to present their versions of the private for each text's distinct purposes. Aside from their differences in form and intention, another notable distinction between these two portrayals of Sarah Palin is their temporal relationship to her rise to fame. On *SNL*, the sketch character evolves concurrently with the real Sarah Palin, with each new media event in the unfolding campaign (including the sketches themselves) adding to the narrative of Palin's media image and popular understandings of Palin in the political landscape shaped by entertainment culture. *Game Change*, however, is a retrospective in both its production and reception, albeit a very recent retrospective with the film premiering on HBO less than four years after the events it depicts took place. In addition to the more nuanced portrayal of public and private selves available to the television docudrama film through its extended narrative space and lack of comedic intent when compared to the sketch, the retrospective approach to events lends itself to approaching Palin with a more sympathetic eye than allowed by (or desired by) topical satire. In short, docudramatic representation has space to elicit sympathy through the demarcation of public and private selves, where we see "another side" to the public figure we thought we knew. The intentions of the sketch, however, collapse public and private into a single frame so that the affective response to the character is based on a more restrictive alignment. The allegiant response is intended to be one of mockery, or satiric criticism. The goal is laughter, and the character is constructed in such a way that the audience's affective response to the character will be to laugh at her, and through that laughter, endorse the sketch character's satiric critique of the actual public figure. The affective understanding of the subject that sketch comedy offers is one that is heavily colored by the spectator's laughter response, generated by the version of the character to which the viewer is granted access.

With this comparison between the adaptation of a public figure to a screen character in docucomedic and docudramatic contexts, the similar processes of re-creation, creation, and access become evident, despite the nuances of how the characterization is executed that are afforded by different media forms with different intentions. The next chapter continues the examination of the textual process of creating characters from real people in forms beyond the biopic with a consideration of celebrities playing themselves in film and television comedy. While the sketch comedy texts examined here are written and performed by third parties with the goal of satirical critique, the following chapter considers the agency of the celebrity subject in the creation of a fictionalized self and the ways such a performance can add to the star image through good-natured self-parody, or the production of authenticity in a fictionalized frame.

5

Beyond the Biopic: Celebrities Play Themselves

Not too long ago, while leading a tutorial discussion in an Introduction to Film and Television Studies class on the topic of performance, a student asked me what I thought about how we can evaluate "good" and "bad" performances when celebrities are playing fictionalized versions of themselves. After all, if public figures are always performing some kind of persona, how do we evaluate their performance when that persona is deliberately designated as a fictional(ized) character? I went to the easy answer first: the comedic, parodic celebrity performance of self, the usually quick cameo where the celebrity is being a "good sport" and making fun of themselves and their public persona. Perhaps we can evaluate those as being good performances because it shows a celebrity is self-aware enough of their own status in their industry, and the way they are perceived by the public that they can do a perfect imitation of a self that is not-quite-them. Then, I paused for a while. I wanted to answer the student's question by giving an example of a celebrity appearing to "play it straight," who played a fictional version of themselves that was not purposefully disavowing their own persona or making fun of it. I told the student that and said, "The only example I know a lot about is Louis C.K., and the fictional version of himself he played in his TV series. But that example raises a lot more questions about performance than it answers."

As a world-famous stand-up comedian and the writer, director, and producer of a television series where he played a version of himself as a slightly less world-famous stand-up comedian, Louis C.K. built his career on performing authenticity through confessional-style material. In November 2017, in the wake of sexual assault and sexual misconduct allegations against powerful Hollywood figures like Harvey Weinstein and Keven Spacey, allegations of Louis C.K.'s own coercive sexual behavior came to light when reporting from the *New York Times* revealed that C.K. was accused of asking numerous women over whom he held a position of professional power to watch him masturbate (Ryzik, Buckley, and Kantor 2017). After having denied rumors of these allegations in the past, including just two months earlier to the *New York Times* (Buckley 2017), C.K. released a statement following publication of the November 2017 *Times* article confirming that the stories were true. The industry response was swift and defiant: C.K. was dropped by his management company, Netflix canceled the planned second comedy special in C.K.'s deal with the streaming platform; FX, the network that aired C.K.'s series *Louie* and with whom he had an overall deal, cut ties with him, including removing him as an executive producer of *Baskets* and *Better Things*; the distribution of his about-to-be-released film *I Love You, Daddy* was withdrawn; and HBO removed his previous comedy specials from their platform and canceled upcoming appearances on the network (Goldberg 2017). C.K.'s career, which had been built on the back of confessional comedy that often joked about his own compulsive sexual behavior, was effectively over now that it had been proven that those jokes were not "just jokes." And this is where the problems lie in unpacking C.K.'s performance of his fictionalized self on television: was it a performance that revealed a true self that permitted his unacceptable private behavior to hide in plain sight? Was it an inauthentic role that, by playing a version of himself that was less successful, endeared him to the audience as an empathetic everyman? Or was it, as I eventually suggested to my class with a somewhat defeated shrug, one of the most consistent performances of self both in and out of fiction, because it had, like the myriad of other predatory figures in entertainment who had been exposed over the past several years, been believable for long enough to garner success and silence those who tried to speak out?

This chapter will consider the docucharacter as it exists through celebrities performing themselves as characters in fictional contexts and, by focusing in particular on the figure of the stand-up comedian, the performance of a semi-fictionalized self in the liminal context of the stage persona that is both the most publicly visible self and the purported revelation of the private self. Throughout this book, the literal front- and backstage spaces occupied by celebrities such as musicians, actors, and politicians have helped the application of Erving Goffman's (1956) dramaturgical metaphor for self-performance. When the actor is on camera, whether in character or as their public persona, they are in an on-stage space. When a politician or CEO speaks publicly, in a television appearance or press interview, they are in an on-stage space. Likewise, when a stand-up comedian enters the stage, it is literally on-stage space where they perform their public stage persona. Trying to demarcate public and private selves within these spaces, however, introduces complications. Kate Warren terms the performance of self within a fictionalized frame as "parafictional personas," and notes that their fictionality "threatens the truth status of their referents" allowing "multiple levels of fiction and reality to co-exist" where the multi-leveled persona is shrouded in "irresolvability" (2016: 56). Warren's characterization of these performances points to complications such as: when the camera is trained on an actor performing what is proposed to be a staged version of their private self, does the fictional frame obscure a "real" self, or does it reveal a truth that can be disavowed by a claim to fiction? What about the stand-up comic who draws on their personal life and private self to construct their public persona? Reflecting personal experience through a comedic lens inherently introduces a degree of fictionality to the comedian's persona as it reveals a private self that must be crafted and honed in a way that is funny. Some performers may present a public image that encourages their audience to ignore the boundaries of back- and front-stage. Recent stand-up comedy specials dealing in personal material, such as Hannah Gadsby's *Nanette* (2018), Patton Oswalt's *Annihilation* (2017), and Bo Burnham's *Inside* (2021), acknowledge and disrupt the comedic frame of front-stage space to reveal aspects of the comedian's private self and life experience with serious intentions. Louis C.K. has consistently also been one such performer, and how his stage persona and on-screen fictionalized self authenticated, and was authenticated by, his eventual confession of sexual misconduct, will be considered in this chapter.

First, however, as I did in conversation with my students, I will look at the broader context of some of the different functions of celebrities playing fictionalized selves, many of which play with persona in deliberately comedic and self-parodic ways. Here I draw on several films and television shows which fictionalize some aspect of the entertainment industry and the types of people that populate it, whether that is Hollywood film, network television, or stand-up comedy. All the texts under consideration in some way satirize or mock the entertainment industry, and the verisimilitude of celebrities appearing as themselves lends documentary evidence to the film or television show's satirical point of view. A celebrity performing as their recognizable self gives a sense of plausible resemblance to what the audience understands, knows, or assumes about the entertainment industry. This sense of recognition and plausibility allows the audience to entertain the possibility that the text's satirical commentary on the industry is a true one. As with the other forms of docucharacter examined throughout this book, audience recognition and expectations are triggered in order to create that plausible connection to actuality and believability. By approaching these texts as examples of self-docucharacterization, I consider the effects that celebrity cameos and fictionalized selves have in granting simulated access to a "real" self of the performer, as well as the claims such characterizations make about the truth and validity of the celebrity's public image. I identify several different functions of the self-performed docucharacter and argue that celebrities appearing as versions of themselves in screen texts can serve to enhance the plausibility of a fictional world, to comedically undermine an established celebrity persona, to demonstrate a celebrity's self-awareness of their established persona, and to authenticate the public persona as a form of "true self."

I begin by examining celebrity self-docucharacterization with texts that take a more two-dimensional approach which does not intend to craft a fully formed character, much like the sketch comedy characterizations discussed in the previous chapter. In the case of a celebrity playing themselves in a caricatured version, there is not an imperative to uncover the speculated "really" behind the public image as a more long-form characterization might. When playing a caricatured version of themselves, the celebrity does not participate in the direct revelation of a "true" self. The revelation of part of a "true" self may be a by-product of the performance: we find out that the celebrity can make a joke at their own expense, or that they endorse the idea that their public image is a farce. But we do not get the impression of a real self directly from the performance of the fictionalized self. Here, I outline some of the functions that a celebrity appearing as themselves can serve in a comedic screen text, and how the varying aims of these functions can alter the way a celebrity persona is adapted to be performed as a fictionalized character.

Narrative Functions of Celebrities Playing Themselves on Screen

Enhancing the Believability of a Fictional World

The appearance of a celebrity performing as themselves in an otherwise fictional text can serve to locate the diegesis within our recognizable world. Not only can this imbue a sense of verisimilitude to the world being depicted, but the audience can take pleasure in seeing recognizable elements of their own world reflected in the world on screen, playing with the paradoxes of the real becoming fictional, and the fictional becoming real (Sobchack 2004: 263). Unsurprisingly, we tend to find celebrities performing as themselves in self-reflexive film and television texts that fictionalize the behind-the-scenes world of film and television production. The appearance of real-world celebrities within the constructed version of "Hollywood" (or whichever segment of the entertainment industry the text focuses on) on screen helps the screen world to resemble ours. While the main characters may be made up, this verisimilitude asserts that the type of people they represent are grounded in actuality. Roles where the celebrity cameo is played relatively straight with little reference to the actor's off-screen persona beyond their physical presence typically serve this function.

Funny People (2009) has several examples of such celebrity cameos. In the film, Adam Sandler plays George Simmons, a hugely successful comedic actor who re-evaluates his personal life when he is diagnosed with leukemia. Simmons' career and public persona shares numerous parallels with Sandler's actual career, both having started in stand-up comedy to become stars of comedy movies with an often-ridiculous premise (compare Sandler's *Billy Madison* [1995], about an immature heir who goes back to elementary school to secure his inheritance, with Simmons' *Re-Do*, about a workaholic lawyer who is given a second chance at youth and finds himself transformed into a baby). While Sandler's extra-textual persona is referenced in the construction of the George Simmons character, there are other comedians in the film whose brief appearances as themselves rely solely on extra-textual reference for the viewer to recognize who they are, and the function of their character in the story.

One scene with multiple celebrity cameos takes place after George finds out that his experimental treatment has worked, and he is now cancer-free. George gathers at a bar with other comics in celebration, including Sarah Silverman, Dave Attell, Ray Romano, and one non-comic, rapper Eminem. There are some jokes that rely on the audience knowing who the celebrities are, such as the verbal altercation between Romano and Eminem, to which Ira (an aspiring comedian and George's assistant, played by Seth Rogen) remarks to Romano, "I thought everybody loved you?," referencing Romano's long-running sitcom *Everybody Loves Raymond*. However, throwaway jokes such as this one aside, the brief celebrity cameos in *Funny People* could presumably have been fulfilled by any other recognizable celebrities who could serve the function of adding a sense of verisimilitude to the George Simmons character and the world he inhabits. For example, Sarah Silverman's role in the film is not specifically dependent on the fact that she is Sarah Silverman. If Silverman had been unable to make the shoot due to a scheduling conflict and it was necessary to cast another comedian in the scene in Silverman's place, there would have been no change to the narrative. The only requirement of whoever performed the cameo was that they be a recognizably famous actor/comedian. The interchangeable nature of celebrities in the scene is made possible by the way the George Simmons character surrounds himself with celebrities that exist in our actual world and carries on largely superficial interactions with them.

This superficiality ties in with the premise that George Simmons is a hugely successful, yet isolated and lonely celebrity lacking significant human connection. By situating George in a version of the real world through his interactions with real-world celebrities, the film also asserts the claim that this is a kind of celebrity personality that could plausibly exist in contemporary Hollywood culture. The verisimilitude turns the cliché of the miserable comedian, the rich and famous man who seems to have everything but is personally unsatisfied, from something that could be written off as a well-worn trope into something that could be a plausible consideration of what entertainers are actually like. Not only is there pleasure for the audience in recognizing elements of our world that have been fictionalized in the references to similarities between Simmons and Sandler and the celebrities making cameo appearances, but there can also be pleasure in a well-worn cliché rendered believable. After all, there is some pleasurable poignancy to the image of the tragic comedian, as evidenced by cultural moments such as reactions to the death of Robin Williams. In the wake of Williams' 2014 suicide, public discourse surrounding his death often dwelled on the disparity between his history of depression and his celebrity image, posthumously searching for the sorrow in his joyful performances. In the case of Williams, this kind of "tragic clown" duality continues to circulate in popular discourse about his life and death, even after his declining health due to Lewy body dementia was revealed as a contributing factor to his suicide, rather than his history of depression and addiction as was first assumed in public reporting.

Although the backstory of *Funny People*'s George Simmons contains numerous references to the Adam Sandler public persona—including the film's opening actuality home video footage of a younger Sandler (recontextualized as Simmons) making prank phone calls, accompanied by other comics such as Janeane Garofalo—actor and character are generally not conflated in a way that implies that Sandler is performing a version of himself. Even so, the way Simmons is presented as a fictional celebrity allows the film to explore ideas of disconnection and a lack of authenticity between the public persona and the private person, much like many of the adaptations of actual celebrities to fictionalized characters addressed in this book—and multitudes that have not been specifically examined here—have done.

Funny People's celebrity cameos, due to their brief screen time, do not develop the celebrities as characters beyond the audience's recognition of them. The visual signifier of their extra-textually recognizable face is the only information the audience is given about the character and their function in the story. In writing on fictionalized celebrity self-performance in comedy, Brett Mills draws on the work of Barry King to argue that celebrities playing a character with their own name goes against the principle of fictional screen characters, that "the character could be played by a large (but not infinite) number of actors" (King qtd. in Mills 2010: 193-4). However, "it makes no sense," Mills argues, "for someone else to play Jerry Seinfeld in *Seinfeld* as the performance's meaning rests on the notion that, while this is a performance, it is one which draws upon the reality of the performer more than is the case for actors and stars who play characters" (2010: 194). There is a limited pool of actors who could play a particular fictional character. But when the character in question is intended to be understood as the self-performance of a recognizable celebrity, that role is only open to one actor. In a celebrity cameo performance such as those in *Funny People*, however, the function of the role could still potentially be played by a wider pool of performers who fit the same basic criteria of the role. In the case of a cameo like Silverman's, the only requirement is being a recognizable stand-up comedian. These are performances that draw less on the reality of the performer as based on their individual persona, rather than the reality of the performer's position in the industry. What is important is that they are a recognizable performer whose presence fits with the fictional world of the screen text and serves a particular function in the textual narrative.

I would argue that the majority of celebrity self-docucharacterizations in screen fiction serve the function of enhancing the verisimilitude of the fictional world. However, for celebrity cameos that do not build a character with depth beyond the real-world recognizability of the celebrity in question, this may be their primary or only function. The opportunity for stunt casting, or the pleasure the audience finds in the recognition of the unexpected appearance of a familiar celebrity, is another element to this kind of celebrity cameo. In *Top Five* (2014), where, like Sandler in *Funny People*, Chris Rock plays a fictional celebrity with some echoes of his own persona, there are numerous celebrity cameos that anchor the fiction of the film to a believable reality. The appearance of Jerry

Seinfeld in a scene at a strip club, however, provides the additional pleasure of seeing a contradiction between the on-stage public image and the off-stage self being performed. Another comedian could have appeared in the scene alongside Rock (as well as Adam Sandler and Whoopi Goldberg playing themselves) in Seinfeld's place and achieved the same function of enhancing the verisimilitude of the film and locating it within our recognizable understanding of actor/comedian celebrity. There is, however, not only the pleasure and surprise for the audience of recognizing Seinfeld's cameo, but the incongruity of seeing Seinfeld's clean and uptight public image transplanted to the context of the strip club. The fictionalized self that Seinfeld is best known for, the "Jerry Seinfeld" of *Seinfeld,* would never have gleefully thrown hundred-dollar bills at the stage, and we would never have heard his familiar stilted cadence accuse a stripper of stealing his wallet. Nor is this behavior something that would be expected from Seinfeld's stage persona and clean, observational comedic material. This kind of incongruous presentation of a private self versus the public image of other performances is another function of the celebrity-as-themselves performance.

Comedically Undermining the Established Persona

In the case of a fictionalized celebrity self-performance that undermines audience expectations about their persona, the function is a primarily comedic one. The comedic effect comes from what Robert Chambers identifies as "parodic banging," a technique he describes as "contrasted material [that appears] to be distinctly and directly at odds" (2010: 7). In a comedically undermining celebrity self-performance, the audience brings their own expectations of what the celebrity persona should be based on how it has been extra-textually established outside of the context of the fictional self-performance. These expectations are then placed at odds with how the celebrity performs as themselves in the fictional frame, embodying a new and unexpected private persona. Here, in terms of Smith's structure of sympathy, the initial formation of character in the recognition stage is subverted by subsequent alliance with the character. In other words, the re-creation of the actual celebrity is recognizable through their physical presence (or drawn resemblance, if it takes place in animation), but the created private self that we are presented with in the text subverts our expectations in unexpected ways.

An extended example of this can be seen in Michael Cera's performance in *This Is the End* (2013). Cera's persona has been established as boyish, innocent, and awkward, through his breakthrough role as George-Michael Bluth in the Fox single-camera comedy *Arrested Development* and subsequent film roles where he plays characters in the same vein, such as *Superbad* (2007) and *Juno* (2008). In his cameo as "Michael Cera" in *This Is the End*, however, Cera is depicted as a drugged-up sex maniac, playing the celebrity gossip trope of the child star gone off the rails. During his brief appearance at the party sequence at the beginning of the film, Cera still retains some of his awkward, dorky persona through elements such as costume and his physical appearance. These are incongruously juxtaposed with "Michael Cera" snorting cocaine, becoming increasingly intoxicated, and being depicted as both an object of sexual desire and a sexual aggressor. His reaction to being caught in a threesome by Jay Baruchel is to stare Jay down and casually invite him to continue using the (currently occupied by Cera and two women) bathroom. There is none of the awkward or embarrassed response that would be expected of a Michael Cera-type character. This character is the opposite of how the audience would likely expect Michael Cera to behave off-screen, considering the expectations audiences bring to the film based on their prior knowledge of Cera's career and public persona. While the child star gone wild narrative is a recurring story in celebrity culture, there has not been any publicized evidence to suggest that Cera has actually followed that trajectory. The comedic effect of Cera's character and performance in *This Is the End* would be considerably different if the drugged-up sex maniac cameo had been performed by an actor who was *known* to the public to have engaged in similar off-screen behavior in defiance of their child star persona (e.g., Lindsay Lohan).

Another example of comedically undermining the established celebrity persona is Brian Williams' recurring role as himself in *30 Rock*. The NBC Nightly News anchor appears multiple times throughout the series for brief cameos. Williams' public persona as the anchor of the (at the time) number one network news broadcast in the United States is one that is endowed with gravitas not only by the position, but also by his manner of address during newscasts: a perpetual slight frown, and the steady, reassuring cadence expected of a news anchor. The *30 Rock* cameos serve to comedically undermine his news anchor role by depicting the Williams character as a juvenile bully. Williams' cameos include him auditioning for a role on *TGS with Tracy Jordan*, the *Saturday Night Live*-esque sketch show within the show, telling terrible jokes with a broadly stereotypical New Jersey accent, worlds away from the measured, neutral "Nowhere, USA" accent of news reading. Another episode shows Williams as an aggressive jock type, taunting the employees of NBC's cable affiliate CNBC. The bully role comes up again when Williams teams up with NBC News reporter Andrea Mitchell to harass *30 Rock*'s lead character Liz Lemon with gossip about her love life.

This is not to argue that a celebrity appearance as themselves in a fictional text can easily be categorized by one function. Williams' *30 Rock* appearances also serve additional functions, such as connecting the world of *30 Rock* to the real world and authenticating its satirical view of television production at NBC. It also serves the function of lightening up Williams' persona, and demonstrating that he can make fun of himself, or have a sense of humor about himself, traits which can make the celebrity likable to their audience. In a role like Williams', where he was (at the time) a prominent face of the network and part of the network brand in his position as Nightly News anchor, his likeability could help foster audience loyalty and attract younger viewers to the network with his image as the "cool" news anchor, particularly through the vehicle of a media-savvy, self-reflexive sitcom like *30 Rock*. Williams has an established history of making fun of himself through numerous appearances on late-night talk shows such as *The Daily Show with Jon Stewart* and *The Tonight Show starring Jimmy Fallon*, and a turn as host of *Saturday Night Live*. The lighter side of Williams' anchor persona is so well established that it has become part of his intertextual public image and is therefore perhaps less comedically outrageous or jarring than a performance like the Michael Cera role mentioned above. The off-screen self of the fictional Williams *character* in *30 Rock* is at odds with Williams the news anchor who is most often seen on screen in the real world. The Williams *performing* the role on *30 Rock*, however, is in line with his public persona outside the text of NBC Nightly News.

As is the case with Louis C.K., the meaning made from a fictionalized celebrity self-performance can change, however, as real-world scandal encroaches on the public persona of the celebrity and alters public perception. This was the case with Williams after it came to light in 2015 that for years, he had been untruthfully embellishing a story about coming under fire while embedded in Iraq. Williams' credibility was destroyed, and his reputation for self-parody was re-examined as an uncomfortable mix of entertainment and news. The perception of Williams-as-Williams became less the sign of a likeable newsman who knew how to have fun at his own expense and more a symptom of a man who had little regard for the trust the public placed in his position, a news reader who was more interested in being an entertainer than a journalist (Burrough 2015;

Saraiya 2015). A fictional self-performance that had once been beneficial for the Brian Williams public persona became a detriment, further evidence to support a negative understanding of Williams after the scandal was revealed.

An additional example of fictionalized celebrity self-performance that serves multiple functions in the text is Bob Saget as himself in *Entourage*. Best known for his wholesome roles in the 1980s and 1990s in *Full House* and as host of *America's Funniest Home Videos*, Saget was also a stand-up comedian whose stage work was notoriously filthy and completely at odds with his television persona. Through several cameos in *Entourage*, Saget is depicted as an off-stage version of his on-stage stand-up persona, a foul-mouthed womanizer. This heightened version of Saget's stand-up persona serves a similar role to C.K.'s fictionalized self-performance in *Louie*: it asserts that the stand-up material comes from an authentic place of who the comedian is off stage. With Saget, however, there is the additional parodic bang of the television work he became most known for: his wholesome television persona incongruously clashes with his stage material, and his performance of his off-stage self in *Entourage*. The incongruity between Saget's stage and television work has become deeply embedded in his intertextual public persona, and it is something that is being parodied by depicting his *Entourage* self as an even more extreme version of his stage persona. Saget's fictionalized self-performance simultaneously authenticates the fictional Hollywood world of *Entourage*, authenticates his stand-up persona, undermines his television persona, and parodies the known disparity between the two that has become a significant element of his intertextual public persona. The confluence of these functions allows Saget's fictionalized self-performance to become a self-aware mockery of established celebrity persona.

Self-aware Mockery of Established Persona

Like the parodic contradiction of the established persona, the comedic effect of mocking a persona relies on audience expectation and extra-textual knowledge of the celebrity subject. But unlike the comedic undermining of persona discussed above, the self-aware mockery of persona confirms these existing audience expectations and heightens them to a level of absurdity. The effect often results in a celebrity persona so ridiculous that it can, like other forms of adaptations of celebrity persona to fictionalized media and the access to various simulated selves they provide, serve to highlight the disconnection between the front-stage performed persona and the "real" or backstage, private self. The celebrity performing commonly known and easily recognizable aspects of their persona in a heightened or ridiculous way gives the impression that the celebrity themself finds representations of these aspects of their public persona to be inherently absurd and false. By embracing a mocking attitude to the popularized cultural understanding of themselves as a celebrity, they achieve both an ironic distance from the public persona as any accurate representation of their "real" self and give the impression that they do not take themselves or their media image too seriously.

James Franco's performance in *This Is the End* is an example of the self-aware mockery of an established media persona. The popular understanding of Franco's celebrity image could be considered a wealth of contradictions. As an actor, he has performed in both serious, dramatic roles that have garnered critical acclaim, awards, and nominations, such as *127 Hours* (2010) and *Milk*; action blockbuster roles such as *Rise of the Planet of the Apes* (2011) and Sam Raimi's *Spider-Man* trilogy (2002–2007); as well as films of the ilk of *This Is the End*'s stoner, bromance humor, such as *Pineapple Express* (2008) and *Your Highness* (2011). In addition to his work as an actor, Franco has published a collection of short stories, held exhibitions of his artwork, taught filmmaking and screenwriting at NYU and UCLA, has pursued master's degrees in writing and filmmaking, and a doctorate in English at Yale. The variety of Franco's work both on- and off-screen has lent itself to a somewhat contradictory persona as an overachieving, yet laid-back, renaissance man. The "James Franco" character of *This Is the End* follows this template of the stoner intellectual. In the film, Franco hosts a star-studded party that gets interrupted by the apocalypse. His house, the private space that becomes an object of humor for the private self of this version of Franco, is filled with bizarre artwork, including some he painted himself (twin paintings of his and Seth Rogen's names hanging above the living room, which, in a self-reflexive twist, the actual Franco painted for the production). The star narrative of James Franco as the intellectual is heightened in the film to the point of pretention, a self-aware acknowledgment of how Franco's celebrity image is perceived, exaggerated to a state of self-mockery.

The functions of fictionalized celebrity self-performance discussed above all treat the celebrity persona as an inherently false character that differs from the celebrity's "real" self to varying degrees. When a celebrity appears in a fictional world, the fictional world can be endowed with verisimilitude. At the same time, though, the inverse also occurs as the celebrity's existence alongside fictional characters can suggest there is a degree of fictionality to the persona.

For the most part, fictionalized celebrity self-performance in film and television has been comedic, or in some way distanced from reality, such as in animation like *The Simpsons* or *BoJack Horseman*, or a fantasy world like *Being John Malkovich* (1999). Even though Louis C.K. plays himself in *Louie* as a stand-up comedian in a series that is ostensibly intended to be a comedy, the fictionalized Louie character as closely aligned with C.K.'s public and stage persona in a way that does not intend to shed light on the disparities between the public and private selves of entertainers. While it may seem like C.K.'s performance in *Louie* is perhaps an irrelevant case study to consider at this point given that his mainstream visibility and influence has been significantly curtailed since November 2017, the cancelation of C.K.'s career has not been as complete as some of the other celebrities whose predatory behavior was revealed in the wake of the #MeToo movement. For an actor such as Kevin Spacey, for example, there are industry gatekeepers preventing the continuation of his career: if casting Spacey in a film is an obviously publicly unpopular decision, he will not be working in the industry, and his public visibility and reach to an audience is blocked. C.K., although he no longer has access to an audience through distribution channels such as Netflix, FX, or HBO, still has the pre-existing infrastructure of his self-distributed comedy specials through his website and e-mail list. Having successfully started this direct-to audience-distribution method in 2011 with *Live at the Beacon Theatre*, C.K. released his first post-scandal special in 2020, titled *Sincerely, Louis C.K.* Sales figures and measures of success that were publicly revealed for *Live at the Beacon* are not available for *Sincerely*, and there was mixed discussion about the special—and the question of whether it is appropriate for it to exist at all—in mainstream press. The special did receive endorsement from the industry, however, by winning the Grammy Award for Best Comedy Album in 2022. In addition, C.K.'s early 2020 and (post-COVID) 2021 tour dates featured multiple sold out shows across major American cities in theaters averaging 2,000–3,000 seat capacity, suggesting that he still has a significant audience willing to pay to see him perform. While C.K. is no longer at the heights of his fame and mainstream visibility, his career as a live performer is still viable, not only in that audiences are willing to pay to see him live, but that major venues, including Madison Square Garden's 5,600 seat Hulu Theatre in New York City, are giving him a stage on which to perform at all.

The post-2017 reception of C.K. as a performer by his remaining audience is arguably tied not only to his performance of self on stage, but his performance of the fictionalized self that purports to be his "authentic" self in *Louie*. A review of a 2020 Louis C.K. show in Washington, DC, quoted audience members being appreciative of C.K.'s comedy remaining in its outlandish, boundary-pushing state, happy to see him "because we know how to take a joke," and describing his "ordeal" as "good for him," suggesting that the revelation of his off-stage misbehavior and subsequent end to mainstream visibility was merely more material in C.K.'s life for him to work with on stage, with no thought given to the women whose careers in comedy had been impacted by C.K.'s coercive sexual abuse (Izadi 2020). This audience reaction suggests that while C.K. has lost a significant portion of his audience who are uncomfortable with his material now that C.K. no longer has "the benefit of the doubt" (Izadi 2020) when it comes to the blurred boundaries of truth and hyperbole in joking discourse, there is still an audience who continue to revel in this aspect of C.K.'s persona and the seemingly authentic congruence between his real-world on-stage self and his fictionalized off-stage self. Additionally, the simulated access to C.K.'s off-stage self that the fictionalization affords can potentially provide a sense of recognition and further authenticity when viewed in retrospect.

In order to consider the stage persona of the confessional and revelatory stand-up comedian as a kind of semi-fictionalized celebrity self performance, as well as the more deliberately fictionalized celebrity self-performance in C.K.'s series *Louie*, I will first consider the role that authenticity plays in understanding the cultural impact of contemporary stand-up comedian persona before moving on to looking at how this authenticity of persona was validated by C.K.'s fictionalized docucharacter in *Louie*.

The Value of Authenticity in Stand-up Comedian Persona

Throughout this discussion, I conceptualize "authenticity" in stand-up comedy in much the same way that the term has been applied to discussion of popular music. In their work on popular music stardom in the biopic, Lee Marshall and Isabel Kongsgaard establish self-expression in popular music as "highly individual selves," creating original art that challenges established traditions (2012: 348). The authentic rock artist's work stems from "personal experience and emotional states" where we "believe that we can find the meaning of the work within the life of its creator" (2012: 350). These ideas of original work stemming from the individualized self are central to understanding authenticity in stand-up comedy. For a comic's persona to be perceived as authentic, material should originate from his or her own lived experience and be shaped by an individualized perspective in ways that mark the comedian's material as being distinctly his or hers. An original, individualized, authentic presentation of material means that even the most well-trodden stand-up topic (such as romantic relationships and the differences between men and women) can be imbued with a new perspective, deriving its uniqueness from the life of the comedian.

With this understanding of stand-up celebrity and authenticity in mind, it is necessary to further define the contemporary stand-up comedian as a type of celebrity. Specifically, what kind of celebrity is the stand-up comedian, whose material is generated from their own life and experience, and how does perceived authenticity facilitate the success of this kind of public persona? Brett Mills argues that "comedy performance can draw on equivalences between assumptions about the performer and that which is performed" (2010: 191). Mills goes on to note that this is undoubtedly the case in all types of performances but suggests that "the specific social roles comedy is understood to fulfil" give a unique inflection to discourses of stardom and celebrity surrounding the comedian as a type of public figure (2010: 191). That is, while the film star may imbue their roles with a sense of themselves, and find a part of their role within themselves, Mills writes that acting generates a version of the star "which is explicitly *not* true," a lie that is acknowledged by performer and audience (2010: 192, emphasis in original). In the case of C.K., or indeed any celebrity who performs a version of themselves under their own name on stage or screen, the usual understandings of stardom are complicated by a failure "to clearly demarcate himself [*sic*] from the performance," creating a situation where it is impossible to know if the performance is an exposure of self, or an acted lie (Mills 2010: 192). Comedic performance is unique, Mills argues, in that the performer is granted permission to conflate the "self-expressive" and "representational" modes of performance. This creates a state that engages in self-revelation without it ever being clear if such a revelation is truly giving audience access to the private self of the comedian (2010: 196). The reception of these modes can be understood as seeing the comedian "acting" as themselves and "being" as themselves (Mills 2010: 200). For example, the stand-up comedian appearing as a panel guest on a late-night talk show often uses modified pieces from their stage act in place of the personal anecdotes that are expected from celebrities in such a forum. The stand-up is ostensibly not performing the "act" of themselves in that moment, yet by bringing elements of their stage performance into the performance of "being" themselves, the two performance modes are conflated. This presentation achieves the kind of everyday authenticity and sincerity of being that Naremore describes as "expressive coherence" (1986: 41).

This conflation of "acting" and "being" of the comedian can be clearly demarcated by a self-representational comic who deliberately calls attention to and temporarily halts the comedic frame. Hannah Gadsby's 2018 special *Nanette* is an example of this kind of performance. Based on the premise of her desire to quit comedy because of her refusal to continue to marginalize herself and her experiences as a queer woman and survivor of sexual assault in order to make the audience comfortable with the light treatment of difficult subjects, Gadsby's special deconstructs the comedic frame to the point where it was labeled (or criticized) by some as being more akin to a lecture than a comedy special (Wired Staff 2018). At one point in the special, Gadsby deconstructs one of her old jokes that was based on a real experience and reveals the lies that were necessary to turn her reality into comedy. In halting the comedic frame, Gadsby reveals her actual, authentic truth in such a deliberately raw way that leaves the audience purposefully sitting with the uncomfortable subject of her assault and without any doubt that there is no joke here, only an authentic revelation that deliberately disavows its formerly comedic context. While the performance reveals Gadsby's authenticity in the moment, it also reveals the inherent inauthenticity of seemingly confessional comedy in that there always has to be some exaggeration or obfuscation of the truth in order to create a joke from lived experience. The popular debate surrounding *Nanette*'s status as comedy-or-not speaks to the idea of the conflation of the "acting" and "being" of the comedian's self as the norm for seemingly confessional stand-up comedian personas. There is a degree of fictionalization of the real self that is inherent to supposedly "revelatory" or "confessional" comedy that is necessary to make a joke work.

The spaces of Goffman's dramaturgical metaphor can be readily applied to stand-up comedy with the presence of a literal front- and backstage. These spaces generate the expectation that, in some way, the stage persona of the comedian is different from the person they are in their off-stage "real life." Confessional comedians who claim to perform as themselves, who claim their material originates from lived experience, and who serve their personal lives up to the audiences for the purposes of humor problematize expectations of personas in on- and off-stage spaces in ways that stage and screen performances based on clearly demarcated fictional characters do not. The curtain between the front- and backstage spaces of the comedy club or theater becomes a porous boundary, the continuity of self-presentation creating a persona that is often still "on," even in what are ostensibly backstage spaces. Confessional comedians of Louis C.K.'s ilk exist in a perpetual state of what could be authentic self-performance or a performance of the authentic. The emerging climate of the "proliferation of the public self" (Marshall 2014a) is in some ways perfect for this kind of stand-up comedian, as their backstage selves are presented in an increasing variety of public, front-stage venues, on- and off-screen, on- and off-line, moving between states of acting and being as themselves without clear boundaries.

It has not always been the case that stand-up comedians were expected to engage in a revealing self-performance on stage. Oliver Double (2005) attributes the origins of "the idea of stand-up as self expression" to the "sick comedians" of the 1950s, such as Mort Sahl and Lenny Bruce. Prior to this, the realm of potentially divisive political and social critique based on the performer's own opinions was considered taboo. Sahl and Bruce's style introduced a more casual and conversational form of delivery and content that injected the comedian's opinions and point of view into their material (Double 2005: 70). The sick comedians became part of the post-Second World War American beatnik counterculture, breaching the previously upheld taboo of politically and socially critical comedy. Sahl and Bruce in particular are credited with "challenging the status quo during a historically conservative time," encouraging both their audiences and other comics to question contemporary social order through comedy that communicated their own truthful points of view (Taylor 2010: 2). In a contemporary context, the rise and fall of the stand-up comedy club boom of the 1980s led to the development of another kind of comedy counterculture. The "alternative" comedy scene of the 1990s featured comedians such as David Cross, Patton Oswalt, Marc Maron, and Janeane Garofalo, performing more "subjective [and] self-referential material" outside of the comedy club system (Clark 2012). With many of the comedians of the 1990s' alternative scene subsequently becoming popular, successful mainstream acts and influencing younger generations of comedians, their self-reflective, personal style of material has a dominant place in the current mainstream stand-up comedy landscape. The revelation of self on stage has spread beyond the literal stage frame to diversified venues for comedian self-performance, such as podcasts, social media, blogs, memoirs, and television shows based on their lives.

As noted in my earlier discussion of *Funny People*, there are long-circulating cultural narratives and questions about the disparity or congruence between the on- and off-stage selves of comedians. This interest, facilitated by the direct-to-audience distribution afforded by online forums such as Twitter and podcasting, perhaps prompted recent interest in consuming off-stage comedian self-performance in both online and traditional broadcast media, in fiction and non-fiction. Tony Moon's (2010) study of representational stage and screen fiction about stand-ups describes how these works have set the tone for cultural narratives about the on- and off-stage selves of comedians, despite the trend toward more autobiographical comedy that has been developing since the 1950s (2010: 202). In terms of screen fiction, Moon cites *Mr. Saturday Night* (1992) and *The King of Comedy* (1982) as examples of works that "have alighted upon the complexities and dichotomies of the comedy performer, seeing it as ripe territory for original drama" (2010: 202). Fictional representations of comedians allow audiences to witness comedy performers in both "performative and social context[s], where their offstage lives inform their onstage personas and vice versa" (Moon 2010: 202). In addition to the works Moon examines, we could add contemporary fictional examples to this category such as the aforementioned films *Funny People* and *Top Five*, semi-autobiographical comedian films such as *Sleepwalk with Me* (2012) and *The Big Sick* (2017), the Showtime series *I'm Dying Up Here* (2017–2018), as well as television series where comedians play versions of themselves-as-comedians, like *Louie*, *Maron* (IFC 2013–2016, with Marc Maron as himself), *Lady Dynamite* (Netflix 2016–2017, with Maria Bamford as herself), and *Crashing* (HBO 2017–2019, with Pete Holmes as himself). In his study of representations of comedians, Moon broaches the idea of diverse niche markets for stand-up comedy and its consumers with regard to the authenticity of a performer and their material. Moon argues that there are some audiences who simply wish to be entertained and give no regard to what the performer's off-stage life is like, and others who wish to see the comedian authentically engaged with their material, and "more than just actors who happen to be delivering a product marked 'humor'" (2010: 202). The latter niche market is not only positioned to be interested in consuming a stand-up comedy persona in a variety of self-performances but has this variety of self-performances available to consume with the diversification of on-stage venues for contemporary comedians. Consistency between these fictional and non-fictional self-performances can generate the impression that the self the comedian performs through their stand-up comedy is their authentic self. It is as Mills, drawing on the work of Joshua Gamson, suggests that in the conflation of "acting" and "being" selves, the continuous public performance becomes the most true and authentic version of the comedian (2010: 197). While the substitute of the fictionalized private self may not entirely deflect questions of "what are they really like?," it generates a perception of authenticity of the public self that invites audiences to accept the public performance as a close approximation of what they are really like, drawn from the comedian's authentic experience and heightened by a comedic framework. Access is provided to a substitute version of the "real" off-stage self.

For the stand-up comedian whose stage material is ostensibly drawn from their own life, their own personal point of view, and their own experience, there is a cultural value in creating the perception that their publicly performed self is an authentic self. Lawrence E. Mintz writes that humor, and, in particular, the form of humor found in stand-up comedy, is a telling sign of the "values, attitudes, dispositions and concerns" of a society or culture (1985: 71). Citing the works of Mary Douglas and Victor Turner, Mintz argues that the shared laughter of the stand-up comedy audience creates a sense of community among individuals in agreement about what constitutes a deserving target of ridicule (1985: 73). The role of the stand-up comedian in forging this shared laughter and sense of community is to act as the "comic spokesman" for the audience, often presenting themselves as "defective in some way" and "represent[ing] conduct to be ridiculed and rejected" (1985: 74). In embodying or calling attention to unacceptable behavior, the comedian forms a relationship with the audience through shared laughter that simultaneously breaks the rules of acceptability and acknowledges that the rules have been broken (Purdie 1993: 3).

I argue that audience perception of a confessional comedian's persona as an authentic representation of themselves is vital in maintaining this relationship. Additionally, to apply Murray Smith's (1995) model of character engagement to audience interaction with the character of comedic persona, the perception of authenticity aids in creating a sympathetic allegiant response in the form of laughter and agreement. This allegiant response allows the audience to recognize parts of themselves in the comedian's persona that they would not normally publicly display or acknowledge. The comedian makes public what is usually considered private, such as Patton Oswalt's day-to-day experience of grief in *Annihilation*, Hannah Gadsby's assault in *Nanette*, Louis C.K.'s sexual compulsions in almost his entire body of work, or Dave Chappelle's controversial alliance with the TERF (trans-exclusionary radical feminist) movement in

The Closer (2021). Through the comedian's public display of transgressive traits or speech, the rules of what is socially acceptable to admit in public are broken. If the audience does not accept the comedian's presentation of self as authentic or truthful of the "real" person behind the persona, this identification process is based on a false premise and violates the audience's trust. This is one element of the value of authenticity in comedian persona that was obliterated for a significant segment of C.K.'s audience with the revelations of his actual private actions in his treatment of some of the women he worked with. C.K.'s transgressive speech in his material dealing with both his own perceived sexual deviance, or his more feminist-leaning material that acknowledges the potential danger that women have to consider when dating men, becomes based on a false premise within a disrupted comedic framework. The social acceptability of C.K.'s transgressions within the comedic frame lose their "saying the unsayable" status when it is revealed that these are not merely thoughts extrapolated to comedic extremes, but actions that have harmed real people.

In some ways, the celebrity of the stand-up comedian is akin to the celebrity of the politician. Both serve as figureheads for a particular worldview or collection of values that are shared by their respective publics. These publics can be deeply divided along ideological lines depending on the comedian's approach to their material, as Louis C.K.'s audience now exists, or as Dave Chappelle's repeated targeting of transgender people in his material and his point of view against "cancel culture" has divided his audience, particularly following his 2021 Netflix special *The Closer*. Both politicians and comedians try to sell the public on themselves and their individual view of the world. The reasons for doing so, the results of doing so, and the rules for doing so are obviously quite different. A politician may say what is necessary to be elected rather than what they truly believe, obscuring their private self. A comedian, particularly a confessional-style comedian, deliberately presents what is claimed to be their private self for the purposes of simultaneously acknowledging and violating the boundaries of public and private frames. This performed private self may be varying degrees of construct, embellishment, or authenticity, but the range of on-stage venues for comedians to perform the state of "being" as themselves leads to a consistency and coherence of self-performance that makes the self appear plausible. As I will discuss with the example of Louis C.K. and his fictionalized self in *Louie*, inviting the audience to witness the fictionalized off-stage life of the stage persona in ways that suggest another function of the celebrity playing themselves in fictionalized contexts: authenticating the public persona.

Louie and Louis C.K.: Constructing and Demolishing Authenticity

There is a congruity between the title character of the television series *Louie*, C.K., and the front- and backstage versions of each that serves an argument for the Louie character being C.K.'s authentic self-performance. Prior to C.K.'s sexual misconduct revelation, authenticity played a fundamental role in attempts to examine the cultural significance of C.K.'s comedy and its value in American popular culture. Andrew Corsello's (2014) *GQ* profile of C.K. discusses the ways that C.K. attempts to defy the boundaries between front- and backstage spaces of performance and artifice, such as the opening to his *Live at the Beacon Theatre* special that has C.K. coming on stage before the house lights have dimmed, and before the audience is fully settled, with no music cue or introduction, simply announcing "Go ahead, sit down, we're just starting." If the audience is granted such access to what seems to be the real, authentic Louis C.K. when he is performing a front-stage self in a front-stage space, what does the fictionalized performance of his off-stage self do to shape his public image? The simulated access to "the authentic self" of C.K. on screen works to reinforce the authenticity of his on-stage persona and complicates any perception of an "authentic self" in his work in the wake of the sexual misconduct revelations.

In addition to performing in the title role of his fictionalized self, C.K. also served as writer and director of every episode of *Louie*. The character of Louie, like C.K. himself, is a stand-up comedian in his forties, divorced, living in New York City, and sharing joint custody of two young daughters with his ex-wife. Both C.K. and Louie share a stage persona that operates in a comedic frame that permits him to say the unsayable, to make confessions about his private self that would otherwise be inappropriate to air in public. In *Louie* we see a version of the backstage self, the social life of the Louie character, the "autobiographical fiction" of C.K.'s off-stage life, which C.K. claims is basically him, minus, ironically, "all [his] good judgement and good luck" (qtd. in D'Allesandro 2012). Through this semi-autobiographical stand-in, we, as an audience, are granted far more access to Louie than the off-stage persona of C.K. himself, despite the sense C.K.'s stage work gives that we are getting a glimpse of his private self through the confessional lens of his stand-up performance. Given the context of the 2017 sexual misconduct revelations, it is clear that our access to the "real" C.K. was, as with any public persona or fictionalization of a persona, selective and constructed.

As a television series, *Louie* is elastic in terms of its narrative structure and continuity in ways that distinguish the show from traditional sitcoms and half-hour comedies based on the stage acts of stand-up comedians that create fictional screen characters out of a stand-up comedian's persona (such as *Seinfeld* or *Roseanne*). Some stories are told in self-contained vignettes that range from five minutes to almost a whole episode, while other stories span multi-part episodes. Some characters or details of Louie-the-character's life are established one way for one story, and then completely changed the next time they are brought up, with details existing to serve the joke or story as necessary. Based on this loose, segmented way of storytelling within and between individual episodes, television critic Matt Zoller Seitz (2012) claims that *Louie* "makes stand-up comedy cinematic," arguing that the lack of consistency between tone and content in the chunks of material that make a stand-up routine is an accepted and unquestioned element of the form. In episodic television, however, this inconsistent and varying structure in a series is unprecedented (perhaps accounting for Zoller Seitz's use of "cinematic" rather than "televisual," conjuring the idea that *Louie* more resembles a series of short films than any existing structure in narrative television at that time). The originality of this structure in television and its relationship to the structure of stand-up comedy contributes to the authenticity of the show and C.K.'s persona as its auteur. The series does not rely entirely on audience knowledge of C.K.'s persona and its extra-textual makeup to generate a two-dimensional rendering. Rather, it offers up C.K.'s on-stage and fictionalized off-stage personas as a rounded character. To use James Naremore's terms, C.K. the actor is playing a "unified front" of his own performative self, the coherent character of Louie who, while he shifts between on- and off-stage performance frames within the diegesis, remains a consistent part (1986: 42).

Louie's narrativization of a stand-up act and its representation of a comedian playing themselves is, of course, nothing new, with *Seinfeld* being the most obvious example of a predecessor to *Louie*. Although these shows both depict comedians playing themselves as working comedians, the singular focus on Louie as the series protagonist, its single camera shooting style, naturalistic performances, absence of laugh track, and the more personal nature of C.K.'s comedy all work together to give the impression that in *Louie*, C.K. is playing a fictionalized version of himself. Stylistically, *Seinfeld* gives the sense that Jerry Seinfeld is playing a fictional character who also happens to be a comedian named Jerry Seinfeld with a tone and sensibility that is derived from Seinfeld's actual stand-up act. *Curb Your Enthusiasm* would be another obvious predecessor to C.K.'s show as it features a naturalistic visual and performance style that is more akin to *Louie* than *Seinfeld*. Indeed, *Louie* and *Curb Your Enthusiasm* do similar work in authenticating the public persona of their protagonist. With Louis C.K. it is as his on-stage self. In the case of Larry David in *Curb*, it is as what he is most famously known for: the other creative voice behind *Seinfeld* and the primary source material for the character of George Costanza. However, although David began his career as a stand-up comic, it is not what he is primarily known for. When compared to C.K., who has amassed a body of stand-up comedy performance on stage and distributed as one-hour specials and album releases, David does not have as much of a visible public/performance persona existing extra-textually to *Curb Your Enthusiasm*. Therefore, *Louie* operates somewhat differently to *Curb* in the extent of the extra-textual stage persona that the show works to authenticate. The presence of stand-up comedy performance in the text of *Louie* and the influence of stand-up comedy on the show's variable narrative structure works to conflate the on-stage persona of Louie with that of C.K. in ways that argue for C.K.'s stage persona as an authentic self to a degree that *Seinfeld* and similar comedian sitcoms do not.

The segmentation demonstrated in *Louie*'s structure is reminiscent of stand-up. Like television, stand-up comedy can be considered a segmented form of entertainment: chunks of material of varying lengths on different topics, and the individual jokes within a chunk. Topics are changed with abrupt transitions: an attitude toward forced segues between jokes as being "hack" (Carter 2005: 138) can mean that without warning the audience is engaging with the comic's ideas on a completely different subject. At the same time, television is a medium of flow, and stand-up could be considered a performance of flow as well. Within the segmentation, there is a consistency that ties discrete elements of material together. Where the branding of a television network ties discrete elements of programming together across a night of viewing, it is the brand of a comedian's persona that works to tie together the discrete elements of an individual stand-up performance. Where *Louie* largely lacks seriality in its storytelling, or the traditional sitcom elements of consistency such as regular recurring characters or key settings, its consistency comes from what P. David Marshall (2014b) describes as the seriality of persona that evolves through repetition and consistency in the performance of a celebrity persona. In this seriality of persona, the "real" C.K. is used as a kind of docudramatic warrant not only through his physical presence in performing his fictionalized self, but also through recognition of the similarities between the stand-up persona (within the series and extra-textually) and the fictionalized character.

For example, in the episode "Subway/Pamela" a pre-credits vignette about Louie's observations and daydreams on a subway ride home is followed by the longer, and unrelated, story of "Pamela," one of the show's few occasionally recurring characters, a fellow single parent who is Louie's friend and object of unrequited love. This story can be broken down into acts: the first, where Pamela establishes that she is not romantically interested in Louie; the second, where Louie gets her permission to tell her just once the extent of his love for her, only to be rejected again; and the third, where in his haste to escape their now-awkward situation, Louie completely misses an impulsive romantic gesture from Pamela. In each of these acts, the source of the humor and how it is presented changes, just as the style of a joke and its target of humor varies throughout a stand-up act. In the first, it is the banter between the two characters; in the second, it is the long set up of Louie's confession for the payoff of his continued humiliation; and in the third, it is the awkwardness between the two and the final punchline of Louie missing his opportunity and losing again. The episode closes with a short segment of Louie/C.K. doing stand-up under the closing credits. In the bit, Louie talks about the skills that middle-aged couples are building so they can become elderly couples that are stuck with each other. He compares a couple he knows to his grandparents, and the tactics the male partners in each use to avoid their spouse that their spouse is unaware of. Louie's explanation for this behavior: "Because he hates you a lot. He hates you more than he loves you." While not directly drawn from the "Pamela" storyline, it is a bitter point of view that, considering Louie's missed opportunity and continued rejection from Pamela, makes sense in the context of the story. The viewer is not expected to take the Pamela story as a literal truth of Louis C.K.'s real life, but it is easy for the viewer to imagine the similar kinds of romantic disappointments that the actual C.K., in his persona as somewhat of an everyman/loser, may have experienced that have informed the perspective of his stage material. In retrospect, the Louie character's easy acceptance of rejection can seem like what is possibly deliberate obfuscation, and not something that is indicated by C.K.'s now publicly known coercive behavior. While the audience sees the authentic connection between Louie's life and stage material, C.K., who shares the same stage material, is now re-read as a fragmented persona.

Although a contemporary viewing of the series can result in seeing C.K. as a fragmented persona that equally as incoherent and contradictory as the series' narrative structure, the series in and of itself maintains consistency through the fictionalized character of Louie, and the viewer's impression of Louis C.K.'s presence as the primary creative producer behind the series: the flow of the persona's brand. There is an interaction between fictional and actual that reinforces this authentic performance across C.K.'s public selves. In its depiction of the fictionalized Louie, the series brings C.K.'s extra-textual stand-up persona into the text through the inclusion of segments of Louie performing on stage alongside the narrative representation of Louie's off-stage life. Rather than existing only as an extra-textual element of C.K.'s persona, C.K.'s on-stage self becomes the on-stage self of the Louie character. The stand-up segments in the series are staged and shot for the specific purpose of being included in the series, rather than arising from a live performance that C.K. would have staged regardless of the needs of the series. Nevertheless, these live performances function similarly to documentary footage in fictional film, as the warrants of actuality that Steven N. Lipkin (2011) writes of in docudrama. Additionally, as Joel Black writes, the presence of documentary footage in fictional film is "a kernel of 'truth' around which the cinematic fiction persistently circles" (2002: 12). Like the storytelling modes of docudrama, and docucomedy that I have discussed, we could perhaps consider celebrities playing themselves as a docucelebrity performance given their blending of the fact of their own real-world celebrity with the fictionalization of their self-as-celebrity performance. The (at the time of its initial airing) seamless overlap between the on-stage selves of C.K. and the Louie character anchors the fictionalized elements of the series to a real-world referent: the actual Louis C.K. as he is known in the real world through his stage persona.

As Louie—and C.K.—openly shares his "tales of excruciating embarrassment and degradation" (Tung 2012) on stage, we witness the debasing events in the life of the fictionalized Louie that the material stems from. Witnessing the correlation between off-stage life and on-stage material encourages the audience to see the actual Louis C.K., the creator of the on-stage persona and the fictionalized self, as a similar authentic voice as his character, comedically commenting on the world through the prism of his own personal experience. This results in the generation of a kind of feedback loop of authenticity reinforcement: Louis C.K. created his on-stage persona; this on-stage persona is the same as the Louie character's on-stage persona; the off-stage life of Louie is created as a plausible stand-in for the "real" off-stage Louis C.K. as he is known through his stand-up persona; and, therefore, we are invited to map the connections of authenticity between C.K.'s fragmented celebrity image onto C.K. and his actual off-stage life.

In C.K.'s personal material, which features specific anecdotes from his life, observations grounded in self-commentary, and jokes made from intimate details of his off-stage life, much of what is regarded as constituting the private self in celebrity culture appears in C.K.'s public persona. As Richard Dyer notes, "cultural assumptions" exist concerning the locus of the most "authentic" and "true [self]" of a person: in the realm of the private and intimate, "when people 'let themselves go,' pour forth their thoughts and feelings in an untrammeled flow" (1998: 122). While C.K.'s stage work is obviously a realm of public performance where material has been prepared and performed on previous occasions, the conversational and confessional nature of his delivery, as well as the often taboo topics that are considered socially unacceptable to broach outside of a comedic frame, makes it appear as though he has "let himself go" and is sharing his innermost thoughts in a public forum. Recontextualizing his stage and screen work post-2017, this raises numerous speculative questions about how much of the "real" or "authentic" C.K. audiences have been seeing in his public performance. C.K.'s work was frequently based in ideas about the nature of hypocrisy—and particularly the hypocrisy of men when it comes to their treatment of women. Topics like this made his work seem confessional and authentic, a representation of a true self, positioning C.K. as a stand-in for the average straight white American man, albeit one who was self-aware enough to realize the power of this position and self-examined enough to tear down this power by making himself the frequent butt of the joke. But as the knowledge of his *actual* private self intrudes upon and breaks down the comedic frame around his stage persona, the full intertextual collage of C.K.'s celebrity image shifts to make new meaning, depending upon who is interpreting the source text. C.K.'s feminist point of view was often couched in him positioning himself as the epitome of the shameful, disgusted, and disgusting male sexual drive. Does this material take on a tone of hypocrisy, or one of speaking from a place of self-reflection and self-awareness? Does what C.K. kept hidden make his material *more* authentic? Or does what it concealed render that authenticity, that place of truth in his personal life, in his private self—no matter how creepy, gross, inappropriate, or objectionable it is—render the authenticity valueless? After C.K.'s sexual misconduct was made public, FX investigated whether C.K. had committed any workplace misconduct during the production of *Louie*. The investigation found no impropriety on C.K.'s part during that time (Libbey 2018). Was C.K.'s sexually coercive behavior a part of his life that he had overcome and adequately reflected upon? Or is it a case of a powerful man who knew exactly what he was doing, who sold sincerity because it sells, and whose hypocrisy between his rhetoric about the way women are treated by patriarchal culture and his contradictory actions makes his behavior even more predatory and abhorrent?

These questions destabilize C.K.'s persona and its authenticity. As C.K. has attempted to make a comeback despite his deplatformization from industry gatekeepers like Netflix and FX, his new material addresses his actions only in terms of how it affected his career and finances, and the embarrassment of having his sexual kinks made public. Rather than atoning for his actions to his more liberally minded fanbase of the past, C.K. seems to be courting a niche of fans who do not see anything particularly wrong with what he did, a deliberately more "anti-cancel culture" crowd: those who, like the audience member quoted by Izadi (2020), see themselves as people who "can take a joke." This tonal shift raises questions of who is and was the "real" Louis C.K., and the answer as it relates to celebrity self-performance in both fictional and non-fictional contexts may be the same as criticisms often leveled at the biopic: that humans are complex, and the ever-changing nature of an individual's life cannot be summed up with just one cohesive narrative. Just like his television series *Louie*, Louis C.K. as a public persona does not have a consistent narrative structure, perhaps, again, and in somewhat of a contradiction, pointing to his fictional self as a version of an "authentic" self.

This chapter has argued that the participation of a celebrity in their own adaptation on screen can work to authenticate their own persona, enhance the believability of fictional worlds, or highlight the implausibility of their own public image by undermining it or heightening it to the point of absurdity. Like the third-party adaptations discussed in previous chapters, the celebrity playing themselves can do so in two- or three-dimensional ways through the re-creation of what we already know and recognize supplemented by the creation of a private self that the general audience does not have access to through the celebrity image alone. In the following chapter, I will consider how audiences and fans approach the appropriation of the celebrity image, and often treat the public persona as another "made up" fictional media text, to narrativize it for communities of fellow fans in the arena of real person fan fiction.

6

Beyond the Biopic: Real Person Fan Fiction

When Jesse Eisenberg hosted *Saturday Night Live*, Andrew Garfield sat at home watching him. What could have been taken as Eisenberg's usual nervous tics, biting his lip, running his tongue along his teeth, were anything but his usual unconscious gestures. They were a purposeful performance meant for Garfield, intended to draw arousal from his co-star, to tease him with their burgeoning off-set relationship. A true story? Almost certainly not. However, for the members of the tsn-kinkmeme LiveJournal community, it's fun to pretend that is how things went, as seen in the request for a story about Andrew's obsession with Jesse's oral fixation kicked off by his *SNL* appearance. The five-part anonymously authored work of fan fiction, "Can't Stand the Heartache" (2011) that fulfilled the request, featured the scene described. Just as the makers of mainstream Hollywood biopic film can take an element of celebrity public image and extrapolate an inner motivation behind it, so too can the fans of a public figure use creative works to speculate upon and invent a private self behind the public face, writing their own access all areas pass to a version of a public figure. When it comes to RPF (real person fiction) fan fiction, however, while moments of public record can be recontextualized in a manner similar to the creations of mainstream film and television, whether biopic, sketch comedy, or celebrity cameo, there is a world of difference in the purpose behind the two forms, the breadth of their distribution, and perceived intention toward factuality. However, is there more in common between the vastly different forms of biopic and RPF fan fiction than first appears when the process of creating a docucharacter is the focus of consideration? Could the ways that small groups of fans adapt a public image as a text have something to say about the ways mainstream audiences at large engage with docucharacters on film or in other media?

This chapter will address these questions by returning to the earlier case study of *The Social Network*. This time, rather than the film, the object of consideration is the online fandom of *The Social Network* (or *TSN*, as is the common fandom abbreviation). This chapter will argue that the process of creating docucharacter remains consistent in its foundational principles—re-creation of the public and creation of the private granting simulated access to the reader or viewer—even when this process is entirely in the hands of the audience. Under examination here are fan works based on the text of the film itself which are about the screen characters depicted in the film, as well as RPF works about the film's actors. In looking at the former, I will demonstrate that the fan production of narratives about characters based on real people further blends the known and the unknown. In creating their narratives, fans draw on the biographies of the actual real person subjects to create characters comprised of intertextual fragments of public image, film character, and fan creation. In looking at the latter, I argue that fan authors engage in a similar process to creating docucharacters as in the biopic, creating plausible characters by fusing documentary evidence with a created private self. Rather than the plausible character purporting to provide insight into a famous figure and their place in the culture at large, though, the plausibility of the RPF character is anchored more in a sense of community play and celebrity fantasy. It is for this reason that I will propose that, like the docudrama mode of presentation in the biopic, the docucomedy mode of presentation in sketch impersonation, or the docucelebrity of the celebrity performance of a fictionalized self, RPF fan fiction can be considered to utilize a docufantasy mode of representation.

There is no single agreed upon interpretation of the characters that *The Social Network* and *TSN* RPF fandoms create and replicate throughout individual authors' works. Attempting to map the scope of the variety of fan fiction manifestations of the film characters of Mark and Eduardo and the RPF characters of the actors Jesse and Andrew is well beyond the abilities of this chapter. It is my hope, however, that by examining works from both the film canon and RPF components of *The Social Network* fandom, I can illustrate the variety of possibilities for individual fan interpretations and the varied forms of character remediation that fan works can create for different purposes, in this and other RPF fandoms. In these differences, however, I argue that there are recurring tropes, elements of characterization, and methods for blending the public with the private that circulate and become part of the celebrity public image within the fan community. These recurring characterizations in turn color the way the fans understand not only the characters of Mark and Eduardo, but the actual people involved: Zuckerberg, Saverin, Eisenberg, and Garfield. I will illustrate this through a consideration of the retention of characterization in works written for the *TSN* kink meme community on LiveJournal, an environment where fulfilling the prompt of a fellow fan is prioritized above adhering to plausibility or the boundaries of canon. I will also look at a case study of two multi-chaptered actor RPF fics (a subset of RPF often referred to as actorfic) that pair Eisenberg and Garfield in a relationship that is facilitated by the fan-perceived queer subtext of the Mark/Eduardo relationship on screen. Before engaging with these case studies, however, it is first necessary to provide some background on the practice of RPF fan fiction and its status as controversial in the arenas of fan studies, fandom, and popular culture at large.

RPF as a Fan Practice

Much like the biopic, RPF has been a relatively understudied subset of its broader academic field, which, in this case, is the literature on fandom, in general, and fan fiction, in particular. Within fan studies, RPF has primarily been written about as an ethical gray area (McGee 2005, Arrow 2013, Thomas 2014), as a fan practice that interrogates the constructed nature of celebrity and the ways fans similarly construct their own online personas (Busse 2006a and 2006b; Arrow 2013), as an increasingly complicated navigation process for fans attempting to maintain the fourth wall as celebrities perform public versions of their private selves on social media (Hagan 2015), and as an example of the intertextual and multimodal possibilities of digital fiction (Fathallah 2018). This oversight may be because, much like the biopic's relationship to film studies, RPF is a maligned and divisive subset of the wider field of fan fiction, both in academia and fandom itself. Despite its divisiveness, however, RPF is a growing area of fandom that can be considered, as Jennifer McGee writes, "the next logical step" in the fannish appropriation of popular culture (2005: 174). Similarly, Amanda Retartha argues for seeing "RPF as powerfully articulating the process by which all fans convert a much-loved text into their own creation," as well as how non-fannish audiences "encounter celebrities as complex fictions shaped by their own perceptions and interpretations" (2014: 14). Much like Retartha, I agree that it is useful to attempt to address the gap in RPF research, not only to achieve a more complete understanding of fan fiction writing and reading for the field of fan studies. It is also useful to consider RPF as a means of further understanding the ways that audiences engage with celebrities as texts, and particularly the imaginative possibilities of celebrities as texts. My focus on RPF here opens further analysis of the process of creating docucharacters by looking at how audiences create and consume the private selves of their favorite public figures.

To begin, I will look at some of the popular scholarly understandings of fan fiction in the field of fan studies with the aim of forming a basic understanding of why fans write and read fan fiction and how this can be applied to RPF fandom. Fan fiction (or fic), as fan scholars have largely understood it, is the work of media fans who appropriate pieces of a favorite text, re-writing and re-presenting it in ways that give themselves and the fellow fans they share the work with something they feel is missing from the original source. Sheenagh Pugh writes that a common understanding of fans' motivations to write fic is a desire for "'more of' their source material or 'more from it'" (2005: 19). For fans seeking more of the source, this could mean writing scenes that are missing from the canon of the source text, extending the timeline of events beyond the canon itself, or reproducing characters the fans have connected with so they can continue to see more of the same kind of interaction. For those who want more from the source canon, this could mean pairing together characters who were not in a relationship in canon, bringing minor characters into the spotlight that fans may feel the canon overlooked, or changing the narrative path or world building of the canon entirely with alternate universe settings. In RPF fan works, the dispersed and often contradictory nature of the celebrity image that comprises the canonical source text intensifies the possibilities for "what if" narratives and variations on characterization. The flexible concept of "canon" in the RPF fic creates endless possibilities for a fan work to simultaneously seek more from and more of the celebrities depicted by fictionalizing elements of public and private life to different degrees.

Canon is something that is more easily defined in most scholarly case studies of fan works that have focused on fictional media texts: television series, films, and books where what fans see on screen (or on the page) is everything that is known about a character. The fan writer's task is to fill in whatever blanks they would like to see filled, based on what the source text contains. With fan works based on real people, though, the spaces between elements of the canonical source text can be wider, and the fragments of self-performance data to draw on perhaps smaller and more dependent on the narrower frame of public performance than those of a fictional character. In this we might note that Richard Dyer's articulation of the concept of the star image is congruent with Cornel Sandvoss' writing on the textual boundaries of fan objects, in that celebrities as fan texts are "constituted through a multiplicity of textual elements;

[they are] by definition intertextual and formed between and across texts as defined at the point of production" (2007: 23). This attempt to define what constitutes canon in the fandom of a real person also bears similarities to what Márta Minier and Maddalena Pennacchia articulate as the source of adaptation in the biopic, finding it to be an intertextual and transmedia body of texts rather than one singular origin text (2014: 7–8). The disparate and intertextual nature of the public figure as a textual fan object can often produce contradictory readings, as fans attempt to define the boundaries of what the celebrity text means to them (Sandvoss 2007: 29–30). The result is a variety of potential interpretations or adaptations of the celebrity as a character, where individual fan authors can choose which elements of the star image to include, emphasize, or disregard. For example, a fan may play up certain characteristics that fit their selected narrative of the celebrity for one work of fiction and disregard those or incorporate other characteristics for their next new fic. Elements of a celebrity's private life, such as a real-life spouse, may be glossed over and erased to write a preferred RPF pairing without having to incorporate infidelity into the narrative. Busse writes that since no single definitive RPF canon exists, fans can define for themselves what constitutes canon and choose to treat any piece of information as truth, regardless of its objectively factual status. In RPF fandom, a piece of tabloid gossip and an officially sanctioned interview carry the same weight of story potential, regardless of either's relationship to actuality (2006b: 215).

This kind of loose treatment of fact in RPF fic is one element of the practice that accounts for its maligned status in fandom. The controversial status of RPF is addressed by Jennifer McGee (2005) in her writing on the ethics of fan fiction and real person fiction. McGee claims that RPF has been "roundly denounced in the fan fiction community," and regarded as possibly illegal and "almost certainly unethical" (2005: 173). Despite the controversial status of RPF in the online fic writing community, McGee asserts that, at the time of writing of her essay published in 2005, the practice was becoming more widely popular and accepted (2005: 173). Nonetheless, in a 2014 essay, Bronwen Thomas describes RPF in similar terms as "highly controversial and contentious" (2014: 171), demonstrating that the fannish division over the practice of "shipping real people" lingers, despite a shift toward RPF acceptance in some circles.

Even with this lingering division, there is evidence of the continued popularization of RPF and a broadening of its range of subjects. McGee notes that the most written about RPF subjects at the time of her essay are pop boy bands, such as the Backstreet Boys, and actors in Peter Jackson's *The Lord of the Rings* film trilogy, with other musicians and actors largely comprising the most written about public figures (2005: 173). In a later published chapter, V. Arrow notes two distinct trends in current RPF fandoms: those that are "an ingrained, central part of media-based fic fandoms" (2013: 323), with RPF existing in fandoms for media texts where the fictional text is also a primary fannish source; and the idea of RPF as a separate entity that has little connection to any fictional characters associated with the celebrity source material. Arrow cites *The Social Network* as an example of the former, with slash fiction about the actors Jesse Eisenberg and Andrew Garfield acting as a "spinoff" of fan fiction about the film's characters, Mark and Eduardo (2013: 323). Arrow adds that RPF fandoms that have a connection to a legitimized narrative or to legitimized writers, directors, or actors (such as *The Social Network*, as a critically acclaimed, award winning, mainstream Hollywood film rather than a more cult or niche genre text) often carry expectations of attracting highly skilled fan authors to their communities, with the legitimacy of the source text contributing a sense of validity to the fandom (2013: 325), further indicating a shift in the acceptance of RPF. However, the majority of RPF fan works are written about celebrities without any connection to a fictional source, Arrow notes, with musician RPF being the most popular sub-category (2013: 323). When looking at the Celebrities and Real People category list of the multifandom fan fiction website Archive of Our Own (AO3), it shows that RPF has been written and shared about historical figures, politicians, athletes, news anchors, comedians, podcasters, and authors, as well as a multitude of musicians and actors from a wide variety of genres and media types. I must note that I refer to AO3 as an example of the variety of celebrity types in RPF fandoms rather than the larger and longer-running archive FanFiction.Net because the latter does not permit the posting of RPF fan works. This absence of RPF in such a prominent multi-fandom fic repository is a major indication of RPF's still relatively contentious status in the online fannish community, despite the growing pool of public figures being fictionalized in RPF works.

To illustrate the divisive nature of RPF in fan spaces, I offer comments from a thread from the anonymous LiveJournal community (or anonmeme) Fail_Fandomanon (FFA) as an example ("Things You Wouldn't Admit" 2012). The thread discussed the reasoning behind some fans' objections to RPF, and the variety of personal boundaries they set in their RPF reading or writing practices. In this thread, the fans' objections can be largely divided into two categories. First is the invasion of privacy, such as writing about non-celebrity significant others or children. Second is the perceived removal of the RPF subject's agency, such as characterizing them as something negative not in the public record (like a rapist or abuser) or writing fictional sexual relationships in explicit detail. The discussion demonstrates the wide variety of boundaries that individual fans often draw regarding their own RPF reading and/or writing practices. Some individual fans acknowledge the contradictory nature of their boundaries. Anonymous commenter A states they would prefer it if RPF featuring non-celebrity spouses could be banned but acknowledges their own slightly contradictory view by stating they find RPF including a real-life spouse who is not a celebrity but part of the entertainment industry working as a publicist to be acceptable. Anonymous fan B writes that they are more comfortable with RPF that is lighthearted "silly fluff and AUs [alternate universes]," but admits they find well-written RPF of the darker, angstier variety to be "compelling." Some in the discussion claim to find the private lives of celebrities boring and don't understand the appeal of RPF, while others find writing fic based on fictional canons to be uninteresting and prefer RPF. As commenter C states, their preference for the latter is "because real people don't follow a specific narrative" ("Things You Wouldn't Admit" 2012). Despite its increasingly visible presence and growing association with fictional media canons as a "spinoff" of the fandom, these comments demonstrate the nature of RPF fan practices as a matter of personal taste with individual fans continually renegotiating their reading and writing boundaries.

The arguments that cast RPF as a removal of the agency of a real person could be summarized, as commenter D in the FFA thread puts it, as the view that RPF is "by its very nature dehumanizing and immoral" ("Things You Wouldn't Admit" 2012). In writing RPF, the fan regards their celebrity of choice as an object that needs to be personalized and made real (McGee 2005: 175–6), much like the way fan fiction about fictional characters works to make the character more real and identifiable to the fan (McGee 2005: 165). Here the agency of the fan author is privileged over the agency of the celebrity subject. The fan author creates an alternate reading of the canonical text of the celebrity public image, choosing which aspects of what is known about the celebrity to add to the composition of a fictional character. Through this process of creating the world of the RPF work, the fan writer also creates the celebrity subject as a character composed of the known public and invented private. By speculating about the private self of the celebrity, their actual private self is encroached upon by strangers who do not know the celebrity as a real person and disregard who the celebrity actually is in favor of the fannish invention that is infinitely more accessible and able to be engaged with. As McGee (2005) argues, many of those who view RPF as an unethical practice see the creation of a character from the text of a celebrity as the negation of the celebrity as a real person. By appropriating the name, image, and personality of a public figure for use in a work of fiction that caters to whatever the author's whims may be, the fan author "denies [the celebrity] their personhood" (McGee 2005: 175–6).

The counterargument to this point claims that the mediated source text of a celebrity public persona does not itself constitute a real person. Some fan writers see this public persona as a constructed commodity that is readily available for fictional adaptation just like any media text that features fictional characters (McGee 2005: 177). Busse goes so far as to argue that RPF can potentially act as a means of rehumanizing the textual object of the star image through the fan activity of "inventing backstories and inner lives" (2006a: 256). In the case of some RPF subjects, the public persona is more readily acknowledged as something closer to a fictional character, such as the heavily constructed boy band personas that Busse writes about (2006a, 2006b). For other kinds of RPF subjects, such as athletes, the boundaries between how much the private self has in common with the public persona may be far less distinct and more akin to the everyday public performance of non-famous selves, or is, at the very least, able to be constructed that way by fans. Regardless of the type of celebrity, though, the one-sided nature of a parasocial relationship remains consistent. The fan is distanced from truly engaging with their object of fandom. The need to forge this connection can be considered a similar process with similar purposes to the personalization of history in the biopic, or the affective understanding of characters based on real people that a film can construct. The process of the fan re-writing the celebrity based on their own points of view and desires creates a character that can be more easily recognized as a relatable person than the distant celebrity image alone (even if the correlation between the constructed and fictional "relatable person" and the actual celebrity's private self the character purports to represent is tenuous at best).

While keeping these general ideas about fan purposes for writing and reading RPF fic in mind, it is important to note that they are only general ideas. Daria Pimenova (2009) writes that fan fiction can be categorized as a certain type of writing with shared characteristics: produced by fans, for fans, based on characters and situations found in existing media texts, and, presumably, not for the purpose of financial gain. It cannot, however, be classified as a genre in the literary sense, as it is not "based on common formal and thematic features," and there are a multitude of diverse ways that fans approach their fan works, encompassing numerous genres (2009: 46). Pimenova's observation of fan fiction as unclassifiable as a singular genre indicates that there is no singular homogenous entity called "fandom," or even a homogeneity existing in the fandom of a particular media text. There is no singular way of "doing fandom," and no singular objective, reason, or process for the way individual fans create their fan works. I argue, however, that one approach to writing RPF fan fiction—recontextualization—is particularly useful for uncovering the ways that the process of crafting characters from the source material of a celebrity public image shares similarities across vastly different forms of media.

Recontextualization is one approach to writing fan fiction and fan fiction characters described by Henry Jenkins (1992: 162). When RPF is considered in terms of the recontextualization approach to fan fiction writing, consistencies in the process of creating characters from public personas become clear. As Jenkins describes it, recontextualization in fan fiction writing sees fan writers working to fill the blanks left in the original canon, such as with a missing scene, an episode coda, or a piece of character backstory. In doing so, writers invite other fans to reread the original media text in light of the context that the fan work establishes (Jenkins 1992: 162). Recontextualization in fan fiction writing can perhaps be further examined alongside Abigail Derecho's (2006) classification of fan fiction as a form of archontic literature, where the relationship between the official canonical text and various fan-created "fanon" texts is an open, unfinished, and non-hierarchical one. Recontextualization in fan writing involves the repetition of existing canon and the addition of fanon material that builds the archive of related, interconnected texts among fan works and canonical works, encouraging side-by-side readings of these official and unofficial texts (Derecho 2006: 65–6). Often, recontextualization-based RPF fic uses existing textual fragments of the star image, such as part of an interview, screen performance, or public appearance, to create an imagined or fantasized private moment attached to that specific public moment. By recontextualizing the public moment within the fiction, the author invites fellow fans to reconsider the public text in light of the imagined private one. The repetition of archontic literature occurs as the original element of the star image exists in the mind of the readers as they consume the fan fiction. Likewise, if they revisit that element of the star image, the fan fiction continues to exist in their mind, and in the archival body of texts related to the subject. The fan can choose to conflate the two variations on the celebrity's star image and imagine the star image in light of the fiction, or keep the two compartmentalized, acknowledging the invented, separate status of the fiction and not indulge in the fantasy reimagining that the fan author has proposed.

In this way, the possibilities of RPF are similar to those of the biopic. Both have the ability to bring a distant public figure closer to viewers, readers, and writers, through "fictional narratives that supplement and enhance those disseminated by the media" (Busse 2006a: 254). The public record becomes personalized for the spectator/reader/writer, and a simulation of otherwise unattainable access is granted to a version of a public figure's private self. The differences, however, between RPF and mainstream Hollywood biopic are far more obvious than their similarities. As a legitimized commercial form, the Hollywood biopic is branded with much higher assumptions of a significant grounding in truth than RPF fan fiction. Consider, for example, how each form presents their disclaimers denying any connection to actual persons, living or dead. The practice of using disclaimers in fan fiction originates in hopes of avoiding legal action for copyright infringement in fic based on existing intellectual property such as television shows or books. This norm of disclaimers is often likewise applied to RPF fic, with a brief statement at the beginning of a fan work clarifying that the work is intended to be fiction and not an actual representation of the public figures it depicts. In mainstream biopic film, similar disclaimers denying a resemblance to the actual people it depicts attempt to avoid legal claims of defamation in ways that "[suggest] an alternate universe in which there is a recognizable fact-based figure leading a different existence" (Aquino 2005: 28). While these disclaimers come at the end of the closing credits, such films often market their narratives as based on true stories and include title cards stating the same at the beginning of the film. This practice foregrounds the film's truth claims while the legally required denial of representing the actual appears to be just a formality.

As a for-profit venture, the Hollywood biopic is assumed to have enough adherences to truth in dealing with the likeness of a real person to avoid accusations of defamation. Indeed, the audience pleasures of watching a film based on a true story are depleted if they are not able to believe that the events on screen bear some resemblance to what happened in actuality: if the public image is not re-created faithfully, the created private image can become less plausible. However, it is understood that the biopic is not a documentary, and thus some degree of fictionalization or invention, such as composite characters or the compression of time, is to be expected (Bingham 2010: 25). Even so, the biopic carries the weight of an intended connection to actuality that RPF fan fiction does not similarly claim. John Aquino notes that "a widely shown movie based on that event may be the last word on the subject for a very long time" (2005: 4). By contrast, the readers of RPF fan fiction are a small community who are aware that the works they are enjoying are the products of their authors (who are primarily known only as their screen names and are presumed to be ordinary fans, just as their readers are), representing a version of the public figure that will not enter wider circulation. There is less of an expectation that the biopic viewer will strictly compartmentalize versions of the real person from their actual self than there is with the RPF reader. The use of the public image to depict an imagined private self in the biopic is less of an invitation to play when compared to RPF, and more of a docudramatic argument for plausible actuality.

In line with this, the biopic subject—or their representatives if the subject is no longer living—can choose to participate in the production of the film, as the remaining members of Queen did with *Bohemian Rhapsody*. At the very least, the living biopic subject who did not participate in or authorize the film can choose to publicly respond to it or denounce it, as biopic subjects such as Mark Zuckerberg and Sarah Palin have. The biopic is widely distributed, intended to spark discussion and contribute to public discourse about its subject, is open to criticism about the ways it does or does not adhere to truth, and open to having its inaccuracies corrected in the public sphere by people involved in the actual events. Conversely, RPF fan fiction is written by fans for fans to share among a small, specific community. There is no money at stake, and no permission is sought from the subjects of the fiction. Indeed, as Pugh notes, if RPF writers could attempt to gain permission from their subjects, "[the subjects] in most cases would be unlikely to give it" considering some of the sexual exploits their fictional selves get up to (2005: 231). RPF fan writers often go to great lengths to keep their work hidden, such as "locking" their fic so that it is only visible to members of a specific community, such as registered members of Archive of Our Own, or writing under a second fannish pseudonym so that not only is the work not connected to their real name, but also separated from their main fandom identity. In fact, the two examples of Jesse Eisenberg and Andrew Garfield actorfic that I will consider later in the chapter are both now only available through limited access: one was deleted by the author but continued to be distributed as a PDF between fans on platforms such as Tumblr; the other remains posted on Archive of Our Own but is locked to be viewable by members only (for this reason, I will not mention the usernames of the authors of either of these fan works in the text of this chapter). Attempts to hide RPF works aim not only to protect the RPF subjects or their associates from finding fic about themselves but to also protect the writers and their communities from mainstream public attention and derision. Such public focus happened in *The Social Network* fandom when the blogs *Dvice* ("The Strange and Scary" 2012) and *Gawker* (Tate 2012) posted articles directly linking to *TSN* fic and fic communities with mocking commentary.

The process of recontextualizing a public self with the depiction of a fictionalized private self is shaped in both biopic and fan fiction by their respective formal conventions, and their creators' purposes. Similar to the way screen biographies of public figures are shaped by the genre's history of repeated tropes and narrative structures, so too the fictionalization of public figures in fandom is a form of creative work developed through a long tradition of conventions, character tropes, and narrative premises. Given fan fiction's lack of commercial imperative, though, the pool of conventions and tropes that stories draw from is far more diverse than those available to mainstream Hollywood film. An individual story does not need to appeal to everybody in the community to find some form of readership. As Busse writes, "fandom is big enough that we can find someone who wants to read what we write and, if we're really lucky, who writes what we want to read" (2013: 317). Fan fiction can range from G-rated stories that do not focus on romantic relationships to explicit erotica involving diverse sexual kinks. There are narrative tropes such as hurt/comfort, time travel, and amnesia, as well as alternate universes that can transport characters into completely different settings, whether that is a space station, high school, or a neighborhood coffee shop. Just as the makers of mainstream Hollywood biopic may have their own agenda or motivation drawing them to bring a life story to the screen in a particular way, the fan writer brings their own creative needs to their work. Individual writers can range from adolescents working through discovering their sexuality, to professional authors looking to tell stories free from commercial imperatives (Jamison 2013: 17), all of which shape the story being told and how its characters are reimagined.

Recontextualization in both biopic and RPF involves recreating what is known to anchor the unknown to plausibility. In the biopic, this involves techniques such as re-staging public events, incorporating archival footage, and using make-up and costume to enhance an actor's resemblance to a public figure. Likewise, RPF invokes the physical body of the subject through description, often through repetition of features that the fan community collectively fixates on, such as Jesse Eisenberg/Andrew Garfield RPF that references Garfield's "Bambi eyes" and "ridiculous hair." As well as conjuring the body of the subject in the minds of readers, the subject's physicality is also reproduced in fic as a means of expressing the emotional state of the fictionalized inner self of the character, through the description of gesture and facial expression. Busse describes the way that RPF writers use existing media footage of their subject to search for subtext that hints toward their desired RPF pairing, looking for "cracks in the 'façade' of the official star text" to reveal what the fan imagines as the "more genuine 'reality' underneath" (2006a: 259). In this process, fan writers take the celebrity's recorded public self-performance and recontextualize it, searching for meaning in body language or facial expression that can be applied in different ways to their fictional work, disregarding any possible original intent or context surrounding something the celebrity has done. This bears similarities to the discourse of celebrity gossip blogs, websites, and magazines, where the celebrity body is a "crucial piece of evidence to be read and negotiated" in perpetually seeking a glimpse of the celebrity's "real" self (Meyers 2010: 181). In the context of RPF, however, the celebrity's "real" self is a clearly signaled fiction which can be pleasurable to consider as a possibility that is "backed" by photographic or video "evidence": for example, photographs from *The Social Network* press events where Eisenberg and Garfield appear to be interacting as a separate entity from the rest of the cast and filmmakers, encouraging fans of the pairing to conjure up a relationship between them that does not exist in actuality. As I will further discuss later in this chapter, elements of the textual star image of the subject are also replicated in an effort to recontextualize them, as fan fiction premises are built around specific public appearances.

Despite their differences in form, medium, mode of production, subject matter, and intended audience, RPF fan fiction and Hollywood biopic both use the material of a public image to write an unknown private self. If, as Steven Lipkin (2011) argues, this constitutes a docudramatic mode of representation in film and television based on real people and events, RPF fan fiction could perhaps be considered a docufantasy mode of representation. In this mode, fans imagine and create who they want the celebrity to be, integrating this fantasy with known elements of the public image to anchor the story to the existing reality of the mediated celebrity. To illustrate how the docufantasy mode manifests in select case studies from *TSN* fandom, I will first consider how fan writers draw on a variety of intertextual source materials and the collective knowledge of the community to ground their fantasy representations in documented actuality.

The Docufantasy Mode in *The Social Network* Fan Fiction

Members of *The Social Network*'s online fan community engage in both creating and attempting to untangle the crossed wires of fiction and reality involved in the constant remediation of the public figures and docucharacters they write. The *TSN* Kink Meme LiveJournal community (the kink meme concept and examples from *TSN* fandom will be further discussed later in this chapter) includes a research post among its resources for writers and readers ("Research Questions" 2011). In this post, community members have considered questions such as whether film character Christy Lee, Eduardo's possessive girlfriend, is based on a real person. In answering the question, responding fans draw on sources including Ben Mezrich's book *The Accidental Billionaires* (from which *The Social Network* was adapted) and the memories of a person who knew the actual Zuckerberg and Saverin circa the formation of Facebook. The fans determine that Saverin did have a girlfriend at the time who did do some of the things depicted in the film, such as sending him excessive amounts of text messages, but her name was not Christy and she was likely a student at Wellesley, not Harvard. One fan speculates that, based on the film's characterization of Eduardo, the actual Saverin may "[have] a bit of a codependent personality" and "could be one of those people who 'can't be alone'" and may have gone through a number of relationships during the time that were merged into a single character, Christy, in the film ("Research Questions" 2011). This is an example of the multiple remediations of a real person and the blurred boundaries of actuality and fiction that can lead to an understanding of various manifestations of the docucharacter that are incorporated into the public image of the actual person. However, as part of a locked post in a fan community, this example is obviously taking place on a much smaller scale than a docucharacter reading taken directly from the film that becomes part of the broader public discourse of a celebrity's persona. In addition to questions of character details based on real people, the kink meme's research questions post includes discussion of other potential story elements, from Harvard exam scheduling to the process of business shareholder meetings, that rely on real-world sources of information to anchor these fictional stories of already remediated public figures to a plausible actuality.

The Mark_Eduardo LiveJournal community has a similar post that seeks to define the lines between fact and fiction for the purposes of further playing with their porous boundaries in the fandom. The "Canon and Fanon" (2011) discussion post raises questions about details in fan works to attempt to separate those that have a basis in either the film text or in reality from those that have been invented by fans and repeated often enough that they have begun to seem factual. As the Mark_Eduardo community includes RPF works about Eisenberg and Garfield, the questions in this post of what is canon and what is fanon also involve the actors and their fictionalized fandom versions. Questions range from topics such as whether the ubiquity of Mark drinking Red Bull in *TSN* fic has any basis in the film's character or the real Zuckerberg, to whether the recurrent Jesse/Andrew narrative of the two actors living together during production of the film actually happened or is merely a fan invention. Once again, the answers are intertextual, drawn from multiple sources that do not rely on a strict definition of "canon," particularly in the case of fan works based on the film characters where answers come from both the text of the film and from sources about the real Zuckerberg and Saverin. Regarding the actors, in response to questions about Eisenberg and Garfield's actual living arrangements during production, some commenters note that what they have read in fic and what they have read in interviews has merged and become hazy to the point where they are unable to pinpoint a specific source for the idea. Other responders, though, manage to source the idea as far as recalling a comment from Eisenberg about him and Garfield waking up and "be[ing] the only people [they] knew in the whole world" while shooting on location in Boston and Baltimore. This serves as an example of the ways fans can choose to recontextualize the words of a celebrity and extrapolate them into a plausible scenario: the actors being isolated from their usual networks of friends and family becomes the two co-stars having only each other to turn to and engage with, possibly to the extent that their relationship is made closer through shared living space. Knowing for sure whether or not the two were sharing accommodation can make a fic scenario that much more enjoyable for the fans, as the fantasy comes a little closer to possibility.

In discussing the argument made by some that RPF is not a moral quandary, Pugh (2005) compares the real-world and fictional versions of public figures to the ways that cities and places are used in literature. Just as a geographical location where a novel (or film, or television series) is set "may not be identical with the place on the map on which it is based," the characters sharing the same name as a real-world public figure do not occupy the exact same space as their real-world referents (Pugh 2005: 231). While it is clearly understood by the vast majority of RPF writers that their versions of characters do not and are not intended to occupy the same space as the public figures they are based on, the desire to align with reality in some way or to differentiate between fiction and reality that is exhibited in these community threads indicates that there are fan fic authors who seek to maintain plausibility through connection to factuality. Locating an RPF fan work on a spectrum of blended truth to pure fantasy fiction can enhance the pleasure of the "what if this was true?" game fans play through the recontextualization of existing star images. By connecting their real person fictions to a plausible version of actuality, the fans draw out the subtext they seek in the official star image of publicity and promotional materials and public appearances, with the aim of making the subtext the text: bringing the between-the-lines reading of their favorite celebrities into the spotlight to be considered and enjoyed by fellow fans.

Having established a foundational understanding of RPF as a fan practice and argued for a view of RPF as utilizing a docufantasy mode of representation, I now move on to putting these ideas to work with case studies of two different types of fan works in *TSN* fandom. First, to demonstrate how the remains of film characterization manifest in a type of fan fiction that often does not prioritize adherence to canon, I will look at the continued adaptation of Mark Zuckerberg and Eduardo Saverin as docucharacters in an example fic from *The Social Network* kink meme.

Kink memes became a staple of fic creation in online fic-writing fandom, particularly around the early 2010s when *The Social Network* fandom was at its peak. The typical setup of the kink meme invites fans to post prompts (either anonymously or with usernames attached) involving a particular pairing and a story idea. The prompt can be as simple as a one-word kink or trope (despite the name, not all the "kinks" of the kink meme are of a sexual nature, and may simply be narrative or character tropes), or a more elaborate story premise. Jamison describes the kink meme as a "game," a "writing underground where stories start and percolate" (2013: 8). Stories developed in kink memes may be perpetually unfinished works in progress, they may be the anonymous works that authors would never dare attach their name to, or they may be rescued from the often difficult to navigate arena of the meme and archived elsewhere, such as AO3 or the author's personal fic archive. As Jamison writes, the aim of the kink meme game is to fill the requests of fellow fans, regardless of how out of character the scenarios may seem: "the writings it produces aren't sacred, nor are they put up to be. It is really no place for purists" (2013: 9).

Here, my aim is to briefly investigate the ways that the film versions of Mark and Eduardo retain elements of their characterization in the context of the kink meme. If the kink meme is to be understood as a game of fannish collaboration between prompters and writers that abandons a more traditional sense of adherence to canon or characterization in favor of the id-driven desires of the fan community, then examining how these characters manifest in that context can shed light on the fundamental core of characterization. By examining what vestiges of canon characterizations remain in works where characterization is often secondary to fulfilling the wishes of the prompter, it can perhaps be revealed that even in the creation of docucharacters that deviate from truth in the most extreme ways, there remain certain hallmarks of characters that are consistent throughout. These are the hooks of actuality from which any scenario can be hung in order to preserve some sense of plausibility or recognizability to an original, actual, source.

There are certain traits of both Mark and Eduardo that regularly motivate prompts and recur throughout the fic that fulfills them. The two characters are often explored in the ways that they differ from each other: Mark's casual dress sense, social awkwardness, and disdain for almost everyone in his life versus Eduardo's immaculate suits, his air of perpetual put-togetherness, and charm and physical grace. As we shall see, fic characterizations of Jesse and Andrew also tend to hinge on the ways they are constructed as different from each other, yet similar to their screen characters: Jesse as overly anxious and awkward versus Andrew as relaxed and easily sociable. The fan-read motivations of the characters also form the basis of kink meme characterization. Because the dynamic between the characters shifts throughout the film's chronology, *TSN* kink meme requests tend to be specific about what point in the timeline they would like to set the story. For example, Harvard-era Mark and Eduardo tends to generate requests for Eduardo as a caretaker, who in various ways prevents Mark from being entirely consumed by his hacking work: reminding Mark to perform the basic functions of eating and sleeping; luring Mark away from the computer with his sexual prowess; or bringing Mark medicine when he ignores a cold and keeps working. The deposition-era Mark and Eduardo is often the sandbox for writers and readers to play up the destruction of their relationship, through angst-ridden, urgent hate sex- or revenge-driven BDSM; or, alternatively, to play fix-it with various manifestations of a reconciliation between Mark and Eduardo, rekindling their friendship or the past romance many fans want to see in the subtext of the film's relationship between the characters.

For example, the story "It's Not a Big Deal" fills a request for Eduardo/Mark eating disorder fic, with the specific prompt: "College era, Eduardo is bulimic (because I'm a horrible person), and Mark finally pays attention to the signs"

("Eduardo/Mark, ED Fic" 2010). It is a prompt that has no basis in the canon of *The Social Network* (there is no indication in the film that Eduardo suffers from an eating disorder), yet it retains elements of canon characterization: Eduardo as image-focused, Mark as somewhat oblivious yet capable of acknowledging a problem with a friend when forced to. Following the timeline-anchored nature of *TSN* fic, it requests a specific era that dictates the dynamic between the characters. This prompt also demonstrates the anonymous, anything goes nature of kink meme culture in general. The anonymous prompter acknowledges that they are "a horrible person" for wanting to see Eduardo not only in a situation that deviates significantly from canon, but one that inflicts the pain of a very real problem on a fictionalization of a character based on a real person. The fic locates the seed of Eduardo's eating disorder in the pressure placed on him by his father, a relationship that the film hints at and a common element of *TSN* fic. Eduardo is characterized as needing to be in control and maintaining his sense of control by hiding his bulimia from people. The fic incorporates canon events in a way that Eduardo's eating disorder becomes the extrapolated unknown private behind the known public image of the canon. Canon events are recontextualized to invite the readers to re-view them in light of the possibility that Eduardo could have had an eating disorder. The scene in which Mark and Eduardo meet Sean for the first time, for example, is represented in the fic from Eduardo's point of view as "Mark totally thinks this Sean guy is a God. It makes him feel sick. He excuses himself from the table" ("Eduardo/Mark, ED Fic" 2010: Part 5). The fic concludes with a scene set post-deposition, with Eduardo returning to the United States from Singapore to attend a Facebook shareholders meeting. Here, Mark realizes Eduardo's problem which leads to an angry confrontation between the two that reveals Eduardo's feelings of betrayal and characterizes Mark in ways that merge with the portrayal of Mark toward the end of the film (remorseful and matured) as he attempts to reconcile by taking care of Eduardo:

> "You know, a lot of teenage girls get this permanent food poisoning also known as an eating disorder." Mark is relentless. "For you, I'd say 40% anorexia, 60 % bulimia. You're a control freak and an overachiever. You're a perfect candidate for an eating disorder."
>
> Eduardo flinches but doesn't bother denying it. Mark is usually right and he is brutal when he is. "Fuck you. You never cared. You don't care. You want to be right. Fine, you're right. I'm fucked up. Be happy and leave me alone." Eduardo turns to go but Mark latches onto his arm, feeling Eduardo's bony wrist under his tailored jacket.

"Well I do now," Mark says. "Eduardo. Wardo. Look at me. I was in love with you too. I still am. I was wrong, I miss you and… I'm sorry." ("Eduardo/Mark, ED Fic" 2010: Part 8)

Here there is evidence of some of the recurring tropes of Mark and Eduardo's characterization: Eduardo as image-obsessed and wanting to be in control, Mark as blunt with a need to be heard and a need to be right. There is the almost taken-for-granted in fandom notion that there was a romantic element between the two in college (whether consummated, unspoken, or unrequited), and the need for a happy ending reconciliation between the two that the film (or reality) does not provide. It is a story crafted for the specific purposes of the fannish audience, with elements of popular fan fiction hurt/comfort tropes, internal angst, external conflict, the revelation of romantic feelings, and reconciliation. Also, as one reader comments, "I know all these feelings so well," indicating that seeing Eduardo struggling with an eating disorder and being helped by Mark personalizes the characters in ways that may be familiar to the readers. This enables the readers to form a sympathetic allegiant response with the characters for new and different reasons that do not exist in the film canon or the reality canon alone.

In addition to retaining elements of the film's characterization of Mark and Eduardo, the fic also blends details from the actual Saverin's life. At the end of "It's Not a Big Deal," Eduardo comes back to the United States from Singapore. The actual Saverin relocated to Singapore after the timeline the film covers, but this detail is not something mentioned or hinted at on screen. This kink meme fic demonstrates not only the ways known elements of the film canon are recontextualized (such as the scene described that recreates Mark and Eduardo's first meeting with Sean Parker), but it also blends in factual elements outside of the film canon. In doing so, the characters become something more than strictly fictional interpretations based on a fictionalized source. Rather, they become hybrids of fictional and non-fictional sources, blurring fandom's traditional boundaries between real person fiction and fan fiction based on fictional source texts. Incorporating intertextual elements of what fan readers know to be true in both fictionalized and actual versions of the public figure's lives further anchors the otherwise unfounded and completely fantastical scenario of the fic to a plausible possibility.

To further examine how documentary evidence is incorporated into the fan fantasy characterization of RPF, I move now to examining two longer works of *TSN* actorfic. The fics in question use different kinds of documentary evidence of the star image from *The Social Network*'s publicity materials to craft the imagined private selves of Jesse Eisenberg and Andrew Garfield as they embark on a romantic relationship during filming of *The Social Network*. I have chosen these particular fics, "The Long Affair" (2012) and "Carry it in My Heart" (2011), for close reading as, in addition to their use of documentary evidence and connection between the relationship and the film, both fics imply a significant degree of character bleed from the on-screen relationship between Mark and Eduardo to the relationship between the actors Jesse and Andrew. This kind of psychic melding between the life of the actor and the desires of their character is a common trope of actor RPF, which Amanda Retartha credits to the prevalence of the Method in popular discourse about screen performance (2014: 28). The popular understanding of Method acting is the actor "committed to inhabiting their character, to finding themselves in their role and the role in themselves" (Retartha 2014: 27). The degree to which this discourse dominates the layman's comprehension of screen acting sees audiences reading all performances through the lens of the Method, regardless of whether the actor is known to be an avowed practitioner or not (Retartha 2014: 28). Through this popular understanding of the actor's work, in *TSN* RPF the on-screen dynamic between Mark and Eduardo plays a significant role in the development of an off-screen relationship between Jesse and Andrew. As such, these works continue the remediation of Mark Zuckerberg and Eduardo Saverin begun by the filmmakers and actors themselves and rework it into a fictionalized account of the production of the film and the actors' relationships to their own inner selves, as well as the real people they portray on screen.

Different methods of using documentary evidence and recontextualizing the star image are central to crafting docucharacter in these two examples of Jesse/Andrew RPF. "The Long Affair" goes to great lengths to anchor its fictionalized narrative to actual points in the real-world public record of the actors' respective star images. The story structures the fictionalized relationship between the two actors in parallel with what is known about the production and promotion of the film. The fic is a particularly clear example of the recontextualization approach as it incorporates specific fragments of the star image both within the fiction and as an extra-text to the fiction. The source canon of the public star image and public knowledge about the production of *The Social Network* is scattered across various texts, such as interviews, behind-the-scenes DVD extras, broadcasts of awards ceremonies, press junket appearances, and film festival schedules. The gaps in the canon that the writer fills in are the moments that are not part of any publicity canon: the actors at home, on the set away from the gaze of making-of documentary cameras, or in hotel rooms during location shoots and trips to awards ceremonies. By fitting the romantic relationship between Jesse and Andrew into the gaps of public record, the fan writer invites their fellow fans to recontextualize these existing publicity materials by viewing them through a perspective established by the fiction. The fic becomes an invitation for fans to think "there could have been a relationship happening behind the scenes, and here is how it might have fit around what we know." In doing so, the fan work appropriates a portion of the star image, based on various publicity materials and public appearances during a set timeline, and uses its status as actuality to lend an air of credibility to the fiction, a persuasive docufantasy for the fan to readily imagine what could have been true.

For example, "The Long Affair" is structured around Jesse and Andrew's relationship in different cities, such as the production locations of Boston, Baltimore, and Los Angeles, or post-production locations such as Garfield's home in London, Eisenberg's home in New York, and a film festival in Berlin. Each chapter, titled for the location in which it takes place, opens with an actual quote from Eisenberg or Garfield that somehow relates to the content of the chapter. Chapter 1, "Boston," begins with the quote that was mentioned earlier as the basis for the fanon assumption that Eisenberg and Garfield shared living space during the on-location production of the film: Eisenberg's comment on *The Social Network*'s DVD commentary that "when we were in Boston it was like we'd wake up, and we'd be the only people we'd know." This extratextual epigraph to Chapter 1 of "The Long Affair" omits the rest of the quote that mentions Garfield's girlfriend and how the two actors spent less time together once production moved to Los Angeles, in order to better suit the purposes of the fictional account.

Judith Fathallah (2018) notes that this blending of extra-textual evidence around which a story is constructed in RPF is a feature unique to the medium specificity of digital fiction. Like the multimedia nature of the celebrity image as it exists in the digital archive, the RPF fan fiction can draw on numerous sources, blending them with varying degrees of reality and fiction, in ways that are not possible in traditionally "analog" literature (2018: 6). In Fathallah's work, she studies the integration of photographs in crafting an RPF narrative, and this visual signifier functions in a way that is not possible in a form like the biopic. In the RPF, it is a photograph of the actual subject that has been integrated into their fictionalization, rather than a re-staging or re-embodiment of the subject by an actor. Likewise, with the textual chapter epigraphs in "The Long Affair," these are the reprinted words of the actual Jesse Eisenberg and Andrew Garfield merged with the fiction of the Jesse and Andrew RPF characters. In her case study of RPF about the band Panic! At The Disco, Fathallah writes that these oscillations between the actual and the imagined within a single work of fiction give the sense that "since both the people and the images this story features are taken from the real world, we have no way of knowing with certainty that the story's events did *not* happen in it" (2018: 13, emphasis in original), adding to the game of what-if among fans and the pleasures of plausibility in a work that all involved know to be fictional.

While the "documentary evidence" of the real can play a role in generating this pleasure of plausibility, fabricated evidence can do much the same, as seen in "Carry it in My Heart." This Jesse/Andrew fic takes a different approach to the documentary evidence that structures the fictional relationship that it creates between the two actors. There is an epistolary component to this fic, with the text of the story augmented by documents such as screen captures of text messages between Jesse and Andrew, post-it note shopping lists from the two sharing a house during production of *The Social Network*, handwritten track lists of mix CDs Andrew makes for Jesse, and even a Polaroid photograph of a hand on the neck of a guitar that claims the subject to be Jesse and the photographer to be Andrew. These documents are, of course, as fabricated as the romance between the two actors that the story depicts, and the epistolary components of this work can be considered a kind of fictional behind-the-scenes "mockumentary" of *The Social Network*'s production. As "The Long Affair" weaves its behind-the-scenes moments of the relationship as a supplement to moments of the public record, "Carry it in My Heart" creates its own private record with mocked up "evidence"—such as photographs or handwritten notes—that are coded as being documentary "fact." Much in the same way that screen mockumentary utilizes the codes and conventions of documentary, such as handheld camerawork and voice-over narration, in order to situate a fiction within factual discourse (Roscoe and Hight 2001:16), the epistolary material of "Carry it in My Heart" encourages the reader to suspend their disbelief and play on the boundaries between truth and fantasy. The reader is invited to accept these documents as artifacts of Jesse and Andrew's relationship as the fiction presents it. It plays with the extrapolated private self of the fan fiction character to bring fabricated documents into the public record: the fan-fictional mediations of Jesse and Andrew's private selves are made public by the public revelation of these private documents. While the public revelation of these documents is not a plot point in the fiction (their text messages to each other are not, for example, revealed in a public scandal that outs the two actors), they are revealed to the public of the fan readers. The fan readers gain access to these intimate, private moments between the fictionalized versions of the actors, and once again it is documentary evidence that heightens the fun of believing the fiction. These are the artifacts of the private life and relationship that the fandom can collectively imagine for the two actors, extrapolated from their public appearances.

In these two fan works, the development of Jesse and Andrew's relationship is deeply dependent on the relationship between Mark and Eduardo as characterized by David Fincher, Aaron Sorkin, and the two actors. The evidence for how the film's creatives approached the characters and understood their relationship exists in the kinds of intertextual publicity materials that RPF works so often reference, or, in the case of "The Long Affair," directly incorporates into its narrative. The way the fan authors continue remediation and reinterpretation of the screen relationship between the characters of Mark and Eduardo can be considered a further remediation and characterization of the actual Zuckerberg and Saverin. As discussed earlier, *The Social Network* fan works that focus on the Mark/Eduardo relationship often draw on the lives of the actual people to fill in personal details that are not contained in the film or use the actual lives of the people depicted in the film to fill in details or speculate about what happens to them after the film's end.

With Mark and Eduardo firmly, if temporarily, implanted in the psyche of the actors portraying, them, Jesse and Andrew are guided into a relationship by the subtext of the one envisioned for their characters. In "The Long Affair," this first arises in a conversation between Jesse and Andrew shortly into the fic's first chapter. After the first day of shooting, the two actors discuss the relationship between their characters. According to Andrew, David Fincher claims that there are "secrets in the margins" he needs to look at to find Eduardo's motivations. Andrew's reading of this is that "'Eduardo is in love with Mark... really, for real, in love. Emotionally, intellectually, physically. He wants him. But he can't have him'" ("The Long Affair" 2012: 3). On considering what that means for whether Mark is in love with Eduardo, Jesse's response is

> "I don't know. I, uh, don't think Mark has the wherewithal to get into love. At least when it's complicated." He smiles and looks away. "But do something adorable and I'll let you know how Mark likes it." (2012: 3)

Here the fan author is working to remediate the motivations of Mark Zuckerberg as imagined by the filmmakers of *The Social Network*, read through the lens of a fan seeking subtext in the film that indicates feelings of romantic love in the relationship between the screen characters of Mark and Eduardo. At the same time, the fan author is extending this search for subtext to the paratexts of the film (publicity appearances, interviews, the making-of documentary, and so on) to uncover the subtext between the screen characters as imagined by the actors. Their characters, in turn, trigger the actors into uncovering a romantic relationship of their own—a relationship the fan author finds in the subtext of the film's publicity paratexts. The way the docucharacter transforms the private self of the actor is reminiscent of James Naremore's argument that in performing a real person, the actor uses both techniques of imitation and of projecting psychological interiority to bring the character to life (2012: 38–42). Not only does the actor's self become projected onto the character, but the character's self—the self of the real person as the actor understands it within the context of the film—is experienced by the actor drawing on Stanislavskian technique. If, as Francesca Coppa argues, media fan fiction is more a performative endeavor than a literary one (2006: 226), in the act of appropriating and creating the actor-as-RPF-character, fan authors could be engaging in similar processes of connection to their object of desire. In "directing" the body of the RPF subject in the mind of the reader (Coppa 2006: 225), the fan author makes their own imitative connections with the object of their fandom. The version of the celebrity that the fan brings to life in their writing simulates a closing of the parasocial gap between star and fan, as the star/character "speaks" to the fan through the course of rendering them in fiction.

Both "The Long Affair" and "Carry it in My Heart" use the actors' consideration of the possible romantic subtext of Mark and Eduardo's relationship as a catalyst to forging a romantic attraction between Jesse and Andrew. With Eisenberg and Garfield serving as the physical embodiment of the fictionalized Mark and Eduardo, the fictionalization of a relationship between the actors continues the process of remediating the docucharacters. In these fan works, the bodies of Jesse and Andrew temporarily belong to the screen versions of Mark and Eduardo and in that temporary surrender to character, extend the fan interpretation of the on-screen relationship. This further works to not only invent private lives for the public figures of the actors but to re-interpret the screen versions of the real public figures they play in the film.

In order to participate in fic writing and reading fandom, fans need to engage in processes of compartmentalization. Writers and readers often need to be able to hold multiple fictionalized versions of the same characters in their mind at once. There are their own characters that differ among stories, the characterizations produced by other fans in their writings, interpretations that individuals may or may not agree with, or ones that become so widely repeated as to become a dominant reading of a character within a community. There is also the compartmentalization that must occur when holding these fictional versions of a real person against the media text of the actual person. The fun of the game comes from allowing the two to overlap, to watch, for example, the public appearance of a celebrity and fit it into the timeline of a particular fic written or read, to imagine the fictional behind-the-scenes goings-on that are made textual in the fic as the fantasy subtext of the actual public artifact. The multiple, compartmentalized versions of real people created in RPF fan communities, while they often play with the truth and, more often than not, aim to anchor themselves to a plausible version of actuality, are not intended as truth. They are fictions that are used to re-imagine the public personas of actual people for no purpose other than the enjoyment of their fans. The seeming frivolity of this, plus the secretive nature of RPF that is intended to be hidden from the celebrity subject, can be cited in arguments on both sides of the debate over whether RPF is nothing more than harmless fun for fans playing with the text of a star image, or a morally dubious practice that denies the personhood of a public figure.

There is unlikely to ever be any kind of universal consensus in fan communities on the ethical questions of RPF, and the practice will remain a matter for individual fans to decide their preferences and boundaries. Though it may continue to become more accepted in fan spaces, the limited scope of its distribution means that RPF fan fiction is not something as culturally pervasive as the biopic, and the influence of its docucharacters is not as far-reaching or prominent in shaping the public image of a celebrity. However, studying RPF as a fan practice and the processes of interpretation in making these characters demonstrates how some audience segments connect with public figures through fictionalization. While a comparatively niche media form, the study of RPF in conjunction with more widely distributed film and television texts that are under consideration throughout this book can reflect the liminal spaces between fact and fiction that audiences occupy as fan fiction writers and readers, as well as consumers of mainstream dramatizations of public figures.

Conclusion: Defined by Docucharacter

"People like stories. They help them make sense of things." So says Chris Darden in response to Marcia Clark's derision of defense narratives in *The People v. O.J. Simpson: American Crime Story*. Narratives and the consequences of our desire for stories, regardless of a strict adherence to raw facts, are a running theme through the re-presentation of the Simpson trial as the series attempts to make sense not only of those events but also of the continuing cultural resonance of the narratives they spun. Although *The People v. O.J. Simpson* was used in Chapter 1 of this book to illustrate how the docudramatic mode of representation re-creates the real in order to ground itself in actuality, that is, of course, not the only way the series functions as a work of adapting real people and events to the screen. As I have argued, like all media texts that feature a process of docucharacterization, *The People v. O.J. Simpson* takes known public events and uses them as a recognizable foundation to argue for the unknown behind-the-scenes. It is in this unknown, backstage story of the events where sense is made. The thematic concerns of the big-picture issues that the series raises—racism, sexism, celebrity, corruption—are anchored to the private selves of its characters. Johnnie Cochran's desire to further the civil rights causes of African Americans and bring to light the LAPD's race-motivated corruption becomes the reason the defense turned the focus away from O.J. Simpson himself to the idea of a police conspiracy. Marcia Clark's helplessness at being unable to adequately represent Nicole Brown as a victim of domestic abuse is tied to her own back story as a rape survivor and the public distractions about her personal life generated by the sexism of the tabloid press. Of all the characters, it is O.J. Simpson who remains the biggest enigma as the series tells its story of a trial that became so disconnected from the specificity of the crime and the accused criminal at hand. The audience cannot come to know Simpson from this series, because the series is not only telling a story, but also about the stories: stories that were so entwined with the American cultural zeitgeist that they still resonate twenty years on, stories so well constructed as to obscure the reality of the man they were supposedly about. The access we have to Simpson is primarily through others: both the characters in the drama, and in the history upon which it was based. The stories, the series posits as its docudramatic argument, is where sense is to be made.

Stories help us to make sense of things, and characters are central to that sense-making process. Characters can serve as a human proxy for thematic concerns, as a means of identification for viewers to situate themselves in the narrative, as the affective core of a story that supplements and enhances cognitive comprehension. Characters help to give an affective dimension to the raw material of known fact. When the characters and stories of our known world are presented to us in ways that make sense to our existing points of view, or to the way we wish to see the world, or even give a new, intriguing spin on the events we thought we knew, the literal facts at the heart of the story may be lost in translation. Often, the raw material of the world as it is, and of human nature as it is, does not make sense. That is why we need fiction, the process of witnessing events on screen, and an imagined, simulated access to the inner selves of our public figures, to gain a different kind of understanding. It is an understanding of witnessing and experiencing that, while it may not rely on the strictest factuality, can make more of a personal connection than facts alone.

The works considered throughout this book, and the multitude of texts like them that were not mentioned or studied here, can all be thought of as metaphors. Robert A. Rosenstone describes historical film in these terms, where the film about real events provides "metaphorical truths" as opposed to literal ones (2006: 9), that what we see on screen is a window into "not a literal reality, but a metaphoric one" (2006: 161). In the recontextualization method of writing RPF fan fiction, stories are created with elements of actuality in mind and encourages readers to re-examine the factual in light of the fictional. Likewise, the satirical sketch impersonation holds up its character for examination in comparison to its original in order to bring to light the gaps between public and private. Stephanie Koziski describes stand-up comedy performance as lies that reveal truths, as the performer recounts stories that have been embellished for performance, but do not depict literal accuracies (1984: 65). In the screen narrativization of these stories, a performer can act as their own metaphorical self, revealing something that may not have happened to them in exactly the way that is depicted, but nonetheless depicts some aspect of themselves. These are all works that compare a creation to its original by encouraging audiences to suspend disbelief and see the creation *as* the original. In doing so, a comparison is made that makes a statement about, or in some way gives insight into, its factual, actual source material.

How these metaphoric versions are constructed and what form they take depends on variables such as genre, medium, mode of production, breadth of distribution, and the author's agenda. These factors will modulate the way Goffman's frames of front and back regions are navigated, whether these frames are maintained or collapsed; whether the selves within them stay within the realms of plausibility or indulge in a loosely recognizable flight of imagination. The mainstream Hollywood biopic will give the sense of a connection to the real through its incorporation of pieces of a public image or elements of documentary fact to claim it tells a truth about its subject: a truth that can potentially simplify the subject and explain their actions through cause-and-effect narrative forms, or that can potentially complicate its subject with ambiguity and the deliberate introduction of the audience's affective response. A piece of RPF fan fiction can create a similar connection to the real through its use of fragments of the public image, but for the intention of a game between the fans who read it, to imagine a "what if" in the life of their desired celebrities. It may be a truth to those fans, but rather than claiming to be a truth about who the subject is and an explanation of their cultural significance, it is a truth that speaks to the audience about what they would like the celebrity to be. A docucharacter in sketch comedy will have public and private selves collapsed into public space, not only due to the restricted time frame of the form but with the comedic goal of externalizing the subject's inner self to satirize the gaps between public and private. In drama, codes of naturalism and an extended screen time allow a private self to be revealed as a behind-the-scenes entity, in contrast or as a complement to the public self. When a celebrity plays themselves in a merging of the documentary fact of their body and the fiction of the self they embody, their purpose may be to mock their public image in caricature, or to embrace their public image and flesh it out, to claim their public performance as an authentic self.

What I have argued by setting out this basic template for how celebrities and public figures become screen characters in contemporary Hollywood biopic and comparing this process with other media forms is that, even with the necessity of change dependent on factors of medium, audience, or mode of production, there is a common process at work here. There is an interest in turning public figures into screen characters of some kind, of being granted access to a recognizable public self that is augmented with a plausible private self to whom we have the kind of access that is unattainable without the frame of fiction. With this basic deconstruction of what makes a screen character out of a public figure established, what follows are several why questions. Why are docucharacters prevalent across such a spectrum of genres, forms, and media? Why are docucharacters appealing and entertaining? Why has the approach to docucharacters shifted in ways that support versions of a story, rather than the definitive telling of a life that characterized the initial stages of the docucharacter in classical Hollywood biopic?

That the texts examined in this book were all largely produced in the late 2000s and through the 2010s is perhaps not just a means of restricting the pool of options for textual analysis. The divisions between public and private are becoming ever more increasingly liminal and questionable for both the famous and non-famous. Celebrities with reality television shows stage their "real" life for the cameras, and ordinary people share their personal stories and public performance of self as reality show contestants. The widespread use of social media also gives ordinary people a platform to construct multiple potential versions of their public self to share with their followers, friends, acquaintances, and strangers alike. With these factors of the contemporary mediascape, particularly the everyday, widespread use of social media, P. David Marshall, Christopher Moore, and Kim Barbour write that the "practise of constructing a public mediated identity is now pervasive and proliferating" (2015: 289). Bernie Hogan (2010) argues that there is a difference between Goffman's dramaturgical metaphor of self-performance and the way we construct public selves in social media, and that difference is the traces that these digital performances leave behind. When thinking of self-performance in terms of drama, it is notable to define the dramatic performance as one that is "perform[ed] in real time for an audience that monitors the actor" (Hogan 2010: 377). The digital performance of self, however, leaves behind an enduring trace, an "artifact" of past performance which functions as an exhibition of self, not dependent on space and time for others to interpret or attempt to understand it (Hogan 2010: 377–81). The permanence of these artifacts and the way they accumulate through continued and constant digital self-presentation has made the ordinary person akin to the celebrity with the expansive, intertextual, often contradictory, and forever unfinished public image. Goffman's idea of the relevant social data one must interpret to understand and navigate social situations is more expansive, less anchored to a specific point in time. It is becoming a more noticeable fact of everyday communication that a "real" self is difficult to pin down. Rather than the metaphoric realities of the texts considered here, everyday self-performance could perhaps be thought of as synecdoche. We see parts of a self-performance attempting to stand in for a whole, complete person, but that whole person becomes more and more difficult to understand as the individual pieces accumulate. The possibilities of fiction, and the plausible comparison to the real, can potentially simplify the task, at least where our public figures are concerned.

The possibilities of fiction are not only a means of simulating access to a more cohesive representation of self, however, but can also offer the pleasures of simulating access to what can seem to be a more authentic version of a self: what happens outside of the front region frame, away from the cameras, beyond the realm of public self-performance. Lemi Baruh points out the voyeuristic pleasures of reality television, taking care to distinguish this contemporary cultural trait of "non-pathological voyeurism" where one "derive[s] pleasure from learning about others' private details" (2009: 191–2). This is opposed to the more established psychiatric definition of voyeurism as a sexual fetish of "covert observation" (Baruh 2009: 191). Baruh writes that the voyeuristic pleasures of reality television, such as the access to personal information about the contestants and witnessing of their actions in spaces coded as private (2009: 194–5), differ from the voyeuristic pleasures afforded by cinema due to "the aura of realism and spontaneity [reality television programs] invoke" (2009: 192). I propose that with the docucharacter, however, these pleasures of non-pathological voyeurism and the sense of realism and spontaneity can be fulfilled by the simulated hyperreality of the fictional world on screen (whether that is the cinema screen of the biopic, or the e-reader screen of the fan fic), where the imagination is engaged and encouraged to accept representation as plausible truth.

Baruh's study deals with reality television featuring ordinary people (like *Survivor* or *Big Brother*) rather than reality television featuring celebrities (like *Keeping up with the Kardashians*, or the versions of formats like *Big Brother* populated with celebrity contestants). When it comes to actual public figures appearing on camera in the reality of their private lives, a documentary that gives an insider perspective can be an enjoyable voyeuristic experience. For example, the documentary film *Weiner* (2016) intended to capture disgraced congressman Anthony Weiner as he redeemed himself through a run for mayor of New York City. The story the documentary ended up telling, though, was about the inner workings of Weiner's life as another sexting scandal came to light during his campaign. The resulting film is a wealth of non-pathological voyeuristic pleasure of witnessing how a scandal can damage both the public and private lives of a known person. However, many public figures are not as fond of cameras as Anthony Weiner, and most of the time, a public figure does not have cameras documenting those moments of their private lives that the public is most curious about. Even with the degree of access *Weiner* has to its subject, however, it is not without its moments when the documentarians are asked to leave the room, where private conversations between Weiner and his (then) wife, Huma Abedin, play out behind closed doors. Not only does the frame of fiction provide simulated access to those kinds of moments, but to the imagined interiority of the subject, making visible private thoughts and actions that further engage the need to know that is such a prominent focus of contemporary media culture. Through its metaphorical engagement with actuality, the docucharacter in its various forms can offer insights into the personal and private: even if it is not literal truth, there is still the pleasure of access, and, through its plausibility or the appeal of a revelation, the pleasure of believing it could be true.

I do not claim there is a direct line of correlation between social media or reality television and the ways public figures are adapted to screen texts. I do propose, however, that both are symptoms of the same cultural moment. It is a cultural moment that carries with it the expectation of knowing everything about everyone, an expectation that is shaped by media-savvy consumers who recognize that the knowledge in question may very well be carefully constructed, purposefully orchestrated to give a specific performance of self. There is always an inaccessible aspect to a public figure, and there is always something that will be unknown about people in our everyday lives. In crafting a fiction that is connected to recognizable or verifiable fact, not only does fact anchor a fiction to the real to create a plausible argument about its subject, but there is also a pleasure in its plausibility. Whether the fiction exists only in our imaginations or is committed to film in a multi-million-dollar Hollywood production, possible and plausible truths can be an enjoyable substitute for actual access and insight. In a cultural moment not only dominated by continuous self-performance, but the destabilization of truth and fact, believable fictions, whether they are harmless speculation about a favorite celebrity's private life, or the misleading treatment of factuality for dramatic purposes in a popular film, hold the appeal of "alternate" realities that may be preferable to objectively factual ones.

Multiple versions of narratives, characters, and real people in screen media are another factor that shapes the contemporary approach to and reception of docucharacters. While the multiple versions of stories and characters that adaptation creates is not a new phenomenon, the speed and frequency at which stories and characters are being remade, rebooted, and recycled across screen media is. The popularity of comic book movies has given us multiple takes on characters like Batman and Spider-Man within the space of just a few years. The need for relatively low-risk content with an established audience and a recognizable brand not only gives way to sequels and franchises but reboots and remakes of existing properties. The easy availability of older film and television content in the digital archive makes the original version just as accessible as its remake, allowing multiple interpretations of a character or story to circulate simultaneously and readily exist in the mind of the viewer, should they so choose. Once again, I do not argue that there is a direct correlation between something like multiple screen versions of a superhero character, and the multiple screen versions of a celebrity or public figure. The popularity and prevalence of both, however, indicate that the re-creation and reimagining of multiple versions of the same characters and stories are becoming increasingly normalized in screen media. Much like the contested nature of biopic characters that are criticized for not representing a "true" or "real" version of their subject, there are remakes and reboots that face similar criticisms. Films like the female-fronted *Ghostbusters* reboot (2016), the spurned *Point Break* remake (2015), or the murderous characterization of Batman in *Batman v. Superman: Dawn of Justice* (2016) see audiences holding the newer versions up to comparisons of the versions they prefer and finding them lacking. As an actual public figure, or one characterization of a public figure over another, may be taken as the "true" version, so too can other versions of remade and reimagined media properties be contested as truer than others, regardless of the equally fictional status of all of them. Audiences are becoming accustomed to navigating multiple co-existing versions of the same stories, of finding faults and choosing favorites.

The expectation of customized content is also a part of contemporary media consumption that is perhaps related to the ways public figures are adapted to screen characters. Eli Pariser (2011) has articulated the concept of the "filter bubble" to describe the ways the algorithms of online platforms such as Google, Facebook, and Netflix learn our behavior and preferences through use, then use that behavior to deliver the content we wish to see at the exclusion of other subjects or points of view. The process of the filter bubble often happens without our knowledge, with these kinds of personalization filters "indoctrinating us with our own ideas, amplifying our desire for things that are familiar" (Pariser 2011: 15). The way the world is reflected back to us online as we wish to see it, customizing content for our own needs, is echoed in the creation of docucharacter. RPF fan fiction is the most obvious evidence of this, as fans follow the tradition of textual poaching to remake media texts in ways that cater to their various individual or collective wants and desires. Ezekiel Kweku (2017) writes about the culture of political memes in much the same terms, referring to the characters created from parody characterizations, Twitter accounts, and memes (such as the Texts from Hillary meme, or *The Onion*'s characterization of "Diamond Joe" Biden) as "liberal fan fiction." Kweku argues that there is a place for fun and humor in the consumption of politics, but as these comforting idealized or comedic characterizations are recirculated among the same ideologically connected publics, the perception of reality is distorted when "as with any other metaphor ... you return to it so often that you start projecting the characteristics of the *metaphor* back onto *reality*" (emphasis in original). There is not that same sense of audience power for creating a customized filter bubble in mainstream Hollywood film as there is with audience-generated content like fan fiction or memes. However, the approach to contemporary biopic that Rebecca A. Sheehan (2013) describes, the "instant biopic" that quickly serves up modern history for dramatization or takes the more distant past and frames it in ways that resonate with contemporary issues, does work to customize historical or contemporary events in ways that enable the audience to make a more personal connection with them, potentially transferring the understanding gleaned from the metaphor—the cinematic representation—onto the actual event. Instant biopic films or television series like *United 93* (2006); *The Social Network, Game Change, The Big Short* (2015); *Patriots Day* (2016); or *The Comey Rule* (2020)—to name just a few—become a means through which to engage with a subject in popular discourse that is often colored by its own place in an individual's filter bubble, dictated by their existing ideological perspective, or the filmmakers' particular motivations, agendas, or ideological position. Additionally, through the instant biopic the audience gains access to events that they may or may not remember, and if they do, it is likely to only be the memory of an outsider's point of view. By connecting with characters, the viewer can place themselves in the story as they engage with the affective experience of the film. This creates personalized memory that supplements the public memory of events that they did not directly experience.

This personalized memory no longer needs to make a claim to being the definitive story of the life of its subject. Once again, the digital archive enables supplemental information to any viewer who seeks it out and allows space for dialogic unpacking of what is fact and what is fiction, and which fictions manage to reveal a truth that fact alone could not reach. For instance, a television series like *The People v. O.J. Simpson* comes with weekly recaps that include fact checks of major moments in the online versions of publications like *Vanity Fair* and *Rolling Stone*. As discussed when considering the critical reception of *Bohemian Rhapsody* and its tenuous relationship to factuality, in the internet age a popular based-on-a-true-story films rarely goes by without a consideration of the truth claims of the film, what really happened, what has been left out, and what was made up for dramatic purposes. It is again a case of having the media space for multiple versions of the story to exist at once: not only multiple fictionalized versions, but also those metaphorical fictions and their comparative relationship to literal fact.

This book has not only introduced a character-focused approach to the expected based-on-a-true story texts like docudramatic television series and biopics but also proposed that this character-focused approach can be applied to other media forms that play with the textuality of celebrity persona. This character-focused consideration can perhaps open new critical and scholarly avenues for approaching both the traditional and non-traditional media forms that adapt public figures to characters. For instance, we could consider questions such as how does the internet age and the easy availability of biographical information on platforms like Wikipedia, or archival footage for comparison on YouTube potentially change the production and reception of biopics and docudramas? Is there a move toward a "Character Study" style of biopic, exemplified by examples from this book of *Jackie* and *Chappaquiddick*, as well as other films like *Steve Jobs* (2015), *Vice* (2018), *Judy* (2019), and *Rocketman* (2019)? These "Character Study" style of biopics tend to exhibit characteristics of a restricted narrative time frame, do not attempt to give a complete life narrative of their subject but allow the story presented to act as an notably illustrative part of their subject's life and who they are, or use reflexive techniques in order to depict their subjects outside of pure life narrative, such as the integration of surreal musical sequences in the Elton John biopic *Rocketman*, or the deliberate breaking of the fourth wall and acknowledgment of Dick Cheney's secretive nature and unknowability in *Vice*.

What other ways has convergence culture, the proliferation of public selves, and the rebooting/remaking/reviving of content in popular entertainment potentially shaped characters based on real people? Does the easy availability of information made it possible to tell only a part of a subject's story, rather than intending it to be the definitive final word on their cultural position, as it was in the classical Hollywood era? Is visual mimesis prioritized as a means of authenticating docudramatic representation because archival footage is so readily available, as exemplified by *Bohemian Rhapsody*'s adherence to verisimilitude in its climactic concert sequence? How does a long-form, multi-season television narrative such as *The Crown*, or season-long television anthologies such as *American Crime Story* and *Feud*, or limited series like *When They See Us* utilize characterization in ways that are potentially different to the medium specificity of television versus the restricted time frame of a biopic film?

This book has only just touched on the possibilities for what a character-focused consideration of the adaptation of real people can uncover about the ways audiences engage with versions of their world by considering the idea of the illusion of access. There are several avenues for further research into this topic. The most prominent of these avenues would be to move from considering docucharacters in texts to studying the reception of docucharacters to understand exactly how characters based on real people can shape popular understanding of a public figure or alter the direction of their extra-textual public image. There are a multitude of questions that a character-focused approach to fact-fiction media can potentially shed light on, and these are obviously far outside the scope of this present work. However, it is my hope that perhaps the ontological category of the docucharacter established here can be applied to considering these and other questions related to fact-fiction media and the ways they shape our understanding of public figures.

Viewing metaphorical representations of the real as lies that tell a truth is a useful way to combat the literalist interpretations often used to malign fictionalized media based on true stories. A "lie that tells a truth" is frequently used as a way of referring to something that is purely fictional, but it is equally applicable to the biopic and other stories based on real people and events: those lies are based in truth, and in doing so, they can access other kinds of truths. As these stories based on real events are lies that tell a truth, so too are the characters adapted from real people. The lie is in what is invented, the truth is communicated by making the lie plausible enough to believe. What truth it tells, and whose truth it tells, can be deconstructed by considering the various factors at work throughout the analysis conducted in this book's case studies: who is producing the content and how is it produced? What is included and what is left out? How is fact supplemented by fiction? How are producers, audiences, genre, medium, and performance offering explanations through their storytelling? RPF fan fiction may tell a truth about its writers and readers. A contemporary biopic may tell a truth about the culture of the past in relation to the present.

A sketch character may tell a truth about the unspoken subtext of a public image. These truths are experienced and exposed by the ways audiences connect with characters and stories that help explain the real world in which they were first staged. Stories help explain things, and when the light shines on that silhouetted image, what we see gives us an understanding of something. Its factuality may be a fixed, objective state, but the truth we each take away from it can become something entirely new.

Bibliography

Allen, R. (1995), *Projecting Illusion: Film Spectatorship and the Impression of Reality*. Cambridge: Cambridge University Press.

American Splendor (2003), [Film] Dir. Shari Springer Berman and Robert Pulcini, USA: Fine Line Features.

Aquino, J. T. (2005), *Truth and Lives on Film: The Legal Problems of Depicting Real Persons and Events in a Fictional Medium*. Jefferson: McFarland.

Arrow, V. (2013), "Real Person(a) Fiction," in A. Jamison (ed.), *Fic: Why Fanfiction Is Taking over the World*, 323–31, Dallas: Smart Pop.

The Aviator (2004), [Film] Dir. Martin Scorsese, USA: Miramax.

Barry (2016), [Film] Dir. Vikram Gandhi, USA: Netflix.

Baruh, L. (2009), "Publicized Intimacies on Reality Television: An Analysis of Voyeuristic Content and Its Contribution to the Appeal of Reality Programming," *Journal of Broadcasting and Electronic Media* 53 (2): 190–210.

Batty, C. (2014), "Me You and Everyone We Know: The Centrality of Character in Understanding Media Texts," in B. Thomas and J. Round (eds), *Real Lives, Celebrity Stories: Narratives of Ordinary and Extraordinary People across Media*, 35–56, New York: Bloomsbury.

The Big Short (2015), [Film] Dir. Adam McKay, USA: Paramount Pictures.

Bignell, J. (2010), "Docudrama Performance: Realism, Recognition and Representation," in C. Cornea (ed.), *Genre and Performance: Film and Television*, 59–75, Manchester: Manchester University Press.

Bingham, D. (2010), *Whose Lives Are They Anyway?: The Biopic as Contemporary Film Genre*, New Brunswick: Rutgers University Press.

Bingham, D. (2013), "The Lives and Times of the Biopic," in R. A. Rosenstone and C. Parvulescu (eds), *A Companion to the Historical Film*, 233–54, Oxford: Blackwell.

Black, J. (2002), *The Reality Effect: Film Culture and the Graphic Imperative*. New York: Routledge.

Boggan, S. (2010), "The Billionaire Facebook Founder Making a Fortune from Your Secrets (Though You Probably Don't Know He's Doing It)," *Mail Online*, May 21.

Bohemian Rhapsody (2018), [Film] Dir. Bryan Singer, Dexter Fletcher, USA: 20th Century Fox.

Buckley, C. (2017), "Asking Questions Louis C.K. Doesn't Want to Answer," *New York Times*, September 11. Available online: https://www.nytimes.com/2017/09/11/movies/louis-ck-rumors-wont-answer.html (accessed October 21, 2021).

Bueno, A. (2016), "Exclusive: Angelina Jolie Spotted for the First Time since Filing for Divorce from Brad Pitt," *ET Online*, October 17. Available online: https://www.etonline.com/news/200573_exclusive_angelina_jolie_spotted_for_the_first_time_since_filing_for_divorce_from_brad_pitt (accessed February 16, 2017).

Burrough, B. (2015), "The Inside Story of the Civil War for the Soul of NBC News," *Vanity Fair*, April 7. Available online: https://www.vanityfair.com/news/2015/04/nbc-news-brian-williams-scandal-comcast (accessed July 15, 2016).

Busse, K. (2006a), "'I'm Jealous of the Fake Me': Postmodern Subjectivity and Identity Construction in Boy Band Fan Fiction," in S. Holmes and S. Redmond (eds), *Framing Celebrity: New Directions in Celebrity Culture*, 253–67, London: Routledge.

Busse, K. (2006b), "My Life Is a WIP on My LJ: Slashing the Slasher and the Reality of Celebrity and Internet Performances," in K. Hellekson and K. Busse (eds), *Fan Fiction and Fan Communities in the Age of the Internet*, 207–24, Jefferson: McFarland.

Busse, K. (2013), "Pon Farr, Mpreg, Bonds, and the Rise of the Omegaverse," in A. Jamison (ed.), *Fic: Why Fanfiction Is Taking over the World*, 316–21, Dallas: Smart Pop.

"Can't Stand the Heartache" (2011), *tsn-kinkmeme LiveJournal*, February 1. Available online: https://tsn-kinkmeme.livejournal.com/1522.html (accessed January 26, 2017).

"Canon and Fanon" (2011), *mark-eduardo LiveJournal*, 7 May. Available online: https://mark-eduardo.livejournal.com/271286.html (accessed March 31, 2014).

"Carry It in My Heart" (2011) [Fan Work], *LiveJournal*, restricted access (accessed March 31, 2014).

Carter, J. (2005) *The Comedy Bible: From Stand-Up to Sitcom*. Sydney: Currency.

Casting JonBenet (2017), [Film] Dir. Kitty Green, USA: Netflix.

Chambers, R. (2010), *Parody: The Art That Plays with Art*. New York: Peter Lang.

Chappaquiddick (2017), [Film] Dir. John Curran, USA: Apex Entertainment.

Citizen Kane (1941), [Film] Dir. Orson Welles, USA: RKO.

Clark, A. (2012), "How the Comedy Nerds Took Over," *New York Times*, April 20. Available online: https://www.nytimes.com/2012/04/22/magazine/how-the-comedy-nerds-took-over.html (accessed March 11, 2014).

The Colbert Report (2005), [Television Program], Comedy Central, October 17.

The Comey Rule (2020), [Television Program], Showtime, September 27–28.

Commoli, J. (1978), "Historical Fiction: A Body Too Much," *Screen* 19 (2): 41–54.

Confessions of a Dangerous Mind (2002), [Film] Dir. George Clooney, USA: Miramax.

Coppa, F. (2006), "Writing Bodies in Space: Media Fan Fiction as Theatrical Performance," in K. Hellekson and K. Busse (eds), *Fan Fiction and Fan Communities in the Age of the Internet*, 225–44, Jefferson: McFarland.

Corsello, A. (2014), "Louis C.K. Is America's Undisputed King of Comedy," *GQ*, May 14. Available online: https://www.gq.com/story/louis-ck-cover-story-may-2014 (accessed February 6, 2015).

Custen, G. F. (1992), *Bio/Pics: How Hollywood Constructed Public History*. New Brunswick: Rutgers University Press.

D'Allesandro, A. (2012), "Emmys: *Louie*'s Louis C.K," *Deadline*, June 17. Available online: https://deadline.com/2012/06/emmys-louies-louis-c-k-287592/ (accessed May 16, 2013).

Day, A. and E. Thompson (2012), "Live from New York, It's the Fake News! *Saturday Night Live* and the (Non)Politics of Parody," *Popular Communication* 10 (1–2): 170–82.

Denton Jr., R. E. (2010), "Preface," in R. E. Denton Jr. (ed.), *Studies of Identity in the 2008 Presidential Campaign*, ix–xiii, Lanham: Lexington.

Derecho, A. (2006), "Archontic Literature: A Definition, a History, and Several Theories of Fan Fiction," in K. Hellekson and K. Busse (eds), *Fan Fiction and Fan Communities in the Age of the Internet*, 61–78, Jefferson: McFarland.

Desjardins, M. (2004), "The Incredible Shrinking Star: Todd Haynes and the Case History of Karen Carpenter," *Camera Obscura* 19 (3): 22–55.

Double, O. (2005), *Getting the Joke: The Inner Workings of Stand-Up Comedy*. London: Methuen.

Dyer, R. (1987), *Heavenly Bodies: Film Stars and Society*. Houndmills: MacMillan.

Dyer, R. (1998), *Stars*, new ed, London: BFI.

"Eduardo/Mark, ED Fic" (2010), *tsn-kinkmeme LiveJournal*, December 24. Available online https://tsn-kinkmeme.livejournal.com/390.html?thread=164486#t164486 (accessed March 31, 2014).

Ellis, J. (1991), "Stars as a Cinematic Phenomenon," in J. G. Butler (ed.), *Star Texts: Image and Performance in Film and Television*, 300–15, Detroit: Wayne State University Press.

Entourage (2004–11), [Television Program] Creat. Doug Ellin, USA: HBO.

Esralew, S. and D. G. Young (2017), "The Influence of Parodies on Mental Models: Exploring the Tina Fey-Sarah Palin Phenomenon," *Communication Quarterly* 60 (3): 338–52.

Fair Game (2010), [Film] Dir. Doug Liman, USA: Summit Entertainment.

Fathallah, J. (2018), "Reading Real Person Fiction as Digital Fiction: An Argument for New Perspectives," *Convergence* 24 (6): 568–86.

Ferris, K. O. (2011), "Building Characters: The Work of Celebrity Impersonators," *Journal of Popular Culture* 44 (6): 1191–208.

Fey, T. (2011), *Bossypants*. New York: Little, Brown.

Fresh Air (2008), [Radio Program] "Tina Fey: Sarah Palin and *Saturday Night* Satire," NPR, November 3.

Funny People (2009), [Film] Dir. Judd Apatow, USA: Universal.

Gaine, V. M. (2010), "Re-Mediated Mann: The Re-Mediation of Public Figures and Events in *The Insider* and *Ali*," *Networking Knowledge* 3 (1): 1–11.

Game Change (2012), [Film] Dir. Jay Roach, USA: HBO Films.

Gamson, J. (1994), *Claims to Fame: Celebrity in Contemporary America*. Berkeley: University of California Press.

Goffman, E. ([1956] 1990), *The Presentation of Self in Everyday Life*. London: Penguin.

Goffman, E. ([1959] 1997), *The Goffman Reader*, C. Lemert and A. Branaman (eds), Maiden: Blackwell.

Goldberg, L. "FX Cuts Ties with Louis C.K. Following Sexual Misconduct," *Hollywood Reporter*, November 10. Available online: https://www.hollywoodreporter.com/tv/tv-news/fx-cuts-ties-louis-ck-sexual-misconduct-1057201/ (accessed October 21, 2021).

Good Night, and Good Luck (2005), [Film] Dir. George Clooney, USA: Warner Independent Pictures.

Guthey, E., T. Clark, and B. Jackson (2009), *Demystifying Business Celebrity*. London: Routledge.

Hagan, R. (2015), "'Bandom Ate My Face': The Collapse of the Fourth Wall in Online Fan Fiction," *Popular Music and Society* 38 (1): 44–58.

Haiduc, S. A. (2020), "Biopics and the Melodramatic Mode," in D. Cartmell and A. D. Polasek (eds), *A Companion to the Biopic*, 23–44, Hoboken: Wiley Blackwell.

Harris, M. (2010), "Inventing Facebook," *New York Magazine*, September 17.

Heidt, S. J. (2009), "'Ça, c'est moi': The Diving Bell and the Butterfly as Autobiographical Multitext," *Adaptation* 2 (2): 125–48.

Hitchcock (2012), [Film] Dir. Sacha Gervasi, USA: Fox Searchlight, 2012.

Hogan, B. (2010), "The Presentation of Self in the Age of Social Media: Distinguishing Performance and Exhibitions Online," *Bulletin of Science, Technology and Society* 30: 377–86.

How Did They Ever Make a Movie of Facebook? (2011), [Film] Dir. David Pryor, USA: Sony.

Hutcheon, L. (2006), *A Theory of Adaptation*. New York: Routledge.

I'm Not There (2007), [Film] Dir. Todd Haynes, USA: The Weinstein Company.

The Iron Lady (2011), [Film] Dir. Phyllida Lloyd, UK: 20th Century Fox.

Izadi, E. (2020), "Louis C.K.'s Sexual Misconduct Tanked His Career. Now He's Selling out Theatres," *Washington Post*, March 11. Available online: https://www.washingtonpost.com/arts-entertainment/2020/03/11/louis-ck-new-standup/ (accessed October 21, 2021).

Jackie (2016), [Film] Dir. Pablo Larraín, USA: Fox Searchlight.

Jacobs, N. (1990), *The Character of Truth: Historical Figures in Contemporary Fiction*. Carbondale: Southern Illinois University Press.

Jamison, A. (2013), "Introduction," in A. Jamison (ed.), *Fic: Why Fanfiction Is Taking over the World*, 2–23, Dallas: Smart Pop.

Jenkins, H. (1992), *Textual Poachers: Television Fans and Participatory Culture*. New York: Routledge.

Jones, J. P. (2008), "With All Due Respect: Satirizing Presidents from *Saturday Night Live* to *Lil' Bush*," in J. Gray, J. P. Jones, and E. Thompson (eds), *Satire TV: Politics and Comedy in the Post-Network Era*, 37–63, New York: New York University Press.

Jones, J. P. (2013), "Politics and the Brand: *Saturday Night Live*'s Campaign Season Humor," in N. Marx, M. Sienkiewcz, and R. Becker (eds), *Saturday Night Live and American TV*, 77–91, Bloomington: Indiana University Press.

Jones, N. (2016), "*The People v. O.J Simpson* Recap: Episode 2 Fact Check," *Vanity Fair*, February 10. Available online: https://www.vanityfair.com/hollywood/2016/02/people-v-oj-simpson-episode-2-recap (accessed February 22, 2021).

Judy (2019), [Film] Dir. Rupert Goold, UK: Walt Disney Studios.

Key and Peele (2012–2015), [Television Program] Creat. Keegan-Michael Key and Jordan Peele, USA: Comedy Central.

Kinsey (2004), [Film] Dir. Bill Condon, USA: 20th Century Fox.

Koziski, S. (1984), "The Standup Comedian as Anthropologist: Intentional Culture Critic," *Journal of Popular Culture* 18 (2): 57–76.

Kweku, E. (2017), "Liberal Fan Fiction: Too Many Memes Will Rot Your Brain," *MTV News*, 7 February. Available online: http://www.mtv.com/news/2979835/liberal-fan-fiction/ (accessed June 30, 2017).

Libbey, P. (2018), "FX Investigation of Louis C.K. Finds No Evidence of Workplace Misconduct," January 7. Available online: https://www.nytimes.com/2018/01/07/arts/television/louis-ck-fx-investigation.html (accessed February 25, 2021).

Lipkin, S. N. (2011), *Docudrama Performs the Past: Arenas of Argument in Films Based on True Stories*. Newcastle upon Tyne: Cambridge Scholars.

Littler, J. (2007), "Celebrity CEOs and the Cultural Economy of Tabloid Intimacy," in S. Redmond and S. Holmes (eds), *Stardom and Celebrity: A Reader*, 230–43, Los Angeles: Sage.

"Live Aid | *Bohemian Rhapsody* (2018) Scene Comparisons," *YouTube*, February 28, 2019. Available online: https://www.youtube.com/watch?v=2cH5htm6T4E (accessed February 22, 2021).

Live at the Beacon Theatre (2011) [Comedy special] Dir. Louis C.K., USA: Pig Newton.

Live in Houston (2001) [Comedy album] Perf. Louis C.K., USA: Circus King Productions.

"The Long Affair" (2012) [Fan work] *Archive of Our Own*, restricted access (accessed October 10, 2013).

Louie (2010–16), [Television Program] Creat. Louis C.K., USA: FX.

Lovelace (2013), [Film] Dir. Rob Epstein and Jeffrey Friedman. USA: Medium Films.

Lucky Louie (2006), [Television Program] Creat. Louis C.K., USA: HBO.

Marshall, P. D. (2014a), "Persona Studies: Mapping the Proliferation of the Public Self," *Journalism* 15 (2): 153–70.

Marshall, P. D. (2014b), "Seriality and Persona," *M/C* 17 (3): https://doi.org/10.5204/mcj.802 (accessed February 10, 2022).

Marshall, P. D., C. Moore, and K. Barbour (2015), "Persona as Method: Exploring Celebrity and the Public Self through Persona Studies," *Celebrity Studies* 6 (3): 288–305.

Marshall, L. and I. Kongsgaard (2012), "Representing Popular Music Stardom on Screen: The Popular Music Biopic," *Celebrity Studies* 3 (3): 346–61.

McGee, J. (2005), "'In the End, It's All Made Up': The Ethics of Fanfiction and Real Person Fiction," in P. M. Japp, M. Meister, and D. K. Japp (eds), *Communication Ethics, Media, and Popular Culture*, 161–80, New York: Peter Lang.

McKinnon, A. (2008), "Even Mud Has the Illusion of Depth: A McLuhanesque Reading of Sarah Palin," *Flow* 8 (10): https://www.flowjournal.org/2008/10/even-mud-has-the-allusion-of-depth-a-mcluhanesque-reading-of-sarah-palin-ann-mckinnon-okanagen-college/ (accessed February 10, 2022).

Meyers, E. A. (2010), "Gossip Talk and Online Community: Celebrity Gossip Blogs and Their Audiences," Diss. University of Massachusetts, Amherst.

Michaud Wild, N. (2015), "Dumb vs. Fake: Representations of Bush and Palin on *Saturday Night Live* and Their Effects on the Journalistic Public Sphere," *Journal of Broadcasting and Electronic Media* 59 (3): 494–508.

Milk (2008), [Film] Dir. Gus Van Sant, USA: Focus Features.

Miller, J. A. and T. Shales (2014), *Live From New York: The Complete, Uncensored History of Saturday Night Live as Told by Its Stars, Writers, and Guests*, Expanded ed. New York: Little, Brown.

Mills, B. (2010), "Being Rob Brydon: Performing the Self in Comedy," *Celebrity Studies* 1 (2): 189–201.

Minier, M. and M. Pennacchia (2014), "Interdisciplinary Perspectives on the Biopic: An Introduction," in M. Minier and M. Pennacchia (eds), *Adaptation, Intermediality and the British Celebrity Biopic*, 1–31, Farnham: Ashgate.

Mintz, L. E. (1985), "Standup Comedy as Social and Cultural Mediation," *American Quarterly* 37 (1): 71–80.

Moon, T. (2010), "Spotlight Kids: The Depiction of Stand-Up Comedians in Fictional Drama: Film, Television and Theatre," *Comedy Studies* 1 (2): 201–8.

Naremore, J. (1986), "Expressive Coherence and the 'Acted Image'," *Studies in the Literary Imagination* 19 (1): 39–54.

Naremore, J. (2012), "Film Acting and the Arts of Imitation," *Film Quarterly*, 65 (4): 34–42.

Pariser, E. (2011), *The Filter Bubble: What the Internet Is Hiding from You*. London: Viking.

Patriots Day (2016), [Film] Dir. Peter Berg, USA: Lionsgate.

Pearson, R. (2014), "Remembering Frank Sinatra: Celebrity Studies Meets Memory Studies," in B. Thomas and J. Round (eds), *Real Lives, Celebrity Stories: Narratives of Ordinary and Extraordinary People across Media*, 187–209, New York: Bloomsbury.

Peifer, J. T. (2013), "Palin, *Saturday Night Live*, and Framing: Examining the Dynamics of Political Parody," *The Communication Review* 16: 155–77.

The People v. OJ Simpson: American Crime Story (2016), [TV program] FX, 9 February.

Pimenova, D. (2009), "Fan Fiction: Between Text, Conversation, and Game," in I. Hotz-Davies, A. Kirchhofer and S. Leppanon (eds), *Internet Fictions*, 44–61, Newcastle-upon-Tyne: Cambridge Scholars.

Pomerance, M. (2013), *The Eyes Have It: Cinema and the Reality Effect*. New Brunswick: Rutgers University Press.

Poncede Leon C. L., (2002), *Self-Exposure: Human-Interest Journalism and the Emergence of Celebrity in America, 1890–1940*. Chapel Hill: University of North Carolina Press.

Pugh, S. (2005), *The Democratic Genre: Fan Fiction in a Literary Context*. Brigend: Seren.

Purdie, S. (1993), *Comedy: The Mastery of Discourse*. Toronto: University of Toronto Press.

The Queen (2006), [Film] Dir. Stephen Frears, UK: Pathe Distribution.

Republican National Convention (2008), [Television broadcast] "Vice Presidential Candidate Gov. Sarah Palin (AK) Full Speech at the RNC," C-Span, September 3.

"Research Questions," (2011), *tsn-kinkmeme LiveJournal*, June 15. Available online: https://tsn-kinkmeme.livejournal.com/8943.html (accessed March 31, 2014).

Retartha, A. G. (2014), 'You're Always Running into People's Unconscious': Public Intimacy and the Imagined Celebrity Self in Fiction, Diss. New York University.

Rhodes, G. D. and J. P. Springer (2006), "Introduction," in G. D. Rhodes and J. P. Springer (eds), *Docufictions: Essays on the Intersection of Documentary and Fictional Filmmaking*, 1–9, Jefferson: McFarland.

Rocketman (2019), [Film] Dir. Dexter Fletcher, UK: Paramount Pictures.

Romano, A. (2019), "*Bohemian Rhapsody* Loves Freddie Mercury's Voice. It Fears His Queerness," *Vox*, January 6. Available online: https://www.vox.com/2018/11/16/18071460/bohemian-rhapsody-queerphobia-celluloid-closet-aids (accessed February 22, 2021).

Roscoe, J. and C. Hight (2001), *Faking It: Mock-Documentary and the Subversion of Factuality*. Manchester: Manchester University Press.

Rosenstone, R. A. (2006), *History on Film/Film on History*. Harlow: Pearson.

Ryzik, M., C. Buckley and J. Kantor (2017), "Louis C.K. Is Accused by Five Women of Sexual Misconduct," *New York Times*, November 9. Available online: https://www.nytimes.com/2017/11/09/arts/television/louis-ck-sexual-misconduct.html (accessed February 24, 2021).

Sandvoss, C. (2007), "The Death of the Reader? Literary Theory and the Study of Texts in Popular Culture," in J. Gray, C. Sandvoss, and C. L. Harrington (eds), *Fandom: Identities and Communities in a Mediated World*, 19–32, New York: New York University Press.

Saraiya, S. (2015), "How Brian Williams Lost His Gravitas to NBC's Relentless Marketing Machine," *Salon*, February 11. Available online: https://

www.salon.com/2015/02/11/how_brian_williams_lost_his_gravitas_to_nbcs_ relentless_marketing_machine/ (accessed July 15, 2016).

Saturday Night Live (2008a), [Television Program segment] "A Non-partisan Message from Governor Sarah Palin and Senator Hillary Clinton," USA: NBC, September 13.

Saturday Night Live (2008b), [Television Program segment] "VP Debate Open: Palin/Biden," USA: NBC, October 5.

Saturday Night Live (2012), [Television Program segment] "Weekend Update: Sarah Palin on *Game Change*," USA: NBC, March 11.

Savage, M. (2018), "*Bohemian Rhapsody:* How Rami Malek Became Freddie Mercury," *BBC News*, 23 October. Available online: https://www.bbc.com/news/entertainment-arts-45939504 (accessed February 22, 2021).

Schechter, J. (1994), *Satiric Impersonations: From Aristophanes to the Guerrilla Girls.* Carbondale: Southern Illinois University Press.

Schwartz, D. (2012), "8 Facebook Privacy Flaps," *CBC News*, 25 September.

Selma (2014), [Film] Dir. Ava DuVernay, USA: Paramount Pictures.

Sheehan, R.A. (2013), "Facebooking the Present: The Biopic and Cultural Instantaneity," in T. Brown and B. Vidal (eds), *The Biopic in Contemporary Film Culture*, 35–51, New York: Routledge.

Shameless (2007), [Comedy special] Dir. Steven J. Santos, Perf. Louis C.K., USA: HBO.

Sicinski, M. (2012), "Truthiness Is Stranger Than Fiction: The 'New Biopic'," in C. Lucia, R. Grundmann, and A. Simon (eds), *The Wiley-Blackwell History of American Film*, 1–21, Hoboken: Blackwell.

60Minutes (2008), [TV Program segment] "The Face behind Facebook," USA: CBS, January 13.

60Minutes (2010), [TV Program segment] "Mark Zuckerberg and Facebook," USA: CBS, December 5.

Smith, C. (2010), "Delete Your Facebook Account: 'Quit Facebook Day' Wants Users to Leave," *Huffington Post*, May 15.

Smith, M. (1995), *Engaging Characters: Fiction, Emotion, and the Cinema*. Oxford: Oxford University Press.

Sobchack, V. (1992), *The Address of the Eye: A Phenomenology of Film Experience*. Princeton: Princeton University Press.

Sobchack, V. (2004), *Carnal Thoughts: Embodiment and Moving Image Culture*. Berkeley: University of California Press.

The Social Network (2010), [Film] Dir. David Fincher, USA: Sony Pictures Entertainment.

Sony Pictures Entertainment (2010), "*The Social Network* Production Notes," *Visual Hollywood*. Available online: https://www.yumpu.com/en/document/view/46852766/the-social-network-production-notes-visual-hollywood (accessed October 8, 2012).

Southside with You (2016), [Film] Dir. Richard Tanne, USA: Miramax.

Steve Jobs (2015), [Film] Dir. Danny Boyle. USA: Universal.
"The Strange and Scary World of Mark Zuckerberg Fan Fiction" (2012), *Dvice*, February 2.
Sully (2016), [Film] Dir. Clint Eastwood, USA: Warner Bros. Pictures.
Tate, R. (2012), "The Most Awesome Homoerotic Mark Zuckerberg Fanfic," *Gawker*, February 2. Available online: https://gawker.com/5881818/the-most-awesome-homoerotic-mark-zuckerberg-fanfic (accessed January 26, 2017).
Taylor, J. M. (2010) "Outside Looking in: Stand-up Comedy, Rebellion, and Jewish Identity in Early Post-World War II America," MA Diss. Indiana University.
"Things You Wouldn't Admit Unanon: RPF Thread" (2012), *Fail Fandomanon LiveJournal*, October 21. Available online: https://fail-fandomanon.livejournal.com/43393.html?thread=196938369#t196938369 (accessed March 31, 2014).
30 Rock (2006–2013), [Television program] Creat. Tina Fey, USA: NBC.
This Is the End (2013), [Film] Dir. Seth Rogen and Evan Goldberg, USA: Columbia.
Thomas, B. (2014), "Fans Behaving Badly? Real Person Fic and the Blurring of the Boundaries between the Public and the Private," in B. Thomas and J. Round (eds), *Real Lives, Celebrity Stories: Narratives of Ordinary and Extraordinary People across Media*, 171–85, New York: Bloomsbury.
Top Five (2015), [Film] Dir. Chris Rock, USA: Paramount Pictures.
Tung, C. (2012), "Revisiting *Shameless*, Louis C. K.'s First Stand-up Special," *Splitsider*, November 13. Available online: https://www.vulture.com/2012/11/revisiting-shameless-louis-cks-first-stand-up-special.html (accessed March 24, 2017).
Turner, G. (2004), *Understanding Celebrity*. London: Sage.
Turner, G. (2016), *Re-inventing the Media*. London: Routledge.
United 93 (2006), [Film] Dir. Paul Greengrass, UK: United International Pictures.
Upchurch, M. (1992), "The Poetics of Sketch Comedy," MA Diss. University of Nevada, Las Vegas.
Van Zoonen, L. (2005), *Entertaining the Citizen: When Politics and Popular Culture Converge*. Lanham: Rowman and Littlefield.
Vargas, J. A. (2010), "The Face of Facebook: Mark Zuckerberg Opens Up," *The New Yorker*, September 20.
Vice (2018), [Film] Dir. Adam McKay, USA: Mirror Releasing.
Vidal, B. (2013), "Introduction: The Biopic and Its Critical Contexts," in T. Brown and B. Vidal (eds), *The Biopic in Contemporary Film Culture*, 1–32, New York: Routledge.
W. (2008), [Film] Dir. Oliver Stone, USA: Lionsgate.
Warren, K. (2016), "Double Trouble: Parafictional Personas and Contemporary Art," *Persona Studies* 2 (1): 55–68.
Weiner (2016), [Film] Dir. Josh Kriegman, Elyse Steinberg, USA: Showtime.
Wilkinson, A. (2018), "*Chappaquiddick*'s Screenwriters on Stumbling Unwittingly into Kennedy Controversy," *Vox*, April 17. Available online: https://www.vox.com/culture/2018/4/16/17234306/chappaquiddick-screenwriters-ted-kennedy-andrew-logan-taylor-allen (accessed February 21, 2021).

Wired Staff. (2018), "Seriously, We Really Need to Talk about *Nanette*," *Wired*, July 31. Available online: https://www.wired.com/story/hannah-gadsby-nanette-discussion/ (accessed October 21, 2021).

WORD: Live at Carnegie Hall (2012), [Comedy album] Perf. Louis C. K., USA: Pig Newton.

Zoller Seitz, M. (2012), "Why Is *Louie* Such a Remarkable TV Show? Because It Makes Stand-Up Comedy Cinematic," *Vulture*, August 23. Available online: https://www.vulture.com/2012/08/why-is-louie-such-a-remarkable-tv-show.html (accessed April 29, 2013).

Index

affective response 3, 9, 44, 55, 64, 94, 130
Allen, Richard 59
The Aviator 34

Baldwin, Alec 2, 75
Batty, Craig 37, 43, 55, 57
Being John Malkovich 107
Biden, Joe 2, 83–7, 90, 92, 156
The Big Short 156
The Big Sick 112
Bignell, Jonathan 45–6
Bingham, Dennis 3, 6, 33–6, 43, 54
biopic
   as adaptation 22, 36
   character construction 22, 26, 29, 32–3, 36–7, 40, 46
   character study 12, 25, 61, 65, 157
   character subjectivity 55–6
   comparison with fan fiction 132–4, 147
   contemporary trends 13, 15–16, 25
   film genre 3, 6, 34, 36, 43
   neoclassical biopic 33–6, 43, 51
   shaping cultural understanding 28–9, 43, 54, 62
Bohemian Rhapsody
   factual inaccuracy 21, 25–6, 28–9
   involvement of Queen 27, 133
   visual mimesis 11, 14, 23–4, 27, 35, 41
BoJack Horseman 107
Branson, Richard 38
Bruce, Lenny 111
Burnham, Bo 97
Bush, George W. 74–6, 79
Busse, Kristina 59, 125, 127, 130, 132, 134–5

Carvey, Dana 74
Casting JonBenet 13
celebrity CEOs 37–8, 49, 77
celebrity culture 57–8, 103, 135
celebrity image: *see* public image
celebrity impersonation 72–4, 88: *see also Saturday Night Live (SNL)*
celebrity politicians 76–7
Cera, Michael 102–3
Chappaquiddick 12, 60–4, 65, 157
Chappelle, Dave 113–14
characters
   in biopic 22, 32, 40
   engagement 59
   in fan fiction 138–9
   identification 3
   meaning making 55, 150
   motivation 31, 43–4
   public/private selves 9
   in sketch comedy 71
Chase, Chevy 74, 76, 78
Citizen Kane 33–4, 48
C.K., Louis 12, 95–6, 104–5, 107–8, 113–21: *see also Louie*
Clarke, Jason 61, 63
Clinton, Hillary 79–82, 88, 156
The Comey Rule 156
Confessions of a Dangerous Mind 57
Connery, Sean 73–4
Cooper, Anderson 89
Couric, Katie 81, 84, 91
Crashing 112
Cross, David 111
The Crown 158
Curb Your Enthusiasm 117
Custen, George F. 22, 32–3, 34, 43–4, 50–1

David, Larry 117
defamation 26–7, 132
The Diving Bell and the Butterfly 36
docucelebrity 119
docucharacter
   definition 4, 5, 6, 7, 13
   engagement 58
   fact-fiction spectrum 10, 27
   in fan fiction: 124, 142, 146
   pleasures 154
   process 11, 68, 70

public/private selves 9, 11, 22, 26, 32, 40, 65
   self-docucharacterization 97–8, 101
   in sketch comedy 70–1, 79, 82
docucomedy 6, 87–8
docudrama
   contextualizing history 16–17
   Game Change 89–90, 92–4
   persuasion 14, 17–18, 53
   theoretical approaches 5, 6, 10–11, 13, 16–17
docufantasy 6, 124, 135–6, 138, 143
documentary 5, 10, 144
Dyer, Richard 7, 8, 23, 35, 57–8, 120

Eisenberg, Jesse
   actor 2, 32, 36, 50, 60, 78
   fan fiction character 123–4, 134–5, 137, 139, 132–46
Entourage 105

factual discourse 10, 57, 144
Fallon, Jimmy 79, 104
fan fiction: *see* real person fiction (RPF)
Fathallah, Judith 143–4
Ferrell, Will 73–6, 78
Feud 158
Fey, Tina
   public image 76, 78–9, 85
   as Sarah Palin 69–70, 74–5, 78, 80–2, 83–6, 89
filter bubble 155–6
Fincher, David 35–6, 145
Ford, Gerald 74
Forte, Will 75
Franco, James 106
Funny People 99–101, 111–12

Gadsby, Hannah 97, 110, 113
Game Change 12, 16, 56, 69, 84, 88–94, 156
Garfield, Andrew
   actor 32, 36
   fan fiction character 123–4, 134–5, 137, 139, 142–6
Garofalo, Janeane 100, 111
Gamson, Joshua 58
Gibson, Charles 80–1, 84, 91

Goffman, Erving
   dramaturgical metaphor 90, 96, 110, 152
   presentation of self 7, 8, 9, 40
   region behavior 8, 9, 35, 84, 151
gossip: *see* scandal

Hammond, Darrell 73–4
Hanks, Tom 73
Hartman, Phil 74
Hitchcock 56
House of Cards 61

idols of consumption and production 33–5
Ifill, Gwen 83, 85–7, 90
I'm Dying Up Here 112
The Iron Lady 57

Jackie 5–6, 11, 56, 60, 65–7, 157
Jacobs, Naomi 10, 59, 71
Jenkins, Henry 131
Johnson, Lyndon B. 53, 65–6
Jones, Jeffrey P. 73–4, 75, 79, 82
Judy 157

Kennedy, Edward M. (Ted) 60–4
Kennedy, Jacqueline (Jackie) 53, 56, 60, 65–7
Kennedy, John F. 56, 60, 61, 65–7
Kennedy, Robert F. (Bobby) 61, 66–7
Kinsey 34
Kopechne, Mary Jo 60–4

Lady Dynamite 112
Latifah, Queen 83, 86
libel: *see* defamation
Lipkin, Steven N. 5–6, 14, 17, 89, 119, 135
Louie 12, 96, 105, 107–8, 112, 115–19: *see also* C.K., Louis
Lovelace 56

Malek, Rami 21, 23–4, 26, 27–8
Mara, Kate 61
Maron, Marc 111–12
Marshall, P. David 57, 111, 117, 152
McCain, John 77, 85, 88–90, 93

McGee, Jennifer 125, 127, 129–30
melodrama 34–5, 53
memory 56, 66, 67, 89, 92: *see also* public memory
Mercury, Freddie 14, 21, 23–4, 25–6, 27–9, 35
metaphorical truth 150–1
Mills, Brett 101, 109–10, 112–13
Moore, Julianne 69, 70, 89

Naremore, James 23, 110, 116, 146

Obama, Barack 2, 24, 86–8, 91
Oswalt, Patton 97, 111, 113

Palin, Sarah
   Game Change character 88–94
   public image 12, 56, 69, 74, 76–8, 133
   Saturday Night Live character 80–7, 89
parody 102, 105
Patriots Day 156
The People v. O.J. Simpson: American Crime Story 11, 14, 15, 16–21, 35, 149–50
performance
   biopic 23–4, 27–8, 50, 63, 66, 91
   celebrities playing themselves 95, 98, 101–2, 105–6
   sketch comedy 73, 75, 79–80
   stand-up comedy 109–10
   Stanislavski method 142, 146
Poehler, Amy 79–82
political celebrity: *see* celebrity politicians
Portman, Natalie 65, 66
presentation of self: *see under* Goffman, Erving
private self 9, 13, 31, 33, 35, 102: *see also* Goffman, Erving
public image
   audience appropriation of 124, 131–2, 143
   intertextuality 22–3
   re-presentation on screen 28, 31, 33, 45–6, 59, 97–8
   on social media 152
   theoretical approaches 7, 8, 9, 14, 21, 59

public memory 6, 14–15, 17–21, 67, 74, 156
public self: *see* public image

real person fiction (RPF)
   comparison with biopic 132–4, 147
   compartmentalization 147
   controversy 127–30
   defining canon 126–7, 136–7, 143–4
   kink meme 138–9
   recontextualization 131–2, 134–5, 138, 140, 142
   The Social Network fandom 123–5, 135–47
   theoretical approaches 125–6, 130–1
reality television 152–3
region behavior: *see under* Goffman, Erving
Retartha, Amanda 58, 59, 125, 142
Rocketman 157
RPF: *see* real person fiction (RPF)

Saget, Bob 105
Sahl, Mort 111
Samberg, Andy 69, 73
Sandler, Adam 99–100, 102
satire 71–2, 74–6, 79, 83–7, 94, 97
Saturday Night Live (*SNL*)
   celebrity impersonation 71–6
   Sarah Palin sketches 69, 78–8, 90–2
Saverin, Eduardo
   biopic character 48, 49–50, 145
   fan fiction character 124, 136–41
scandal
   Anthony Weiner 153–4
   Brian Williams 104–5
   in *Chappaquiddick* 61–2
   gossip and celebrity discourse 34–5, 58, 135
   Louis C.K. 95–6, 107–8, 120–1
Schmidt, Steve 89, 92
screen characters: *see* characters
Seinfeld 101–2, 116–17
Seinfeld, Jerry 101–2, 116
Sheehan, Rebecca A. 2, 15–16, 25, 156
Silverman, Sarah 99–101

The Simpsons 107
sketch comedy 70–1, 87–8, 93: *see also* Saturday Night Live (SNL)
Sleepwalk with Me 112
Smith, Murray
    allegiance 9, 113, 141
    alliance 44–5
    character engagement 55
    recognition 40, 45, 71–2, 87
    structure of sympathy 4, 102
Sobchack, Vivian 54, 66, 99
The Social Network
    character construction 31–2, 39–40, 42–51, 56
    fandom 123, 128, 134–47
    instant biopic 156
    making of documentary 35–6
    neoclassical biopic 34–6, 43
Sorkin, Aaron 35–6, 46, 47, 145
Stand-up comedians
    authenticity 108–9, 110–11, 112–14
    celebrity 109–10, 114
    persona 96–7
    representations of 112
star image: *see* public image
Steve Jobs 157
structure of sympathy: *see under* Smith, Murray

subjectivity 12, 32, 37, 55–7, 60, 65
Sudeikis, Jason 83, 86
30 Rock 79, 85, 103
This Is the End 102–3, 106

Timberlake, Justin 32, 36
Top Five 101–2, 112
Trebek, Alex 73–4
Trump, Donald 2, 10, 75
truthiness 25
Turner, Graeme 35, 57–8, 76

United 93 156

Vice 157

Weiner 153–4
When They See Us 158
Williams, Brian 103–5
Williams, Robin 100

Zanuck, Darryl F. 43
Zuckerberg, Mark
    biopic character 36, 39–40, 42, 44–50, 60, 145
    Facebook controversies 41–2
    fan fiction character 124, 137–41
    public image 31, 37–9, 133